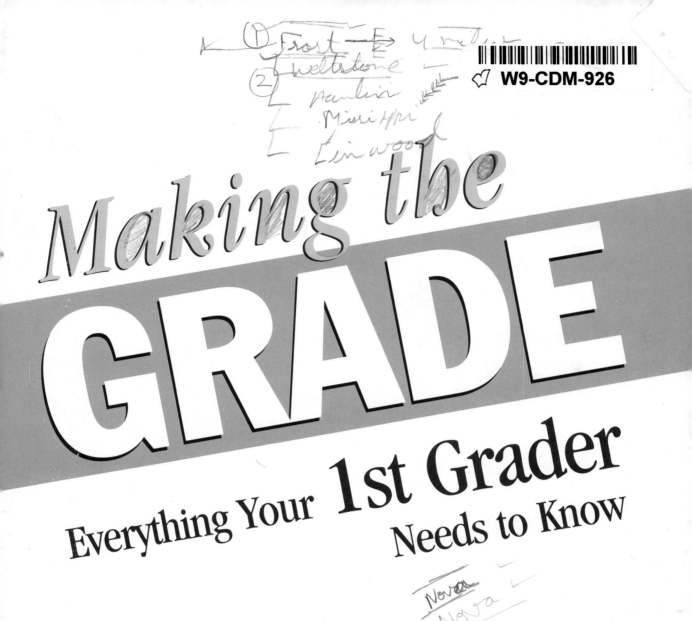

Making the GRADE

Everything Your 1st Grader Needs to Know

by
Laura B. Tyle

BARRON'S

About the Author

Laura B. Tyle has worked in educational book publishing for several years as a researcher, writer, and editor of educational and reference materials for students of all ages. She has contributed to the writing and editing of textbooks and educational materials in math, science, social studies, and language arts. Laura is also the published editor of a series of biographies written for children. She holds a B.A. in history from the University of Illinois at Chicago.

All inquiries should be addressed to:
Barron's Educational Series, Inc.
250 Wireless Boulevard
Hauppauge, New York 11788
http://www.barronseduc.com

Library of Congress Catalog Card No. 2003057775

International Standard Book No. 0-7641-2476-5

Library of Congress Cataloging-in-Publication Data
Tyle, Laura B.
     Everything your 1st grader needs to know / by Laura B. Tyle.
       p. cm. — (Making the grade)
     Includes bibliographical references (p.) and index.
     ISBN 0-7641-2476-5
      1. First grade (Education)—Curricula—United States. 2. Home schooling—Curricula—United States. 3. Curriculum planning—United States. I. Title: Everything your first grader needs to know. II. Title. III. Making the grade (Hauppauge, N.Y.)

LB15711st T95 2004
372.19—dc22   2003057775

Printed in China
9 8 7 6 5 4 3 2 1

Table of Contents

PROMOTING LITERACY 1

MATH

SCIENCE

SOCIAL STUDIES

How to Use This Book

Welcome to the *Making the Grade* series! These seven books offer tools and strategies for hands-on, active learning at the kindergarten through sixth-grade levels. Each book presents real-world, engaging learning experiences in the core areas of language arts, math, science, and social studies at age-appropriate levels.

Who should use this book?

Whether you're a stay-at-home or working parent with children in school, a homeschooler who's guiding your children's education, or a teacher who's looking for additional ideas to supplement classroom learning experiences, this book is for you.

- If you have children in school, *Making the Grade* can be used in conjunction with your child's curriculum because it offers real-world, hands-on activities that exercise the concepts and topics he or she is being taught in school.
- If you're a homeschooler who's guiding your children's education, this series presents you with easy-to-access, engaging ways to interact with your child.
- If you're a teacher, this book also can be a source for additional activities.

This book is your passport to a whole new world, one that gives you enough support to be a successful educator while encouraging independent learning with one child or shared learning among your children. *Making the Grade* offers enriching educational opportunities and encourages a student-directed, relaxed learning environment that optimizes children's interests.

What is Making the Grade?

We're glad you asked! First, we'd like to tell you what it's not. It's not a textbook series. Rather, each book in the series delivers age-appropriate content in language arts, math, science, and social studies in an open-ended, flexible manner that incorporates the "real" world. You can use this book as a supplement to your core learning instruction or use it to get a jump start on the fundamentals.

Each subject section presents lessons comprised of both "teaching" pages and "student" pages. Throughout the lessons, you'll find guidance on giving constructive encouragement and ways to balance educational and recreational pursuits. And each book in the *Making the Grade* series is perforated for flexible learning so that both you and your child can tear out the pages that you're working on and use one book together.

How do the lessons work?

The teaching and student pages work together. The lesson instruction and teaching ideas for each specific lesson appear first. Activities that offer opportunities for your child to practice the specific skills and review the concepts being taught follow. Creativity and imagination abound! Throughout each lesson, hands-on activities are incorporated using concepts that are meaningful and relevant to kids' daily lives. The activities account for all kinds of learners—that is, visual, auditory, or kinesthetic learning. (For more information on learning styles, see the Glossary on page 353.) Be encouraged to allow ample time for discovery of the concepts in each lesson—whether that be a few hours or a few days—and ample time for unstructured independent exploration. Your student can help guide the pace. Follow your child's interests, as it will make learning fun and valuable.

Objective and Background

Each lesson opens with an objective that tells you exactly what the lesson is about. The background of the lesson follows, giving you the rationale behind the importance of the material being addressed. Each lesson is broken down for you so that you and your student can see how the skills and concepts taught are useful in everyday situations.

Materials and Vocabulary

Have you ever done a project and found out you're missing something when you get to the end? A list of materials is given up front so you'll know what you need before you begin. The lessons take into account that you have access to your local library, a computer and the Internet, writing instruments, a calculator, and a notebook and loose paper, so you won't find these listed. The materials are household items when possible so that even the most technical of science experiments can be done easily. The *Making the Grade* series paves the way for your learning experience whether you and your student are sitting side by side on the couch or in a classroom, at the library, or even on vacation!

Following the materials list, vocabulary words may be given offering clear, easy-to-understand definitions.

Let's Begin

Let's Begin is just that, "Let's Begin!" The instructional portion of the lesson opens with easy, user-friendly, numbered steps that guide you through the teaching of a particular lesson. Here you'll find opportunities to interact with your student and engage in discussions about what he or she is learning. There also are opportunities for your student to practice his or her critical-thinking skills to make the learning experience richer.

In the margins are interesting facts about what you're studying, time-savers, or helpful ideas.

Ways to Extend the Lesson

Every lesson concludes with ways to extend the lesson—teaching tips, such as hints, suggestions, or ideas, for you to use in teaching the lesson or a section of the lesson. Each lesson also ends with an opportunity for you to "check in" and assess how well your student has mastered the skill or grasped the concepts being taught in the lesson. The For Further Reading section lists books that you can use as additional references and support in teaching the lesson. It also offers your student more opportunities to practice a skill or a chance to look deeper into the content.

Student Learning Pages

Student Learning Pages immediately follow the teaching pages in each lesson. These pages offer fun opportunities to practice the skills and concepts being taught. And there are places where your student gets to choose what to do next and take ownership of his or her learning. Since reading may be a new skill for your student, be patient as he or she reads the directions and activities on these pages.

Visual Aids

Throughout the book you'll see references to the Venn Diagram, T Chart, Web, Sequence Chain, and Writing Lines found in the back of the book. Many lessons incorporate these graphic organizers, or visual methods of organizing information, into the learning. If one is used in a lesson, it will be listed in the materials so that prior to the lesson you or your student can make a photocopy of it from the back of the book or you can have your student copy it into his or her notebook. See the Glossary for more information on graphic organizers.

What if my student is just learning how to read?

Many children begin to read at this age, so be sure to guide your student in a noncritical and nonjudgmental manner as he or she navigates through unfamiliar territory. Be aware that research has indicated that a child needs to see a word many times (sometimes up to 20 times) before reading becomes automatic. Since this is an average, some words will be learned quicker than others. Let your student guide you as to his or her pace for reading. You may wish to return frequently to the Promoting Literacy section for guidance and strategies to help your new reader.

What about field trips or learning outside the classroom?

One very unique feature of the *Making the Grade* series are the In Your Community activities at the end of each subject section. These activities describe ways to explore your community, taking advantage of your local or regional culture, industry, and environment while incorporating the skills learned in the lessons. For example, you can have your student help out at a farmer's market or with a local environmental group. These unique activities can supplement your ability to provide support for subjects. The activities give your student life experiences upon which he or she can build and expand the canvas upon which he or she learns.

These pages are identified in the Table of Contents so that you can read them first as a way to frame your student's learning.

How do I know if my student is learning the necessary skills?

Although each lesson offers an opportunity for on-the-spot assessment, a formalized assessment section is located in the back of this book. You'll find a combination of multiple-choice and open-ended questions testing your student on the skills, concepts, and topics covered.

Also, at the end of every subject section is a We Have Learned checklist. This checklist provides a way for you and your student to summarize what you've accomplished. It lists specific concepts, and there is additional space for you and your student to write in other topics you've covered.

Does this book come with answers?

Yes. Answers are provided in the back of the book for both the lessons and assessment.

What if this book uses a homeschooling or educational term I'm not familiar with?

In addition to the vocabulary words listed in the lessons, a two-page Glossary is provided in the back of the book. Occasionally terms will surface that may need further explanation in order for the learning experience to flourish. In the Glossary, you'll find terms explained simply to help you give your student a rewarding learning experience free from confusion.

Will this book help me find resources within the schools for homeschoolers?

In Communicating Between Home and School, there are suggestions for how to take advantage of the opportunities and resources offered by your local schools and how these benefits can enhance your homeschooling learning experiences.

I'm new to homeschooling. How can I find out about state regulations, curriculum, and other resources?

In For Homeschoolers at the beginning of the book, you'll find information about national and state legislation, resources for curriculum and materials, and other references. Also included is a comprehensive list of online resources for everything from homeschooling organizations to military homeschooling to homeschooling supplies.

How can I use this book if my student attends a public or private school?

Making the Grade fits into any child's educational experience—whether he or she is being taught at home or in a traditional school setting. Student-selected activities can be found in nearly all lessons, which can enhance and build upon his or her existing school learning experiences. At the end of each subject section, you'll find In Your Community activities that provide ways to discover your local region while incorporating information from the lessons. Many first graders are adjusting to a full day of school for the first time, so be encouraged to work together with your student to choose activities—you may wish to only take advantage of certain lessons, exercises, or components. Let your student guide you!

For Homeschoolers

Teaching children at home isn't a new phenomenon. But it's gaining in popularity as caregivers decide to take a more active role in the education of their children. More people are learning what homeschoolers have already known, that children who are homeschooled succeed in college, the workplace, and society.

Whether you're new to homeschooling or have been educating your children at home for quite some time, you may have found the homeschooling path to have occasional detours in finding resources. Families choose homeschooling for different reasons. This book hopes to minimize those detours by offering information on state regulations, homeschooling approaches and curriculum, and other resources to keep you on the path toward a rewarding learning experience.

Regulations

There never has been a federal law prohibiting parents from homeschooling their children. A homeschooler isn't required to have a teaching degree, nor is he or she required to teach children in a specific location. Each state has its own compulsory attendance laws for educational programs as well as its own set of regulations, educational requirements, and guidelines for those who homeschool.

Regardless of the level of regulation your state has, there are ways to operate your homeschool with success. Here are a few tips as you negotiate the homeschooling waters:

- Be aware of your district's and state's requirements.
- Don't let these laws, rules, and regulations deter you. The National Home Education Network (NHEN) may be able to help. Go to the association's Web site at *http://www.nhen.org*. For even more information on your state's laws and related references, see Homeschooling Online Resources that follow. They can help you find information on your specific state and may be able to direct you to local homeschooling groups.
- Veteran homeschoolers in your area can be a source of practical knowledge about the laws. Consult a variety of homeschoolers for a clear perspective, as each family has an educational philosophy and approach that best suits it.

Homeschooling Military Families

Frequently moving from location to location can be exhausting for families with one or more parent in the military. If you have school-age children, it can be even more complicated. Schools across states and U.S. schools in other countries often don't follow the same curriculum, and states often can have varying curriculum requirements for each grade.

The Department of Defense Dependent Schools (DoDDS) is responsible for the military educational system. There are three options for military families in which they can educate their children:

1. attend school with other military children
2. if in a foreign country, attend the local school in which the native language is spoken, although this option may require approval
3. homeschool

Homeschooling can provide consistency for families that have to relocate often. The move itself, along with the new culture your family will be exposed to, is a learning experience that can be incorporated into the curriculum. Note that military families that homeschool must abide by the laws of the area in which they reside, which may be different from where they claim residency for tax purposes. If your relocation takes your family abroad, one downside is the lack of curriculum resources available on short notice. Nonetheless, military homeschoolers may be able to use resources offered at base schools.

Approaches and Curriculum

If you're reading this book you've probably already heard of many different approaches to and methods of homeschooling, which some homeschoolers refer to as *unschooling* (see the Glossary for more information). Unschooling is not synonymous with homeschooling; it's a philosophy and style of education followed by some homeschoolers. It's important that you choose one approach or method that works best for you—there's no right or wrong way to homeschool!

The curriculum and materials that are used vary from person to person, but there are organizations that offer books, support, and materials to homeschoolers. Many homeschoolers find that a combination of methods works best. That's why *Making the Grade* was created!

Support Groups and Organizations

Homeschooling has become more popular, and the United States boasts a number of nationally recognized homeschooling organizations. Also, nearly every state has its own homeschooling organization to provide information on regulations in addition to other support. Many religious and ethnic affiliations also have their own homeschooling organizations too, in addition to counties and other groups.

Famous Homeschoolers

Many famous people were once homeschooled, including Ansel Adams, Louisa May Alcott, Alexander Graham Bell, Pearl S. Buck, Charlie Chaplin, Agatha Christie, Charles Dickens, Thomas Edison, Benjamin Franklin, Wolfgang Amadeus Mozart, George Patton, and Mark Twain. A number of U.S. presidents also have been homeschooled, including George Washington, Thomas Jefferson, Abraham Lincoln, Woodrow Wilson, and Franklin Delano Roosevelt.

Homeschooling Online Resources

These are some of the online resources available for homeschoolers. You also can check your phone book for local organizations and resources.

National Organizations

Alliance for Parental Involvement in Education
http://www.croton.com/allpie/

Alternative Education Resource Organization (AERO)
http://www.edrev.org/links.htm

American Homeschool Association (AHA)
http://www.americanhomeschoolassociation.org/

Home School Foundation
http://www.homeschoolfoundation.org

National Coalition of Alternative Community Schools
http://www.ncacs.org/

National Home Education Network (NHEN)
http://www.nhen.org/

National Home Education Research Institute (NHERI)
http://www.nheri.org

National Homeschooling Association (NHA)
http://www.n-h-a.org

Homeschooling and the Law

Advocates for the Rights of Homeschoolers (ARH)
http://www.geocities.com/arhfriends/

American Bar Association
http://www.abanet.org

Children with Special Needs

Children with Disabilities
http://www.childrenwithdisabilities.ncjrs.org/

Institutes for the Achievement of Human Potential (IAHP)
http://www.iahp.org/

National Challenged Homeschoolers Associated Network (NATHHAN)
http://www.nathhan.com/

Military Homeschooling

Department of Defense Dependent Schools/Education Activity (DoDDS)
http://www.odedodea.edu/

Books, Supplies, Curriculum

Federal Resources for Educational Excellence
http://www.ed.gov/free/

Home Schooling Homework
http://www.dailyhomework.org/

Home School Products
http://www.homeschooldiscount.com/

Homeschooler's Curriculum Swap
http://theswap.com/

HomeSchoolingSupply.com
http://www.homeschoolingsupply.com/

General Homeschooling Resources

A to Z Home's Cool
http://www.gomilpitas.com/

Family Unschoolers Network
http://www.unschooling.org

Home Education Magazine
http://www.home-ed-magazine.com/

Home School Legal Defense Association (HSLDA)
http://www.hslda.org

Homeschool Central
http://www.homeschoolcentral.com

Homeschool Internet Yellow Pages
http://www.homeschoolyellowpages.com/

Homeschool Social Registry at Homeschool Media Network
http://www.homeschoolmedia.net

Homeschool World
http://www.home-school.com/

Homeschool.com
http://www.homeschool.com/

HSAdvisor.com
http://www.hsadvisor.com/

Unschooling.com
http://www.unschooling.com/

Waldorf Without Walls
http://www.waldorfwithoutwalls.com/

Communicating Between Home and School

For homeschoolers, often there is limited contact with the schools beyond that which is required by the state. Yet a quick glance at your local schools' resources may reveal opportunities that can aid you in creating extracurricular activities that follow your interests and supplement your child's total learning experience.

Special Needs

If you have a child with special needs, such as dyslexia or ADHD (attention deficit hyperactivity disorder), taking advantage of the programs and services your public school provides can expand your support system and give you some relief in working with your child. In many instances, the easy access and little or no cost of these services makes this a viable option for homeschoolers.

Depending on your child's diagnosed needs, some school districts may offer full services and programs, while some may only provide consultations. Some school districts' special education departments have established parent support networks that you may be able to participate in as a homeschooler. States and school districts vary in terms of what homeschoolers are allowed to participate in, so check with your local school administrator and then check with your state's regulations to verify your eligibility.

Two organizations, the Home School Legal Defense Association (HSLDA) and the National Challenged Homeschoolers Association Network (NATHHAN), offer a wide range of information and assistance on services and programs available for special needs children. Check them out on the Internet at *http://www.hslda.org* and *http://www.nathhan.com.* Your local homeschooling group—especially veteran homeschoolers—will have practical information you can use.

Additionally, some homeschooling parents combine the resources of a school with those offered by a private organization to maximize support.

Gifted Children

If your child is considered gifted, your local public school may have programs available for students who require additional intellectual attention. Check with your local school administrator and your state's regulations first. In addition to providing information on special needs children, HSLDA and NATHHAN offer resources for parents of gifted children.

Don't be afraid to check out the colleges in your area, too. Many times colleges, especially community colleges, offer classes or onetime workshops that might be of interest to your child. Check with your local schools to see how you can take advantage of these opportunities.

Extracurricular Activities

Opportunities abound for homeschoolers to get involved with extracurricular activities. Clubs and interest groups allow children and parents to interact and share ideas with other homeschoolers. Extracurricular activities not only enrich the learning experience, they can also provide opportunities for friendship.

You might want to meet regularly for planned activities focusing on a particular subject matter, such as math instruction, science workshops, or pottery classes. You could meet at someone's home or perhaps at a community or religious center. Another enriching idea is to form a theme group or club based on a group's interests. You could gather together as a quilting group, a nature club, a chess club, a play group, and more—let your interests guide you. Or you could just get together to simply share ideas or plan group activities, such as a craft project, a book discussion, or the creation of a newsletter. Parents and children can work together to plan activities and events or to create their own sporting teams, such as golf, water polo, and fencing, to name a few.

If you can't find a meeting on a particular subject area or theme in your region, don't hesitate to form one in your community. One way to begin might be to check out the Homeschool Social Register at *http://www.homeschoolmedia.net*. Here you can find other homeschoolers in your area and homeschoolers who share your educational philosophy and interests.

Other extracurricular activities, such as 4-H, Girl Scouts, Boy Scouts, religious youth groups, arts and crafts, athletics, music, and language or debate clubs, may be offered in your community. They can provide additional opportunities for your homeschooler to interact with his or her peers and have a valuable learning experience at the same time. Extracurricular activities offered at local schools also may prove worthwhile to investigate.

Returning to School

If you plan on having your child return to school, taking advantage of the programs and opportunities offered can help ease the transition back into the classroom. Your child will already experience a sense of familiarity with his or her surroundings and peers, which can help smooth the transition to a different structure of learning.

Meet Your First Grader

Enthusiastic, boundless, silly, contrary, defiant, undecided—do any of these describe your first grader? First-grade children are commonly caught between a newfound desire for independence and an ever-present need to feel secure and accepted, wrestling simultaneously with both. Of course, each six to seven and a half year old is unique and develops at his or her own individual pace. However, getting to know the common characteristics and behaviors of your child's age group can be helpful in navigating a supportive and harmonious journey through his or her learning and development.

Acknowledge Profound Inner Shift

A first grader's world view no longer revolves around you, the parent or primary caregiver. Instead, the self has taken central focus in the world. Your child may now realize that he or she is a separate person and must begin to make some decisions on his or her own. This realization can create feelings of anger and abandonment, which may prompt your first grader to test your power and your love. Six year olds may begin to speak disrespectfully to parents or act contrary to your instructions, even to the extent of becoming impossible or aggressive. A first-grade child also may cry often and for seemingly insignificant reasons. He or she may begin to have periods of not getting along with siblings or friends or complain about not wanting to complete lesson work.

Your first grader is more aware of your flaws than he or she was as a kindergartener and may begin to point them out in sometimes hurtful ways. This criticism is part of the coping mechanism of separation. Ironically, while using his or her words to alienate you, your first grader needs to feel safe and secure in your love and acceptance more than ever. This inner push and pull may become evident in the way your child can cling to you one moment and then dart away with a defaming remark toward you the next.

Parental approval is critical at this age, and any type of criticism may be excruciating to your child and lead to profound mood swings and erratic behavior. However, the behavior of a first grader usually becomes less extreme when he or she feels assured of parental love and approval.

Provide Reliable Schedules and Routines

As your first grader grows through this uncertain stage of self-realization and budding independence, establishing reliable daily routines is essential. Being able to count on your attentive presence within a consistent morning and evening schedule will help promote your child's self-confidence and balance. Perhaps set aside a special time to cuddle and read a book before bed. In the morning, maintain a predictable routine with a warm wake-up greeting and family breakfast time.

When a first grader feels secure and cared for, his or her need to explore is more likely to come out. Excited about new experiences and eager to venture into the outside world, there is also a very light side to a first-grade child. First graders can show great joy for life.

Enjoy Enthusiasm

First graders tend to have a great gusto for discovery and an enthusiasm for all things new. Your first grader may become more adventurous and daring this year and easily do things or go places alone. First graders can also be extremely warm and loving with family and friends during more harmonious moments.

Children at this age are characteristically silly, giggly, and goofy, enjoying nonsense rhyming, made-up words, and plays on words. Your child may also like to hear jokes and laugh easily when you tell them. A first grader often makes a point to remember a joke that was especially funny so that he or she can retell it later—whether everyone has heard it already or not!

First graders love to learn and show off new skills. Your child may be eager to have your attention while he or she reads or counts aloud for you. Riddles and guessing games that challenge your first grader's wit and creativity are also favorites. You may notice that your first grader likes to win—all the time—and may even try to change rules or look for loopholes to come out the winner.

Espouse Eager Intellect

Although eager and quick at many mental tasks, a first grader is not as mentally prepared for making decisions. He or she often bounces back and forth when trying to decide between two opposites, having an equal and conflicting desire to choose each one. Once your first grader chooses the red shirt, he or she may immediately flip and realize he or she really wanted to wear the blue one all along. Allowing your first grader to make his or her own choices is important. However, you can reduce your child's anxiety by presenting a limited number of options to choose from, such as "Would you like peanut butter and jelly or a turkey sandwich for lunch?" or "Shall we read the book about whales or the book about astronauts?"

Children at this age can ask a lot of questions. The questions may focus on why things are the way they are and how things work. Some of your child's questions may be very blunt, difficult to answer, or just plain outside an adult's comfort zone. Do your best to answer in a straight and honest manner. It will be obvious to a first grader if you react with shock, skirt around issues, or try to change the subject. This may confuse or frustrate your child.

Your first grader may take more intimate opportunities to ask you about how babies are made and what parents do together in bed. Your child may also be aware of the aging process and have questions about elderly people and the way older bodies look. Be mindful about the risk of overexposing a precocious child to information he or she isn't ready for, but do answer these questions truthfully. Give simple answers and avoid going into unnecessary detail. If you're careful not to project shame or embarrassment onto your first grader, he or she will most likely continue questioning only to the extent of his or her own comfort limit and stop.

Balance Independence and Security

A first grader is able to do more things alone but still needs a good deal of adult help. Often a first-grade child will become resistant to receiving help from his or her primary caregiver specifically. This age can be a difficult transition for many parents; however, your child's development will be greatly affected by your ability to let out the reigns and embrace his or her newfound independence. Acknowledge the things your child is now ready to do on his or her own, especially self-care tasks such as brushing teeth and getting dressed. If your child gets the feeling that you think he or she is incapable, your child may internalize that feeling.

As your child becomes more self-sufficient, your caregiving time with him or her will decrease. Your first grader is less likely to experience the illusion of abandonment if you are mindful about maintaining emotional and physical closeness. Try replacing the time you previously spent in direct care with an equal amount of time offering attention in other ways, such as playing games, sharing stories, or showing affection. Doing things in the same room with your first grader while he or she works independently will also help minimize the feelings of loneliness so common along the road to maturity.

Honor Privacy and Accomplishment

Provide ample opportunity for your first grader to experience the feelings of accomplishment and approval he or she so eagerly seeks. Allocate age-appropriate tasks that can be easily completed, such as giving the family pet water and setting or clearing the dinner plates. This will give you a chance to offer genuine appreciation and praise. Your first-grade child may also be delighted when you include him or her in adult conversations or when asked to share an opinion about a topic.

It isn't uncommon for a first grader to begin to establish a private life away from parents and begin to withhold details of his or her excursions and activities outside the home. Abbreviated responses to your questions about his or her activities—such as "Just fine," "Nothing big," or "It was OK"—are a sign of your first grader's desire to create some separation. Although it may feel like a slight, this is a positive sign of development. Be understanding and allow your child to take this healthy and normal step. If your first grader doesn't spend much time away from home or with adults other than parents, involving him or her in a community sports, arts, or Scouting program that meets several times a week may be beneficial.

Note Physical Changes

First graders' bodies are growing quickly, and movement abounds. Your child probably moves nonstop through most of the day. Your first grader may have a tendency to be clumsy, run into things, or knock things over. Exuberance at the park, especially doing spins or flips on the bars, is common first-grade behavior.

Although energetic at times, first graders tire easily. After a long day, fatigue can turn into crabbiness or a refusal to mind parents. Frequent illnesses are also common at this age. Most six- to seven-year-old children begin to lose their baby teeth and grow their first adult teeth.

Your first grader is also still developing fine motor skills and may struggle with learning to hold a pencil. Don't be overly concerned if your first grader uses an unorthodox grip. If the writing is legible, then the grip your child is using is probably a good one for him or her at this time.

Provide Encouragement

You may find that your first grader has an ongoing desire to be the best, biggest, and fastest and may brag to you or others about his or her accomplishments. Your first grader is compensating for a new awareness of his or her limits and imperfections. If no one else comments on your child's achievements, he or she will be the one who talks about them. Recognize this as an inadvertent prompt to you for more encouragement and admiration. Go ahead and offer as much extra encouragement and support as possible. If your first grader becomes fulfilled now, he or she won't need to perpetuate this behavior as an adult.

Be Flexible in Learning

You may find that your first grader prefers to do lesson work in a variety of unusual positions, such as kneeling on a chair, standing up, or laying on the floor. Your first grader will probably need to move throughout lesson time, even fidgeting in a chair to the point of toppling it right over. The lessons in *Making the Grade* allow for movement breaks whenever necessary and include many hands-on and kinesthetic activities.

First graders tend to be auditory learners, which means that they absorb information best through sound and hearing. Your child may consistently repeat lesson information out loud in order to process it internally. Similarly, a first grader will usually whisper each word out loud when reading alone to hear the sounds. Phonics, a reading method that focuses on the sounds of letters, is a good fit for the auditory bent of first graders. *Making the Grade* provides fundamental lessons in phonics development in the Promoting Literacy section.

A first grader can be extremely sensitive to criticism, and the academic arena is a place where you may see these sensitivities. Your first grader's emotional, physical, and intellectual world is changing very quickly, and your child will advance at his or her own pace. Set realistic expectations and be patient if your child struggles with seemingly simple material. Some children excel immediately with fundamental materials, such as reading and basic math, while others may need a little more time and understanding.

If your first grader is adjusting to a full school day for the first time, he or she may be more tired than usual, especially at the beginning of the school year. Be flexible and patient as he or she makes this transition. If your child is in a traditional school setting, he or she may not wish to come home and sit through more instructional lessons. *Making the Grade* allows your child to choose what activities he or she would like to do—and how long to spend doing them! If you do sense a need for more practice of a certain skill or in a certain area, you may wish to go to a particular lesson or a particular section for a deeper look. Let your child direct you to his or her interests and needs. Encourage your first grader to explore and learn independently at his or her own pace!

Promoting Literacy

Promoting Literacy

Key Topics

Short Vowels

Long Vowels

Vowel Patterns

Poetry

Fiction

Tall Tales

Consonant Blends

Nonfiction

Writing Sentences

Making the Grade: Everything Your 1st Grader Needs to Know

Exploring the Short *a*

Phonics helps children decode and read words they have never seen before.

OBJECTIVE	BACKGROUND	MATERIALS
To help your student recognize the short /ă/ sound, connect it to the written letter *a*, and blend it with other letter sounds to make words	An important skill that beginning readers must develop is the ability to match sounds to the written letters that stand for them. One of the most common sounds in English is the short /ă/ vowel sound. Short /ă/ is the sound in the middle of the word *cat*. In this lesson, your student will learn to recognize the short /ă/ sound and combine it with other letters to make words.	<ul><li>Student Learning Pages 1.A–1.B</li><li>alphabet flash cards or alphabet blocks</li><li>1 copy T Chart, page 355</li></ul>

VOCABULARY

BLEND to put parts together

VOWEL one of five letters in the alphabet: *a, e, i, o, u,* and sometimes *y*

Let's Begin

1 **INTRODUCE** Begin the lesson by helping your student focus on the short /ă/ sound. Say the words *map, apple,* and *cat*. Say the words slowly so your student can hear the separate sounds. Then have him or her repeat the sounds and **blend** them to make the words. Then ask, *What sound do you hear at the beginning of* apple? [student should sound out the short /ă/] *What sound do you hear in the middle of* map *and* cat? [student should sound out the short /ă/] *Is it the same sound?* [yes] Challenge your student to say other words he or she knows that have the same /ă/ sound in them. As you go through this lesson, be sure to take as much time as needed until your student feels comfortable with what he or she has learned. You may take a few hours or return to this lesson over the course of a few days—let your student be the guide!

2 **EXPLAIN** Write the letter *a* on a sheet of paper. Explain to your student that the letter *a* is a **vowel.** It's one of the five vowels in the alphabet: *a, e, i, o,* and *u.* Sometimes *y* is used as a vowel. Tell him or her that every English word has at least one vowel in it. Then explain that the letter *a* sometimes stands for the short /ă/

sound in *cat*. Write the word *cat*. Have your student say the word and underline the *a*. Ask, *What kind of alphabet letter is a?* [vowel] Now write the words *tap, pan,* and *ant*. Direct your student to say the words out loud, and then underline the vowel in each word.

3 **PRACTICE** Distribute these alphabet flash cards or alphabet blocks to your student: *a, m, p, t,* and *n*. Have him or her read each letter out loud. Tell your student that he or she can build quite a few words with these letters. Say the word *tap*. Have your student repeat the word. Ask, *What is the first sound?* [/t/] Tell him or her to find the card or block with the letter *t*. Ask, *What is the next sound?* [/ă/] He or she should find *a* and put it to the right of *t*. Ask, *What is the last sound?* [/p/] He or she should put *p* next to *a*. Have your student say *tap*. Then have him or her spell the word: t, a, p. Guide him or her in building some or all of the following words in the same manner: *map, man, tan, pan, mat, pat, an,* and *ant*.

4 **EXPLAIN** Explain that there are lots of words with the short /ă/ sound that rhyme. Write these examples: *hat/cat, nap/cap,* and *fan/man*. Have your student say each pair of words out loud. Invite him or her to say other words that fit into these three word families. Then distribute a copy of the T Chart found on page 355. Write the word *cap* at the head of one column and the word *sat* at the head of the other column. Challenge your student to write as many words as he or she can think of that rhyme with each of these words.

5 **DISTRIBUTE** Distribute Student Learning Page 1.A. Read the directions together. Guide your student as necessary as he or she works through the page.

Branching Out

TEACHING TIP

When helping your student with unfamiliar words, be sure to guide in a noncritical, nonjudgmental manner to encourage positive learning.

CHECKING IN

To assess your student's understanding of the lesson, ask him or her questions about each of these words: *rap, ant,* and *fat*. Ask, *What sounds do you hear at the beginning, middle, and end of the word? What is the vowel in the word? Is the vowel the first sound, middle sound, or end sound? How do you spell the word?*

ENRICH THE EXPERIENCE

Read to your student or listen to recorded children's stories, poems, and songs that use the short /ă/ sound in rhymes. A classic example is *The Cat in the Hat* by Dr. Seuss.

FOR FURTHER READING

Caps for Sale: A Tale of a Peddler, Some Monkeys and Their Monkey Business, by Esphyr Slobodkina (Harper Audio, Book and Cassette Edition, 2000).

Phonemic Awareness Songs and Rhymes, by Wiley Blevins (Scholastic Professional Book Division, 1999).

Phonics Learning Games Kids Can't Resist (*Grades K–2*), by Michelle Ramsey (Scholastic Professional Book Division, 2000).

Match Short *a* Words

PROMOTING LITERACY 1.A

Say each word. Write the correct word under each picture.

h	a	t

p	a	n

a	n	t

c	a	n

1.

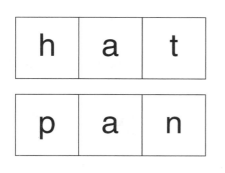

C	A	N

3.

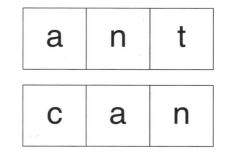

h	a	t

2.

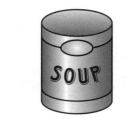

A	N	T

4.

P	A	N

What's Next? You Decide!

Now it's your turn to choose what to do next in the lesson. Read the activities and decide which one you want to do—you may want to try them both!

Draw Pictures with *a*

hat

a MATERIALS

- ❏ several sheets construction paper
- ❏ markers or crayons

a STEPS

Things with *a* in their names are all around you.

- ❏ Find things with *a* in their names.
- ❏ Draw pictures of the things you find on construction paper.
- ❏ Write the name under each thing you draw.

Make a Rhyming Hand

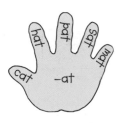

a MATERIALS

- ❏ 1 sheet construction paper
- ❏ markers or crayons

a STEPS

- ❏ Trace your hand on the paper.
- ❏ Write words that rhyme.
- ❏ Write one word on each finger.
- ❏ In the palm, write the "rhyme family," such as –*at*. (The words on the fingers are all members of the same "family.")

Understanding the Short *e*

*Learning vowel sounds will provide your student
with a better understanding of every word!*

OBJECTIVE	BACKGROUND	MATERIALS
To help your student learn to read and write words with the short /ĕ/ sound	Vowels are often difficult letters for students to read because they can't always distinguish the different sounds they make. It's important for your student to understand that vowels can make different sounds, but that they are predictable. In this lesson, your student will learn to recognize the short /ĕ/ sound and read and write words that contain this sound.	■ Student Learning Pages 2.A–2.B ■ 1 egg or 1 picture of an egg ■ 15 index cards ■ 2 shoeboxes ■ 2 paper fasteners

Let's Begin

1 **INTRODUCE** Review with your student the vowels *a, e, i, o,* and *u.* Explain that he or she will be learning about a new vowel today—the vowel *e.* Hold up the egg and invite your student to tell you what it is. Explain that the word *egg* begins with the short /ĕ/ sound. Hold up a sheet of paper with the capital and small letter *e* on it. Invite your student to chant the short /ĕ/ sound and point to the letters.

2 **EXPLAIN** Tell your student that the short /ĕ/ sound can appear at the beginning of a word, such as *egg,* or in the middle of a word, such as *pet.* Invite your student to repeat these words and listen for the short /ĕ/ sound. Then ask him or her to listen to each word you say and decide if it has a short /ĕ/ sound. (Be sure to pronounce all vowels clearly.) If it does, ask your student to stand up and repeat it. If it doesn't, ask your student to remain seated. Provide these words: *cat, elephant, apple, vet, bell, in, red, cot, step, nut, end,* and *den.*

3 **CONNECT** Tell your student that he or she can use the short /ĕ/ sound to form words. Explain that you would like to write the word *men.* Draw three boxes on a sheet of paper. Below them draw an arrow going from left to right. Remind your student that this is the direction in which we read and write words. Ask your student to repeat the word *men.* Ask, *What sound do you hear at the beginning of* men? [/m/] Invite your student to write the letter in the box. Ask, *What sound do you hear next in* men? [/ĕ/] Have

him or her write the letter *e* in the next box. Ask, *What sound do you hear at the end of* men? [/n/] Have him or her fill in the last letter. Repeat this exercise as desired with the words *peg*, *set*, *fed*, and *Ben*.

4 **PRACTICE** Invite your student to play a game to practice using the short /ĕ/ sound. On eight index cards write the letters *b*, *t*, *n*, *y*, *j*, *w*, *l*, and *g*. Place these cards in a shoebox labeled "First Letter." On six more index cards write the letters *n*, *t*, *s*, *g*, *d*, and *b*. Place these cards in a shoebox labeled "Last Letter." Place a card with the letter *e* on the table. Invite your student to form the following words using the letters provided: *bed*, *beg*, *bet*, *ten*, *net*, *yes*, *jet*, *wet*, *web*, *let*, *led*, and *get*. As he or she creates each word, ask your student to point to the letters and blend them to read the word. Then have him or her write simple sentences using rhyming short *e* words.

ENRICH THE EXPERIENCE

Together with your student read some of his or her favorite books. Have him or her identify short *e* words as he or she reads them.

5 **EXPAND** As an additional review of the short /ĕ/ sound, use the letter cards from Step 4 to play a game of Silly or Real? Ask your student to mix up the letter cards in the boxes and select them randomly. Then have him or her create words using the letter *e* and the two selected letters. Ask your student to read the word and decide if it's a real word or a silly word. Or your student can also just choose cards and make nonsense words, which would give you an indication that he or she is paying attention to the letters.

6 **APPLY** Distribute Student Learning Page 2.A. Explain that words with the same letter parts are called word families. Make a copy of the page. Help your student cut out the four circles and connect each pair using a brass fastener. Have him or her turn the bottom circles to form different words. Invite your student to blend and read the word families.

FOR FURTHER READING

Ben's Pens: The Sound of Short E, by Alice K. Flanagan (Childs World, 1999).

Click, Click: Z, X, Short E (*Dr. Maggie's Phonics Readers*), by Margaret Allen (Creative Teaching Press, 1999).

Every Egg: Learning the Short E Sound (*Power Phonics/Phonics for the Real World*), by Lynn Metz (PowerKids Press, 2002).

Branching Out

TEACHING TIP

When learning about the short *e*, your student may become confused about words that have the short /ĕ/ sound with different spellings, such as *said* or *head*. These words might come up while your student is thinking of short *e* words. It's okay to accept these answers without correction, since these words contain the same sound.

CHECKING IN

To assess your student's understanding of the lesson, find some objects around the house whose names have short vowels. Hold up the objects and say the names aloud, and have your student tell you if the name of the object has a short *e*. For additional practice, have him or her write the short *e* words.

Make Word Wheels

Cut out the four circles and connect them. Spin
the wheels to read the words you make!

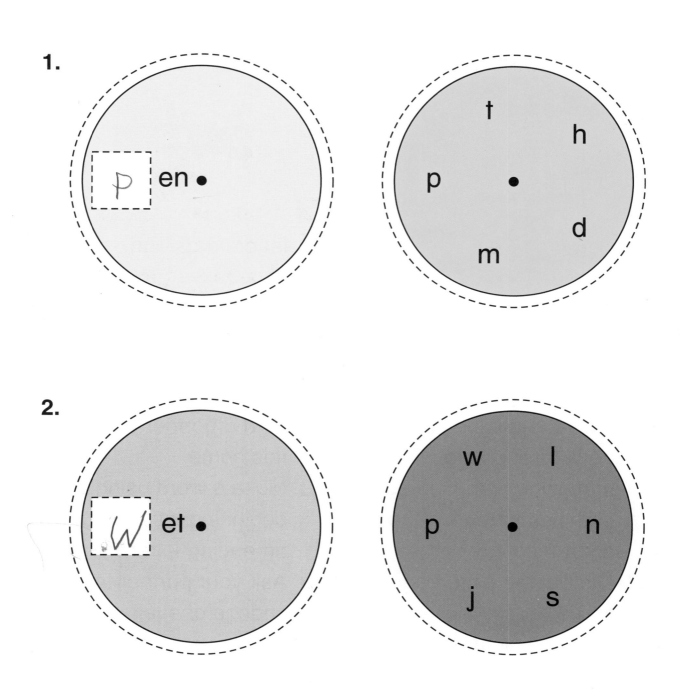

What's Next? You Decide!

Now it's your turn to choose what to do next in the lesson. Read the activities and decide which one you want to do—you may want to try them both!

Make a Short *e* Collage

MATERIALS

- ❑ old magazines
- ❑ 1 pair scissors
- ❑ glue
- ❑ 1 large sheet construction paper
- ❑ markers or crayons

STEPS

- ❑ Draw a big letter *e* on the construction paper.
- ❑ Look through old magazines for pictures of things that have the short *e* sound.
- ❑ Cut out the pictures you find.
- ❑ Glue the pictures on the construction paper.
- ❑ Write each short *e* word below its picture.

Create New Words

jet

MATERIALS

- ❑ letter cards and shoeboxes (from Step 4 in Let's Begin)
- ❑ 4 letter cards (*a, i, o, u*)

STEPS

- ❑ Find a partner to play this game.
- ❑ Make a word using a beginning letter, *e*, and an ending letter.
- ❑ Ask your partner to change one letter to make a new word.
- ❑ Take turns changing letters.

Investigating the Short *i*

Vowel sounds are the foundation for building great words.

OBJECTIVE	BACKGROUND	MATERIALS
To help your student identify and build words with the short /ĭ/ sound	The short *i* can appear at the beginning of a word, such as *inch,* or in the middle of a word, such as *fig.* The short *i* can also be used to build word families with the same letter parts, such as *rim, brim,* and *trim.* In this lesson, your student will learn to recognize the short /ĭ/ sound as well as read and write short *i* words.	■ Student Learning Pages 3.A–3.B ■ 1 copy Writing Lines, page 357 ■ 1 shoebox ■ markers or crayons ■ 2 copies Web, page 356

VOCABULARY
CONSONANTS letters of the alphabet that aren't vowels; *y* can be used as a consonant and vowel

Let's Begin

1 **INTRODUCE** Begin this lesson by writing the letters *b, d, f, g, h, j, k, l, s, t,* and *r* for your student. Have your student say each of these letters out loud. Tell him or her that these letters are called **consonants.** Define a consonant as any letter of the alphabet that isn't a vowel. Next, write the vowel *i* on another sheet of paper and ask your student to say the letter out loud. Remind your student that the letter *i* is one of five vowels. Ask your student to name the five vowels. [a, e, i, o, u]

2 **EXPLAIN** Tell your student that he or she is going to learn about the short /ĭ/ sound. Explain to your student that the short /ĭ/ sound can appear at the beginning of a word, such as *itch,* or in the middle of a word, such as *rip.* Say the words *itch* and *rip* several times while emphasizing the short /ĭ/ sound within each of the words. Ask your student to repeat the short /ĭ/ sound with you. Then help your student blend each letter sound in the word *rip: rrrĭĭĭppp.* Invite your student to repeat the word *rip* three times.

3 **DISTRIBUTE AND PRACTICE** Distribute a copy of the Writing Lines found on page 357. Then tell your student that he or she is going to play a game. Say the words *pet, pig, lift, run, in, up, big, six, dog, pill,* and *hen* aloud. Tell your student that if the

word has a short /ĭ/ sound in it, he or she should repeat the word out loud and write it on the Writing Lines. If the word doesn't have a short /ĭ/ sound, then he or she should say and write nothing. Offer a lot of praise and encouragement throughout the game. Answer any questions your student may have. Then have your student write rhyming sentences with the short *i* words that he or she wrote.

4 **GUIDE** Tell your student that the word *gift* has a short /ĭ/ sound. Explain that he or she is going to make a gift box for short *i* words. Give your student the empty shoebox and crayons or markers. Allow your student time to decorate his or her gift box. Next, help your student brainstorm words with the short /ĭ/ sound. Have your student write each word on individual index cards (possible words include *bib, rib, rim, pig, pill, hill, big, dig, lift, twin, flip, hip, tip, dip, six, sit, fit,* and *clip*). Have your student put the short *i* words into his or her gift box. Invite your student to say each word out loud as he or she places it in the box.

5 **BUILD** Help your student group short *i* words into word families. Give your student two copies of the Web found on page 356. In the center of each Web write: _____*ig* and _____*it*. Then help your student come up with short *i* words that have the letter combinations –*ig* and –*it*. Encourage your student to name some words he or she has learned in the lesson. Also help your student go through various consonants in the alphabet to help him or her form each word family. Ask your student to write the individual words in the surrounding ovals of the correct Web.

6 **REVIEW** Distribute Student Learning Page 3.A. Read the directions and ask your student if he or she has any questions. Allow time for your student to complete the activity.

Branching Out

TEACHING TIP

Tell your student that there is a fun way for him or her to remember the short /ĭ/ sound. Have your student scrunch his or her nose up and make the short /ĭ/ sound over repeatedly.

CHECKING IN

To assess your student's understanding of the lesson, say a word and ask your student to give a thumbs up if the word is a short *i* word and a thumbs down if it isn't a short *i* word. Say the words *sit* [up], *cat* [down], *red* [down], *lip* [up], *still* [up], *ran* [down], *sun* [down], and *rim* [up].

Help Iggy Juggle

Iggy the Clown can only juggle balls with short *i* words. Choose words in the box that have a short *i*. Write the words in the balls. Then color the clown.

win   jump   fox   mix   fish   ship   bug   write

What's Next? You Decide!

Now it's your turn to choose what to do next in the lesson. Read the activities and decide which one you want to do—you may want to try them both!

Make a Short *i* Quilt

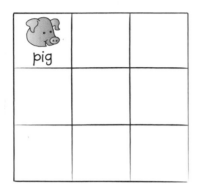

pig

MATERIALS

❑ 1 posterboard
❑ markers or crayons

STEPS

❑ Divide the posterboard into nine boxes with your marker or crayon.
❑ In each box, draw something that has a short *i* in its name.
❑ Write the name of each thing below the picture.
❑ Hang the quilt where people can see it.

Make a Fl*i*pbook

b ill

MATERIALS

❑ 1 sheet yellow paper
❑ 1 sheet green paper
❑ 1 pair scissors
❑ 1 stapler

STEPS

❑ Cut the yellow and green paper into four strips.
❑ Staple the yellow strips to one green strip to make a book.
❑ Write *ill* on the green paper.
❑ Write a different letter on each yellow strip: *b, f, h, w.*
❑ Flip the pages to make different short *i* words.

PROMOTING
LITERACY
LESSON
1.4

Exploring the Short *o*

Short vowel sounds are the building blocks of reading.

OBJECTIVE	BACKGROUND	MATERIALS
To teach your student how to identify the short /ŏ/ sound in reading and writing	In the English alphabet, vowels have many different sounds. Learning short vowel sounds is an important step in helping your student become a successful reader. In this lesson, your student will learn how to read and pronounce the short /ŏ/ sound. Your student will also learn to identify the short /ŏ/ sound in words that he or she hears.	■ Student Learning Pages 4.A–4.B ■ index cards

Let's Begin

1 **EXPLAIN** Review the vowels that your student has studied so far: *a, e,* and *i.* Remind your student that he or she has learned the short sounds for these vowels. Provide examples of words with the short /ă/, /ĕ/, and /ĭ/ sounds. Examples are *cat, set,* and *fit.* Inform your student that in this lesson he or she is going to learn about the short /ŏ/ sound. Write the following words on a sheet of paper: *on, sock,* and *box.* Then pronounce each word as your student repeats after you. Tell your student that the *o* in each word makes a short /ŏ/ sound. Have your student point to the *o* in each word.

2 **PRACTICE** Demonstrate the short /ŏ/ sound for your student. Point out that this vowel sound is made with a slightly open mouth. Be sure to keep the sound short. Don't confuse your student by pronouncing the long /ō/ sound. Repeat the sound over and over. Then have your student join you in pronouncing the short /ŏ/ sound.

3 **INTRODUCE** On a sheet of paper, write several simple words that have the short /ŏ/ sound. Review them with your student by pointing to each letter and sounding it out. For example, use *hop.* Repeat this process using words with which your student is familiar, such as *top* and *hot.* Have your student practice saying these and other words that have a short /ŏ/ sound.

4 **RELATE** Help your student connect the sound of the short *o* with its spelling in simple words. Take apart the word *on.* Write

ENRICH THE EXPERIENCE

The short *o* is all around you. When you're not teaching the lesson, call out the names of everyday household items that have the short /ŏ/ sound. For example, when you're in the kitchen with your student, call out *clock, pot, mop,* and so on. Have your student repeat these words as you say them.

the word on a sheet of paper. With your student identify the two letters in the word *on*. Then break the word into its two sounds, /ŏ/ and /n/. Repeat each sound with your student. Be sure to point to each letter when pronouncing the sound. Then blend the sounds together to say the word: /ŏ/ /n/, *on*. Invite your student to repeat the word several times on his or her own.

5 **BLEND** Expand on the previous step by blending other words that have the short /ŏ/ sound. Begin with the word *dot*. Then identify and review the sound for each letter. Blend the different sounds together: *dddŏŏŏttt*. With your student continue this activity with other short *o* words. Walk your student through a few more examples. Then let him or her try blending words without your help.

6 **BUILD** Help your student build word families that consist of short *o* words. Fold a sheet of paper into three columns. At the top of each column write ＿＿＿＿*ot*, ＿＿＿＿*op*, and ＿＿＿＿*og*. Name different consonants in the alphabet. Challenge your student to decide if the consonants can be added to the letters in each column to make a short *o* word. If so, write each word in the appropriate column. When you are done with the activity, have your student say the words in each column. Listen to be sure he or she pronounces the short /ŏ/ sound correctly.

7 **PRACTICE** Distribute Student Learning Page 4.A. Read the directions to your student and clarify any questions that he or she may have. You may want to read each line of the rhyme before your student works through the page. If you read the rhyme out loud, don't complete the blanks. Just sound out the letters.

Branching Out

FOR FURTHER READING

Hot Pot: The Sound of Short O, by Alice K. Flanagan (Child's World, 1999).

On the Job: Learning the Short O Sound, by Lynn Metz (PowerKids Press, 2002).

Short O and Long O Play a Game, by Jane Belk Moncure (Child's World, 2001).

TEACHING TIP

Come up with some rhymes to help your student learn to identify word families. For example, *I ran and ran for blocks and blocks. I ran so fast, I wore out my socks!* Point out that many rhyming words have the same ending sounds because they end with the same letters.

CHECKING IN

To assess your student's understanding of the lesson, choose a passage from one of his or her favorite stories. Be sure that the passage has several words that have the short /ŏ/ sound. Read the passage out loud. Ask your student to stop you when he or she hears a short *o* word.

Finish the Story Rhyme

Read each line of the rhyme. Fill in the blanks with one of the letters in the box. Then color the picture.

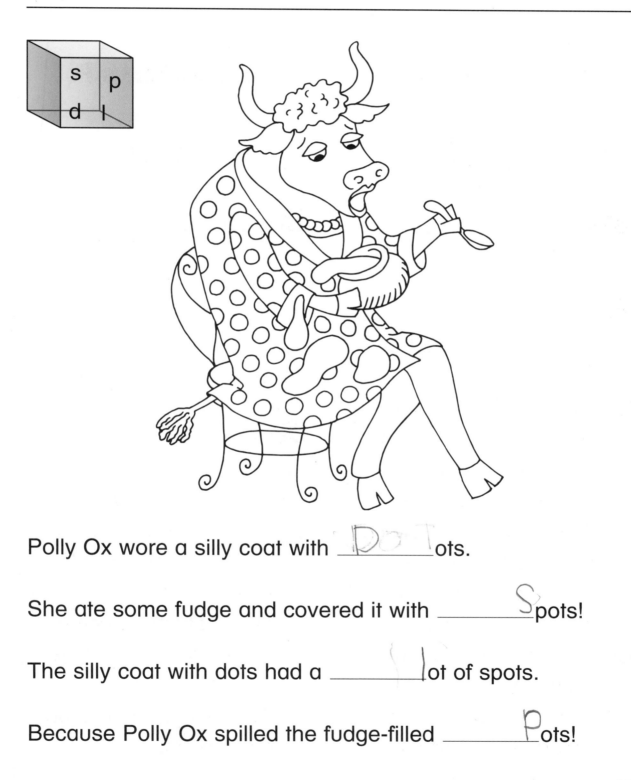

Polly Ox wore a silly coat with ___Do Tots.

She ate some fudge and covered it with ___Spots!

The silly coat with dots had a ___lot of spots.

Because Polly Ox spilled the fudge-filled ___Pots!

What's Next? You Decide!

Now it's your turn to choose what to do next in the lesson. Read the activities and decide which one you want to do—you may want to try them both!

Go on a Short *o* Hunt

 MATERIALS

❏ sticky notes

STEPS

Go on a hunt for short *o* words!

❏ Look around the room.
❏ What are the names of the things you see?
❏ Do the names have a short *o* sound? If they do, write the names on sticky notes. Ask an adult to help you.
❏ Put the sticky note on the thing.
❏ Go into a different room. Try another short *o* hunt!

Make a Short *o* Pot

MATERIALS

❏ several sheets construction paper
❏ 1 pair scissors
❏ glue
❏ markers or crayons

STEPS

❏ Draw a pot on construction paper.
❏ Cut out the pot. Write on the pot "Short *o* Pot."
❏ Draw flowers and stems on construction paper. Cut them out and glue them to the pot.
❏ Write short *o* words on the flowers.

Learning the Short *u*

To make phonics fun, you must jump, hum, and run!

OBJECTIVE	BACKGROUND	MATERIALS
To teach your student to identify, read, and write words that have the short /ŭ/ sound	Your student has learned that every English word contains vowels. He or she has also learned that it's important to recognize vowel sounds when reading and decoding words. In this lesson, your student will practice reading and writing words that have the short /ŭ/ sound.	■ Student Learning Pages 5.A–5.B ■ 1 umbrella ■ 24 index cards ■ 1 copy Writing Lines, page 357 ■ 1 shoebox ■ construction paper ■ crayons or markers ■ 1 copy T Chart, page 355

Let's Begin

1 **EXPLAIN** Tell your student that he or she will be learning about a new vowel sound in this lesson. Hold up an umbrella. Invite your student to tell you what it is. Point out that the word *umbrella* begins with a short /ŭ/ sound. Have your student chant the sound at the beginning of *umbrella*. Remind him or her that this sound may be found in the beginning of words or in the middle of words, such as in *fun*. Invite your student to think of other words that have the short /ŭ/ sound in the beginning and middle letters.

2 **IDENTIFY** Say the following words out loud to your student: *jug, gut, pot, up, fin, hunt, under, cab, ten,* and *fun*. Tell your student to jump each time he or she hears the short /ŭ/ sound. When helping your student with unfamiliar words, remember to do so in a noncritical and nonjudgmental manner.

3 **PRACTICE** Play the following game to practice reading words with the short /ŭ/ sound. Write the following words on index cards and place them in a shoebox: *sun, tub, bug, rug, nut, gum, mug, bun, bus,* and *mud*. Invite your student to select one of the cards. Have him or her blend the letters to say the word out loud. Then ask your student to draw a picture of the word on a sheet of construction paper and write the word below the picture. As your student shows interest in this lesson, you may choose to spend more than a couple of hours on short *u* words and extend the learning over the course of a few days.

PROMOTING LITERACY

LESSON 1.5

4 **DISTRIBUTE AND WRITE** Explain to your student that he or she can write words that contain a short *u* by sounding them out. Act out the word *run*, and ask your student to guess what word you're acting out. Then help him or her write this word. Distribute a copy of the Writing Lines found on page 357. Invite your student to write the letter that he or she hears at the beginning, middle, and end of the word *run*. Repeat this activity with the words *hum*, *rub*, *hug*, and *cut*. Challenge your student to write simple rhyming sentences using these words.

5 **COMPARE** Remind your student that word families consist of words that have the same parts of letters. Write the words *sun*, *fun*, and *run* on a sheet of paper. Invite your student to circle the letters that are the same in all three words. [un] Now write the following words on index cards: *bug*, *lug*, *tug*, *rug*, *mug*, *dug*, *hug*, *but*, *gut*, *cut*, *hut*, *rut*, *nut*, and *jut*. Then distribute a copy of the T Chart found on page 355. At the top of the first column ask your student to write the letters *ug*. At the top of the second column, have him or her write the letters *ut*. Ask your student to sort the word cards by word family and write each word in the correct column. Then ask him or her to blend and read each word.

6 **DISTRIBUTE AND PRACTICE** Distribute Student Learning Page 5.A to your student. Read the directions with him or her. Then assist your student in blending the letters to read each word. Allow time for your student to color each part of the picture.

TAKE A BREAK

If your student seems to be getting tired or restless, take a break and play a version of Simon Says in which your student only acts out words that contain the short /ŭ/ sound. Words that can be used include *run*, *jump*, *tug*, *rub*, *cut*, *hum*, *buzz*, and *drum*.

Branching Out

TEACHING TIP

At this point in the book, your student has learned all five short vowel sounds. To reinforce his or her understanding, review a list of words that contain each short vowel sound. Help your student read and pronounce each example.

CHECKING IN

To assess your student's understanding of the lesson, dictate the following sentence for your student to write: *A bug dug up a nut.* Check to make sure your student spelled the short *u* words correctly.

FOR FURTHER READING

Fun! The Sound of Short U, by Peg Ballard and Cynthia Klingel (Child's World, 1999).

Just Bugs: Learning the Short U Sound (*Power Phonics/Phonics for the Real World*), by Jeff Jones (PowerKids Press, 2002).

Color the Short *u* Words

Color each part of the picture that has a short *u* word.

umbrella

sun

bat

up

cloud

fluff

wet

cut buzz

jump

gum

hug

won

daisy

bud

set

fun

mutt

hit

but

sat

What's Next? You Decide!

Now it's your turn to choose what to do next in the lesson. Read the activities and decide which one you want to do—you may want to try them both!

Write a Poem

MATERIALS

❏ 1 T Chart with word families from lesson

STEPS

Write a poem using your short *u* words!

❏ Choose one of the word families to use in a poem.
❏ Write or say a sentence with one of the words at the end.
❏ Write or say another sentence with a rhyming word at the end.
❏ Keep going until you think your poem is done.
❏ If it doesn't make sense, that's okay—just have fun!

Have Fun with Bugs

Bug Book

MATERIALS

❏ 1 book about bugs
❏ markers or crayons
❏ 1 sheet construction paper

STEPS

❏ Look through a book about bugs. Choose a bug that you like.
❏ How many legs and wings does your bug have?
❏ What is its name?
❏ Draw a picture of the bug that you like.
❏ Share your picture with a friend.

Exploring the Long *a*

Learning words with the long a *will lead to a long vocabulary.*

OBJECTIVE	BACKGROUND	MATERIALS
To teach your student how to identify and pronounce the long /ā/ sound in words	The long /ā/ sound is a common vowel sound in the English language. Many words with the long /ā/ sound also end with a silent *e*. The letter combinations *ai* and *ay* may also produce the long /ā/ sound in some words. In this lesson, your student will practice recognizing the long /ā/ sound. He or she will also practice building long *a* words that follow the consonant-vowel-consonant-*e* pattern.	▪ Student Learning Pages 6.A–6.B ▪ markers or crayons

VOCABULARY
SILENT having no sound

Let's Begin

1 **REVIEW** Tell your student that he or she has learned the short sounds for the vowels *a, e, i, o,* and *u.* Review each sound and ask your student to repeat after you: /ă/, /ĕ/, /ĭ/, /ŏ/, /ŭ/. Say words with these vowel sounds. Examples are *hat, well, fish, mop,* and *bug.* Ask your student to repeat each word after you. Give your student the hint that long vowels say the name of the letter, for example, for *lake,* the vowel sound is /ā/, which is also how we say the letter *a.*

2 **REVEAL** Inform your student that in this lesson he or she will learn the long /ā/ sound. Write the word *ate* on a sheet of paper. Say the word out loud. Ask your student which sound he or she hears at the beginning of the word. [student should sound out the long /ā/ sound] Tell your student that this sound is called the long /ā/ sound. Invite your student to join you in chanting the long /ā/ sound.

3 **EXTEND** Write the words *name* and *race* on a sheet of paper. Say each word out loud. Invite your student to repeat each word after you say it. Ask your student which sound he or she hears in the middle of each word. [the long /ā/ sound] Tell your student that the *a* in each word makes this sound. Then break down the sounds of each letter in the word *name:* /n/ /ā/ /m/.

Ask your student what he or she notices about the sound of the *e* in *name*. [there is no sound] Explain that a letter that is not pronounced is **silent.** Point out that words that have a long *a* and end in a silent *e* usually follow a consonant-vowel-consonant-*e* pattern. Ask your student to point to the vowel, the consonants, and the *e* that form this pattern in the word *name*.

4 **DISTINGUISH** Demonstrate the difference between long /ā/ and short /ǎ/ sounds. Write the word *mad* on a sheet of paper. Have your student sound out each letter in the word: /m/ /ǎ/ /d/, *mad*. Next, add the silent *e* at the end of *mad* to form *made*. Have your student sound out each letter in this word: /m/ /ā/ /d/, *made*. Point out that your student sounded out the same letters in the two words. Ask your student to tell why the words *mad* and *made* don't sound the same. [*mad* has a short /ǎ/ sound, *made* has a long /ā/ sound]

5 **BLEND** Write the word *bake* on a sheet of paper. Identify the sound each letter stands for: /b/ /ā/ /k/. Help your student blend each sound into the next: *bbbāāākkk*. Then invite your student to repeat the word *bake* on his or her own. Next, help your student build word families. Explain that words in the same word family as *bake* all have the letters *a*, *k*, and *e*. Then work with your student to replace the *b* in *bake* with other consonants that would form real words. Challenge your student to come up with one of these words on his or her own. [*cake, lake, make, take,* and so on] Repeat this activity with other consonant-vowel-consonant-*e* words that have the long *a*.

6 **CHALLENGE** Guide your student in making long *a* word jumbles for others to solve. Have him or her choose long *a* words and write the letters in different orders. Then encourage him or her to give the jumbles for someone to solve. For example: e k c a = c a k e. Then have your student choose four long *a* words that he or she learned in the lesson. Have him or her write simple rhyming sentences using the words. Then distribute Student Learning Page 6.A. Explain the directions. Then help your student sound out each word before he or she begins the activity.

Branching Out

TEACHING TIP

Demonstrate how a short *a* word also changes meaning when a silent *e* is added to make it a long *a* word. Show pictures of word pairs such as *cap/cape, plan/plane,* and *man/mane*.

CHECKING IN

Write a list of words that have both the long /ā/ and short /ǎ/ sounds. Read each word out loud. Ask your student to say "Yay!" when he or she hears the long /ā/ sound.

Chase the Cheese

Help the mouse find the path to the cheese!
Color the boxes that have long <u>a</u> words.

start

lake	late	cake	mat	cat
sat	Sam	tale	take	tall
bag	lap	all	made	mad
lag	sack	state	snake	snack
hat	apple	ate	at	snap
as	lack	place	ape	same

What's Next? You Decide!

Now it's your turn to choose what to do next in the lesson. Read the activities and decide which one you want to do—you may want to try them both!

Make a Long *a* Snake

MATERIALS

❏ different colored sheets construction paper

❏ markers or crayons

STEPS

Use long *a* words to make a long snake.

❏ Cut out strips of construction paper.

❏ Think of words that have the long *a* sound.

❏ Write each word on a strip of paper.

❏ Glue the ends of the strips together to make one long strip.

❏ Draw eyes and a mouth for a long *a* snake!

Make a Long *a* Treasure Chest

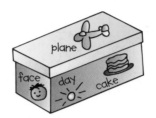

MATERIALS

❏ 1 shoebox with lid

❏ paints

STEPS

❏ Ask an adult to help you find a shoebox with a lid.

❏ Paint and decorate the shoebox and the lid.

❏ Paint long *a* words all over the shoebox.

❏ Keep cards with long *a* words and pictures in the shoebox.

❏ Now you have a long *a* treasure chest.

Examining the Long *e*

A bee, a sneeze, and a tree are things related through the long /ē/ sound!

OBJECTIVE	BACKGROUND	MATERIALS
To help your student recognize the long /ē/ sound and build words with it	Many English words contain the long /ē/ vowel sound. The long /ē/ sound is often found in words that have a silent *e* at the end, such as the first *e* in the word *these*. The long /ē/ sound is also often represented in spelling by the vowel combinations *ee* and *ea*. In this lesson, your student will learn to recognize the long /ē/ sound and associate it with common word families.	<ul><li>Student Learning Pages 7.A–7.B</li><li>alphabet flash cards or alphabet blocks</li><li>1 yellow crayon</li><li>1 copy Web, page 356</li></ul>

Let's Begin

1 **INTRODUCE** Begin the lesson by helping your student focus on the long /ē/ sound. Say the words *he, she,* and *these.* Say the words slowly so your student can hear the separate sounds: /h/ /ē/, *he.* Have him or her repeat the sound segments slowly and then blend them to make the words. It's important to help students with unfamiliar words in a noncritical and nonjudgmental manner. Then ask, *What sound do you hear at the end of* he *and* she? [student should sound out the long /ē/ sound] *What sound do you hear in the middle of* these? [student should sound out the long /ē/ sound] *Is it the same sound?* [yes] Challenge your student to say other words that have the same /ē/ sound in them.

2 **EXPLAIN** Write the words *he, she, be, me,* and *we.* Say each word out loud. Ask your student, *What sound do you hear at the end of each word?* [student should sound out the long /ē/ sound] Explain that the letter e stands for the long /ē/ sound in these words. Then call attention to the pattern of the words. Point out that all these words begin with a consonant and end with a vowel. Have your student underline each vowel and double underline each consonant.

3 **MODEL AND PRACTICE** Use alphabet cards or alphabet blocks to build the word *these.* Say the word slowly and have your student say the word and spell it out loud. Point out that the word pattern is consonant-vowel-consonant-*e.* Ask, *What sound*

> **TAKE A BREAK**
>
> Have your student make up a rhyme that's built around the long /ē/ sound. If he or she is having trouble getting started, read out loud a rhyme from the fun *Ook the Book* by Lissa Rovetch (Chronicle Books, 2001). One of the rhymes in the book, "Eep the Sheep," uses the long /ē/ sound.

does the first e *have?* [long /ē/ sound] *What sound does the second* e *have?* [no sound] Explain that in words with this pattern the first vowel has the long /ē/ sound and the final *e* is silent. Say the words *Steve, Pete,* and *these.* Have your student build these three words with the alphabet cards or blocks. Let your student guide you as to how long to spend on the lesson—you may wish to spend an hour or two, or you may prefer to spend all day learning about long *e* sounds and words!

4 **DISTRIBUTE** Distribute Student Learning Page 7.A next. Read the directions together before your student begins the page.

5 **EXPAND** Explain to your student that there are several long /ē/ word groups or word families. Write these examples: *feed/need, sheep/weep, deal/meal, clean/mean,* and *seat/meat.* Have your student say each pair of words out loud. Ask, *What letters in each pair of words are the same?* [eed, eep, eal, ean, eat]

6 **CHALLENGE** Tell him or her to underline the similar letters in each pair of words from above. Then distribute a copy of the Web from page 356. Have your student choose one of the words from the pairs above and write it in the center of the Web. Help him or her write a word from the same word family in each of the surrounding circles. Guide your student as necessary. For more information on vowel patterns *ee, ea,* and *ie,* go to Lesson 1.12.

7 **INVESTIGATE** Recognize that learning sounds, letters, and words can be challenging. See what works best for your student. Your student may find that hearing and repeating the sound aloud helps, or you may find that it works best to have your student write down letters. You and your student together may find that moving around and pointing and looking at letters makes it easier for him or her to understand phonics. Let your student guide you as to what works best for him or her.

Branching Out

TEACHING TIP

Make learning fun and have your student play "teacher" for the lesson. Have him or her tell you about the long *e* sound and what objects have that sound.

CHECKING IN

To assess your student's understanding of the lesson, observe as he or she completes Student Learning Page 7.A. If you find your student is having difficulties, you may wish to take a break, and then go back through parts of the lesson and be patient as he or she learns about the short *e* sound.

ENRICH THE EXPERIENCE

Encourage your student to walk around your home and find items that have the long *e* sound. For cross-curricular learning, have him or her count the number of items that he or she encounters.

FOR FURTHER READING

Amazing Animals: Level Two: Long-Vowel Sounds (Now I'm Reading), by Nora Gaydos (Innovative Kids, 2001).

Phonics They Use: Words for Reading and Writing (3rd Edition), by Patricia Marr Cunningham (Addison-Wesley Publishing Company, 1999).

Rumpus of Rhymes: A Book of Noisy Poems, by Bobbi Katz (Dutton Books, 2001).

Turn On the Lights!

Look for the windows with long *e* words. Color them yellow to turn on the lights. Start at the bottom and climb your way to the top!

What's Next? You Decide!

Now it's your turn to choose what to do next in the lesson. Read the activities and decide which one you want to do—you may want to try them both!

Make a Word Tree

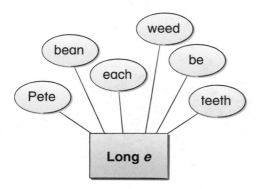

bean

weed

each

be

Pete

teeth

Long e

MATERIALS

❏ 1 sheet construction paper
❏ markers or crayons

STEPS

Make a tree of words that have a long e, such as the word *be.*

❏ Draw a tree trunk. Write "Long e" on the trunk.
❏ Draw circles for leaves.
❏ Write a word with the long e sound in each circle.

Make a Card Game

MATERIALS

❏ 16 index cards
❏ markers or crayons

STEPS

❏ Choose eight long e words.
❏ Write one word on each card.
❏ Make two cards for each word.
❏ Ask a friend to play. Each of you gets four cards.
❏ Play a game like Go Fish.
❏ Make pairs of cards that match.
❏ The first player to make two pairs wins!

Recognizing the Long *i*

Ice cream, kites, and bikes are things a child likes. And learning the long i *brings a way to say these favorite things.*

OBJECTIVE	BACKGROUND	MATERIALS
To teach your student how to recognize the long /ī/ sound and build word families with long *i* vowels	The long /ī/ sound is another common vowel sound in the English language. By understanding the long *i*, your student will be able to build word families with the silent *e*. In this lesson, your student will learn how to identify and pronounce the long /ī/ sound in words. He or she will also build words with a consonant-vowel-consonant-*e* pattern.	■ Student Learning Pages 8.A–8.B ■ crayons ■ 1 audiocassette recorder (optional) ■ 1 audiocassette tape (optional)

Let's Begin

1 **INTRODUCE** Tell your student that in this lesson he or she will learn the long /ī/ vowel sound. To help your student connect this sound to a familiar word, say the word *ice cream*. Tell your student that the beginning sound in this word is a long /ī/ sound. Then invite your student to pronounce the long /ī/ sound in *ice cream*.

2 **REVIEW** Remind your student that he or she has also learned about another sound the vowel *i* can make—the short /ĭ/ sound. Write these words on a sheet of paper: *kit, fin,* and *hid*. Say each word out loud. Sound out each letter in these words: /k/ /ĭ/ /t/, /f/ /ĭ/ /n/, and /h/ /ĭ/ /d/. Then invite your student to pronounce each word after you.

3 **EXTEND** Revisit the short *i* words you reviewed in Step 2. Add an *e* to the end of each word. Write the new words on a sheet of paper: *kite, fine,* and *hide*. Say each word out loud. Sound out each letter as you point to it: /k/ /ī/ /t/, and so on. Tell your student that the *e* at the end of each long *i* word is silent. Remind your student that many words with long vowels follow the consonant-vowel-consonant-*e* pattern. Ask your student to point to the consonants, the vowel, and the *e* in each long *i* word. Then invite your student to alternately pronounce the words with the short /ĭ/ sounds and the words with the long /ī/ sounds: *kit/kite, fin/fine,* and *hid/hide*. Be sure your student is able to clearly distinguish each vowel sound.

4 **BUILD** Remind your student that words in the same word family have the same letter parts. Offer an example, such as the

+

ENRICH THE EXPERIENCE

For research and ideas on teaching phonics, log on to http://teacher.scholastic.com/reading/bestpractices. Click on the Phonics link. This Web site offers features ranging from interactive activities your student can do online to advice from *Instructor* magazine.

words *bite* and *kite*. Point out that these words have both the letters *ite* and the long /ī/ sound. Also point out that the two words rhyme, or have the same ending sounds. Then draw word pies like the ones below on a sheet of paper. In each quadrant, write words that are part of the same long *i* word family. Invite your student to say each word and to underline the letters that are the same in all the words.

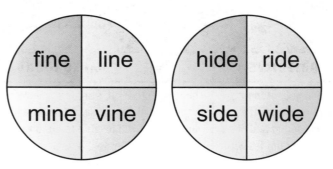

5 **PRACTICE** Distribute Student Learning Page 8.A. Read the directions to your student and assist him or her as needed. Then have your student choose long *i* rhyming words and make simple rhyming sentences. As your student shows interest, encourage him or her to write a poem. You may wish to have him or her make up a poem and tell it aloud to you verbally, and then help him or her write it. Or you can have him or her recite it into a recorder.

Long *i* Haiku
Do you have a dime
To buy five fine limes at nine
While flying a kite?

Branching Out

TEACHING TIP

You might want to point out to your student that one way to remember all long vowel sounds is to think of each letter's name in the alphabet. For example, the long /ī/ sound is the same sound as the name of the letter *i*.

CHECKING IN

Point out different objects in your home and have your student say "i" when you point out something with the long /ī/ sound.

FOR FURTHER READING

The Great Big Book of Fun Phonics Activities, by Claire Daniel, Deborah Eaton, and Carole Osterink (Scholastic, 1999).

Monster Phonics: Special Vowels for Grades 1–2, by Vicky Shiotsu and Lucy Helle, ill. (Lowell House Juvenile, 2000).

Answer the Long *i* Riddles

Use the pictures to answer the riddles. Then write the missing letters in each word.

1. Rhymes with *time*

D i m e

2. Rhymes with *like*

B i k e

3. Rhymes with *nice*

M i c e

4. Rhymes with *bite*

K i t e

What's Next? You Decide!

Now it's your turn to choose what to do next in the lesson. Read the activities and decide which one you want to do—you may want to try them both!

Make a Long *i* Line

MATERIALS

❏ 1 long length clothesline or thick string
❏ markers or crayons
❏ several sheets construction paper
❏ clips for hanging clothes

STEPS

❏ Hang a clothesline or string across a room in your home. Ask an adult to help you.
❏ Name some things with a long *i*.
❏ Draw pictures of those things on sheets of construction paper.
❏ Use the clips to hang the sheets on the clothesline.

Make a Rhyming Rainbow

MATERIALS

❏ 1 sheet construction paper
❏ markers or crayons

STEPS

❏ Draw a rainbow in different colors.
❏ Think of three long *i* words that rhyme.
❏ Write the words in one color of the rainbow.
❏ Do this again for other long *i* words that rhyme.
❏ Draw things around the rainbow.
❏ Make your picture fun!

PROMOTING
LITERACY

LESSON
1.9

Investigating the Long *o*

Learning the long /ō/ sound opens doors to reading and writing.

OBJECTIVE	BACKGROUND	MATERIALS
To teach your student how to recognize the long /ō/ sound as well as build long *o* word families	Another long vowel sound produced by words that follow the consonant-vowel-consonant-*e* pattern is the long /ō/ sound. The letter pairs *oa* and *ow* may also produce the long /ō/ sound in some words. (Your student will be familiar with the *ow* sound in *cow.*) In this lesson, your student will learn to pronounce and identify the long /ō/ sound. He or she will also build words with a consonant-vowel-consonant-*e* pattern.	■ Student Learning Pages 9.A–9.B ■ several sheets construction paper ■ 1 pair scissors ■ tape ■ 1 copy T Chart, page 355

Let's Begin

1 **INTRODUCE** Tell your student that in this lesson he or she will learn a new vowel sound—the long /ō/ sound. Say the word *old.* Invite your student to repeat the word after you. Then sound out each letter in the word while stretching out the vowel *o:* /ō/ /ō/ /ō/ /l/ /d/. Ask your student which sound he or she hears at the beginning of the word *old.* [/ō/] Tell your student that this vowel sound is the long /ō/ sound. Then lead your student in chanting the long /ō/ sound. As you work through the lesson, let your student's needs guide you as to how long to spend on the activities. You may only need to take an hour, or you may find you'd like to spend more time.

2 **BUILD** Tell your student that other words with a long /ō/ sound have the letters *old.* Help your student add different consonants to *old* to build words with the same letter and sound pattern. Write down the following words and say them out loud: *cold, fold, hold, sold,* and *told.* Then sound out each letter to help your student blend each sound into the next: /c/ /ō/ /l/ /d/. Invite your student to repeat the sounds after you. Then have your student pronounce the word on his or her own. Repeat this exercise with each word you listed in the *old* word family. Remember to help your student with any unfamiliar words in a noncritical and nonjudgmental manner.

3 **REVIEW** Remind your student that he or she also learned the short /ŏ/ sound. Write the words *not* and *hop* on a sheet of construction paper. Tell your student that each of these words

has a short /ŏ/ sound. Then sound out each letter in the two words while stretching out the short vowel *o:* /n/ /ŏ/ /ŏ/ /ŏ/ /t/ and /h/ /ŏ/ /ŏ/ /ŏ/ /p/. Invite your student to repeat after you as you sound out each word.

4 **EXTEND** Show your student the sheet of construction paper with the words *not* and *hop*. Then add an *e* at the end of each word to form *note* and *hope*. Sound out each letter and then say each word as your student repeats after you: /n/ /ō/ /ō/ /ō/ /t/, *note*, and /h/ /ō/ /ō/ /ō/ /p/, *hope*. Ask, *What sound does the o make in these words?* [/ō/] Ask, *What sound does the e make?* [no sound] Remind your student that some words with a long vowel sound have a consonant-vowel-consonant-*e* pattern, with a silent *e*. As a review, ask your student to tell you what a consonant is. [a letter that isn't a vowel] Invite your student to point to the consonants in the words *note* and *hope*.

5 **PRACTICE** Cut circles out of construction paper to look like *o*'s. Write these words on each circle: *box, go, no, hot, mop,* and *rope*. Tape the circles to a wall in an area where your student can reach them. Ask your student to say each word out loud. Instruct him or her to take the circle down if the word has a long /ō/ sound. Have your student say "No long *o*!" if the word has a short /ŏ/ sound.

6 **EXPLAIN** Tell your student that some words with the letters *oa* and *ow* have the long /ō/ sound. Use a copy of the T Chart found on page 355. Write the heading "ow" in the left column of the chart and list these words: *low, bow, grow, snow,* and *row*. Next, write the heading "oa" in the right column and list these words: *oat, boat, coat,* and *soap*. Ask your student to read out loud each word listed. Guide him or her as needed. Then have your student choose rhyming long *o* words and make simple rhyming sentences.

7 **PRACTICE** Distribute Student Learning Page 9.A. Read the directions to your student. Be sure your student understands how to carry out the activity. Point out that one example has been done for him or her.

Branching Out

TEACHING TIP

Change some of the words of "Row, Row, Row Your Boat" to help your student practice the long /ō/ sound. For example, "Row, row, row your boat slowly through the snow. Joe, Moe, Flo, and Bo grow cold as their boats go!"

CHECKING IN

Write sentences that have long *o* words. Read each sentence with your student. Then invite your student to circle the words that have the long /ō/ sound.

Help Bo Find His Long *o* Words

Bob took Bo's long *o* words. Find the long *o* words in Bob's box. Cross them out of Bob's box. Write the words in Bo's box.

rope   Boat

oPen   cold

rope	stop
hot	open
boat	cold
mop	ox

What's Next? You Decide!

Now it's your turn to choose what to do next in the lesson. Read the activities and decide which one you want to do—you may want to try them both!

Make a Long *o* Coat

MATERIALS

❑ 1 posterboard
❑ markers or crayons

STEPS

Make a coat with long *o* words.

❑ Draw a person in a long coat on the posterboard.
❑ Draw pockets all over the coat.
❑ Write a long *o* word on each pocket.
❑ Color the coat.
❑ Show your family your new long *o* coat!

Play the Long *o* Toss

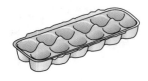

MATERIALS

❑ 1 empty egg carton
❑ 1 marker
❑ 1 penny
❑ 1 pair scissors

STEPS

❑ Ask an adult to cut the lid off an empty egg carton.
❑ Ask the adult to write a different long *o* word inside each cup.
❑ Put the egg carton on the floor.
❑ Toss a penny into the carton.
❑ Which cup did it land in? Say the long *o* word!

Exploring the Long *u*

The wonders of language begin with phonics.

OBJECTIVE	BACKGROUND	MATERIALS
To help your student recognize long /ū/ sounds and build words with them	The long *u* in English can be pronounced in two ways. In some words the long *u* is pronounced /yo͞o/, the sound in *use*. The long *u* can also be pronounced /o͞o/, the sound in *tube*. In this lesson, your student will learn to recognize long /ū/ sounds and associate them with word families and spelling patterns.	■ Student Learning Pages 10.A–10.B ■ 8 index cards ■ 1 copy T Chart, page 355

Let's Begin

1 **INTRODUCE** Begin the lesson by helping your student focus on the two long /ū/ sounds. First, say the word *tube* slowly so he or she can hear the separate sounds: /t/ /o͞o/ /b/. Have him or her repeat the sound segments slowly. Then ask, *What sound do you hear in the middle of* tube? [student should make the /o͞o/ sound] Explain that this vowel sound is called the long *u*. Then repeat the process with the word *use*. Ask, *What sound do you hear at the beginning of* use? [student should make the /yo͞o/ sound] Explain that the long *u* can also sound like the *u* in *use*. Challenge your student to say other words that have the long /ū/ sound in them. As your student learns unfamiliar words, remember to guide in a nonjudgmental and noncritical manner to encourage positive learning.

2 **EXPLAIN** Write the words *rude* and *flute*. Point to each word as you say it out loud. Ask, *What sound do you hear in the middle of each word?* [student should make the /o͞o/ sound] Explain that the letter *u* makes the long /ū/ sound in these words. Now write the word *cube*. Ask, *What sound do you hear in the middle of this word?* [student should make the /yo͞o/ sound] Explain that the letter *u* also makes the long /ū/ sound in this word. Have your student write each of these three words and underline the letter *u* in each. Then have him or her say each word in a sentence, emphasizing the long /ū/ sound.

3 **PRACTICE** Provide an opportunity for your student to practice recognizing long *u* words. Prepare eight index cards. Write each of these words on a card: *tape, huge, robe, use, hide, rule, cute,*

A BRIGHT IDEA

Read aloud one of your student's favorite books (make sure it has long *u* sounds). Have him or her call out each time he or she hears a long *u* sound.

and *pale*. Give your student one card at a time. Have him or her say the word and spell it out loud. If the word has the letter *u* in it, he or she should keep the card. If the word doesn't have a *u* in it, he or she should give the card back.

4   **EXPLAIN AND DISTRIBUTE**   Write the word *cute.* Explain that a lot of the long *u* words in this lesson have the same spelling pattern as *cute*. The pattern is consonant-vowel-consonant-*e*. Guide your student to write *cute* letter by letter. When he or she has written the letters *c-u-t,* tell him or her to pause and say the word. [*cut*] Ask, *Is the* u *sound in* cut *a long* /ū/ *sound?* [no] Then have him or her write the *e* at the end of the word and say the completed word. [*cute*] Ask, *Is the* u *sound in* cute *a long* /ū/ *sound?* [yes] *What sound does the* e *at the end have?* [no sound] Explain that the silent *e* at the end of a word means the *u* has the long /ū/ sound. Distribute Student Learning Page 10.A. Then read the directions together before your student begins the page.

5   **EXPAND**   Explain that there are several word families or patterns of letters that have a long *u* in them. To help your student recognize these patterns, prepare a copy of the T Chart found on page 355. In the first column write these words in a list: *flute, mule, tune, cube,* and *rude.* In the second column write these words in a list: *crude, dune, tube, cute,* and *rule.* Then give the copy to your student. Tell him or her to draw a line from each word in the first column to the word in the second column that has the same pattern of letters. Have him or her underline the letter patterns that match in each pair. [flute/cute, mule/rule, tune/dune, cube/tube, rude/crude]

Branching Out

TEACHING TIP

Make up some sentences that have several words with the long /ū/ sound. For example, *Lucy tuned the flute and tuba.* Then invite your student to repeat the sentences several times out loud. Pronouncing a series of similar vowel sounds will help your student master fluency in speaking.

CHECKING IN

To assess your student's understanding of the lesson, say the words *mule, use, cube, tune,* and *flute.* Have him or her write each word, say the word out loud, and underline the vowel that represents the long /ū/ sound.

ENRICH THE EXPERIENCE

Choose a book that your student knows well and read it out loud. Tell him or her to listen carefully to how you say the words, and stop you if you say a word incorrectly. Whenever you come to a word with a silent *e,* such as *kite,* say the word without the *e* (*kit*). Let your student correct you. See how quickly he or she can catch your mistakes.

FOR FURTHER READING

Phonics Pathways (8th Edition), by Delores G. Hiskes (Dorbooks, 2000).

Short U and Long U Play a Game, by Jane Belk Moncure (Child's World, 2001).

Uu: Sandcastle 3—Long Vowels, by Mary Elizabeth Salzmann (Sandcastle, 2000).

Build Long *u* Words

Read each picture name. If the name should have the letter *e* at the end, write the *e*.

1.

flut*e*

2.

tub*e*

3.

cub *e*

4.

cub

5.

tub

6.

mul *e*

What's Next? You Decide!

Now it's your turn to choose what to do next in the lesson. Read the activities and decide which one you want to do—you may want to try them both!

Write a Long *u* Book

MATERIALS

❑ 4 sheets construction paper
❑ markers or crayons

STEPS

Write a funny book of long *u* words!

❑ Fold the construction paper in half to make a book.
❑ Write a long *u* word on each page.
❑ Draw a funny picture for each word.
❑ Give your book a funny name. Write it on the front.

The Cute Cube

Make a Mule Puzzle

MATERIALS

❑ 1 sheet cardboard
❑ construction paper
❑ crayons
❑ glue
❑ 1 pair scissors

STEPS

Make a picture puzzle of a mule.

❑ Draw a mule on construction paper.
❑ Paste the mule picture to the cardboard and let dry.
❑ Cut the cardboard picture into seven pieces. Make sure to cut each piece in a different shape.
❑ See if a friend can put your puzzle together!

Using *ai* and *ay*

The vowel pairs ai *and* ay *are used each day, and they're
another way to make the sound long* a*!*

OBJECTIVE	BACKGROUND	MATERIALS
To help your student explore how the long /ā/ sound can be written as the vowel pairs *ay* or *ai,* and to build words with *ay* and *ai*	The long /ā/ sound—the vowel sound in the words *ate* and *cake*—is represented by the written letter *a*. The long /ā/ sound can also be represented by the vowel pairs *ay* and *ai*. In this lesson, your student will learn to associate the vowel pairs *ay* and *ai* with the long /ā/ sound and will use these vowel pairs to build words.	■ Student Learning Pages 11.A–11.B ■ 1 copy T Chart, page 355 ■ 8 index cards

Let's Begin

1 **REMIND AND EXPLAIN** Remind your student that the first sound in the word *ate* and the middle sound in the word *cake* are examples of the long /ā/ sound. The single letter *a* represents the long sound in these words. Ask him or her to say other words in which the letter *a* represents the long *a* sound. Then write the word *may.* Say the word out loud and point to *ay.* Explain that at the end of words, *ay* has the sound of long /ā/. In this pair of letters, the vowel *a* has the long sound, and the letter *y* is silent. Write *play* and *say.* Ask your student to say the words slowly and underline the *ay* pairs. Challenge your student to say other words that have *ay* at the end. If you find that *ai* and *ay* words are challenging for your student, be sure to take enough time going through the lesson. You may wish to spend a couple of hours or go back to it over the course of a few days. Let your student be the guide.

2 **EXPLAIN AND DISTRIBUTE** Write the word *wait.* Underline *ai* and explain that the vowel pair *ai* also represents the long /ā/ sound. The *a* has the long sound and the *i* is silent. Write the words *rain, mail, paid,* and *bait.* Have your student underline the vowel pair in each word and say each word out loud. Ask, *What letter in each word represents the long sound?* [*a*] Then tell him or her to cross out the letter that's silent in each word. Ask, *Which letter did you cross out in each word?* [*i*] Distribute Student Learning Page 11.A. Read the directions together before your student begins the activity.

Your student may enjoy learning the memorable lyrics to "The Rain in Spain," a song from the classic musical *My Fair Lady*. Explain to him or her that in the song a language teacher is helping a girl learn to pronounce English words. You can find the lyrics to the song at http://www.stlyrics.com. Your student may also enjoy learning to sing the song. Check your local library for an audiocassette or compact disc of the movie's soundtrack.

FOR FURTHER READING

Hands-On Phonics Activities for Elementary Children, by Karen Meyers Stangl (Jossey-Bass, 1999).

Phonics Through Poetry: Teaching Phonemic Awareness Through Poetry, by Babs Bell Hajdusiewicz (Goodyear Publishing Company, 1998).

A Poem a Day (Grades K–3), by Helen H. Moore (Scholastic Trade, 1999).

3 **EXPLAIN** Tell your student that there are several word families and letter patterns that have *ay* and *ai* in them. Remind your student that words in the same word family often rhyme, such as *rain/train* and *may/play*. Ask your student to say other words that fit into these two word families. Then distribute a copy of the T Chart found on page 355. Write the word *rain* at the head of one column and the word *may* at the head of the other column. Challenge your student to write as many words as he or she can think of that rhyme with each of these words.

4 **EXPLORE** Talk with your student about familiar rhymes that include *ay* and *ai* words. A rhyme that he or she may know is: *Rain, rain, go away, / Come again some other day, / Little Johnny wants to play*. Discuss the long /ā/ sounds and how the words are spelled. Then have your student write a rhyme of his or her own using the *ay* and *ai* word families. Provide guidance as necessary. Encourage him or her to say the rhyme out loud to make sure the words rhyme.

5 **EXPAND** Discuss with your student the difference between the short /ă/ sound and the long /ā/ sound. Say these two words out loud: *pal* and *pail*. Have your student say the words slowly, focusing on the different vowel sounds. Then write the two words. Ask, *What is the difference in spelling between* pal *and* pail? [*pail* has an *i* in it] Then prepare a word game. Write the following pairs of words on index cards. Write one word on each side of a card: *ran/rain, pad/paid, mad/maid, bat/bait, lad/laid, pan/pain, man/main,* and *pal/pail*. Show your student one side of a card. Have him or her read the word and say it out loud. Then your student should guess the word on the back of the card and spell it. Give your student one point for every correct answer.

Branching Out

TEACHING TIP

Make sure your student understands that reading involves paying attention to the meaning of the words, not simply sounding out letters to blend words. Every so often, ask your student to tell you what a word means. Also, encourage him or her to guess what new words mean from their context in sentences.

CHECKING IN

To assess your student's understanding of the lesson, observe as he or she completes Student Learning Page 11.A. If you find that your student is having trouble, review portions of the lesson. Remember to help him or her with unfamiliar words in a noncritical and nonjudgmental manner.

Discover Long *a* Words

Read each clue. Complete the word that fits the clue. Use *ay* or *ai* to spell the word.

1. It moves on tracks

tr __a i__ n

2. Do things for fun

pl __a y__

3. One part of a week

d __a y__

4. Water from the sky

r __a i__ n

5. Letters in the post office

m __a i__ l

6. Horses eat it

h __ay__

7. What *ai* words did you write that rhyme?

train rain

8. What *ay* words did you write that rhyme?

hay day

What's Next? You Decide!

Now it's your turn to choose what to do next in the lesson. Read the activities and decide which one you want to do—you may want to try them both!

Make a Bookmark

MATERIALS

- ❏ 1 sheet cardboard
- ❏ markers or crayons
- ❏ 1 pair scissors

STEPS

- ❏ Draw a bookmark on the cardboard. Cut out the bookmark.
- ❏ Write *ay* and *ai* words on both sides of the bookmark.
- ❏ Color the bookmark with markers or crayons.
- ❏ Use your bookmark the next time you read!

Make a Comic Strip

MATERIALS

- ❏ 1 sheet paper
- ❏ newspaper comics
- ❏ glue
- ❏ 1 pair scissors

STEPS

- ❏ Cut out pictures in newspaper comics.
- ❏ Paste the pictures on the paper.
- ❏ Write a funny story about the pictures using words that have a long *a.*

 Ray got mail.

 The mail was from Mr. Snail.

 He wrote Ray to say good day.

Comprehending *ee*, *ea*, and *ie*

Words with vowel pairs can make long /ē/ sounds.
In bee, beat, *and* believe *this sound abounds!*

OBJECTIVE	BACKGROUND	MATERIALS
To help your student associate the vowel pairs *ee*, *ea*, and *ie* with the long /ē/ sound and build words with *ee*, *ea*, and *ie*	The long /ē/ sound is represented by the written letter *e*. The long /ē/ sound can also be represented by the vowel pairs *ee* and *ea*. A few irregular words with the vowel pair *ie*—such as *chief*—are also pronounced with the long /ē/ sound. In this lesson, your student will learn to identify long *e* words with the vowel pairs *ee*, *ea*, and *ie*. He or she will also build words using these three vowel pairs.	■ Student Learning Pages 12.A–12.B ■ alphabet flash cards or alphabet blocks ■ 1 copy Web, page 356 ■ 17 index cards

VOCABULARY
VOWEL PAIR two vowels next to each other in a word

Let's Begin

1 **REMIND** Tell your student that in this book he or she has learned that the vowel sounds in the words *he, feed, me*, and *deal* are examples of the long /ē/ sound. Say the four words slowly. Have your student repeat the sight words and emphasize the long /ē/ sound in each word. Ask, *Which words have the long /ē/ sound at the end?* [*he, me*] *Which words have the long /ē/ sound in the middle?* [*feed, deal*] Then write the words and have him or her underline the letters that represent the long /ē/ sound. Combining phonics concepts with usage of sight words can aid in developing your student's reading capabilities. Then ask your student to say other words that have the long /ē/ sound.

2 **REVIEW** Write the words *need, see*, and *keep*. Point out that the **vowel pair** *ee* represents the long /ē/ sound. Remind your student that when these two letters are together in a word, the first *e* is usually the long *e*. The second *e* is silent. Say some or all of the following words one at a time: *speed, teeth, green, bee, tree*, and *wheel*. Say aloud other *ee* sight words that he or she is familiar with, such as *feet, meet, beep*, and *sleep*. Have your student write each word and underline the vowel pair. Then have him or her write three sentences using three of the *ee* words he or she just wrote.

3 **PRACTICE** Distribute these alphabet flash cards or alphabet blocks to your student: *e, e, d, p, w, h,* and *s.* Tell your student that together you are going to build some words with the vowel pair *ee.* Say the word *deep.* Have your student repeat the word. Ask, *What is the first sound?* [/d/] Tell him or her to find the card or block for *d.* Ask, *What is the next sound?* [/ē/] *What letters represent that sound?* [ee] Your student should put *e* and *e* to the right of *d.* Ask, *What is the last sound?* [/p/] He or she should put *p* next to *ee.* Have your student spell the word and say it out loud. In the same manner guide him or her in building some or all of the following words: *weed, seed, see, sheep, sweep,* and *speed.*

4 **REVIEW** Remind your student that the vowel sound in the word *deal* is the long /ē/ sound. Write the words *peach, seat,* and *meal.* Point out that the vowel pair *ea* represents the long /ē/ sound. Remind him or her that when these two letters are together in a word, the first vowel, *e,* has the long /ē/ sound. The second vowel, *a,* is silent. Say some or all of the following sight words one at a time: *real, clean, teach, wheat, bean,* and *eat.* Then give your student clues to arrive at these other sight words: *heat, neat, dream,* and *meat.* Have your student write each word and underline the vowel pair. Now have him or her write a sentence using each word.

5 **PRACTICE** Have your student fill in the missing *ea* vowel pair in a series of words. Write the list of words below on a sheet of paper. Write the words with letters missing as shown. Have your student fill in the vowel pair to build each word. Then challenge him or her to tell the meaning of each word.

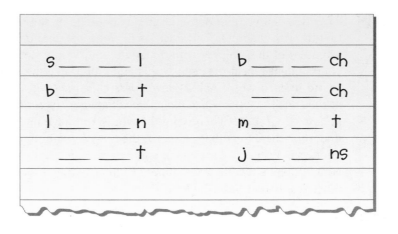

6 **EXPLAIN** Say the word *chief.* Ask, *What vowel sound do you hear in the word* chief? [/ē/] Write the word *chief.* Point to the vowel pair *ie* and underline it. Explain that the word *chief* doesn't follow the rule about vowel pairs. In the word *chief,* the second vowel (the *e*) has the long /ē/ sound. The first vowel (the *i*) is silent. Remind your student that usually the first vowel has the long vowel sound and the second vowel is silent. Write these four

words that are also exceptions to the rule: *belief, field, piece,* and *believe.* Ask your student to say the words slowly and then spell them. Have him or her underline the *ie* vowel pair in each word. Then have your student use each of the words in sentences.

7 **REINFORCE** To help your student remember the *ie* word exceptions, distribute a copy of the Web found on page 356. Have him or her write the word *chief* in the center of the Web. Say the following words one at a time: *brief, field, believe, piece,* and *belief.* Tell him or her to write a word in each of the circles. Ask, *How are the words in the circles the same as the word* chief? [all have the letters *ie* and the long /ē/ sound] Then challenge your student to spell the words out loud. Have him or her turn the paper facedown. Say each word and have your student spell it. After each word, have your student turn the paper over and check his or her spelling.

8 **REVIEW** Play a game with your student called Match the Vowel Pair. Use index cards to make 12 playing cards. Write one of the following words on each card: *queen, teeth, cheek, wheel, peach, bean, wheat, clean, field, believe, piece,* and *belief.* Then prepare two identical three-column charts (one for each player) with these column heads: "feed," "deal," and "chief." Shuffle the cards. To play the game, players take turns drawing one card at a time. A player writes the word he or she picked in the correct column of the chart. Continue drawing cards and writing words in the correct columns. The first player to write three words in each column wins.

9 **DISCUSS** Talk to your student about the difference between the short /ĕ/ sound and the long /ē/ sound. Say these two words out loud: *bet* and *beat.* Have your student say the words slowly and focus on the different vowel sounds. Write the two words. Ask, *What is the difference in spelling between* bet *and* beat? [the word *beat* has an *a* in it] Then use index cards to make a word game. Write the following pairs of words on the cards, with one word on each side of a card: *fed/feed, step/steep, set/seat, men/mean,* and *bed/bead.* Show your student the short *e* side of a card. Have him or her read the word and say it out loud. Then ask your student to guess the long *e* word on the back of the card and spell it.

10 **EXPLAIN** Tell your student that one way to figure out which word belongs in a sentence is to see how it fits with other words. Write this sentence for your student: "She will _____ us in the park." Ask, *Which word belongs in this sentence,* meet *or* meat? [meet] Discuss the different meanings of *meet* and *meat.* Then write this sentence: "Lily found a _____ on the

ENRICH THE EXPERIENCE

Show your student how to use a dictionary to check the spellings of words with vowel pairs. If your student hasn't used a dictionary before, introduce him or her to a picture dictionary. A beginner's book is *Richard Scarry's Best Picture Dictionary Ever* by Richard Scarry (Golden Books Publishing Company, 1998). Or your student might prefer *The Oxford Picture Dictionary* by Norma Shapiro and Jayme Adelson-Goldstein (Oxford University Press, 1998). Be sure to point out the part of a dictionary entry that shows how to pronounce the word.

bus." Ask your student whether *set* or *seat* fits the sentence. [*seat*] Invite your student to talk about how he or she knew which word fit.

11 **EXTEND** Invite your student to practice the concept he or she studied in Step 10. Write some or all of the following sentences and the related word choices. Have your student write the correct word in each blank.

Billy goes to _____ early each night. (*bed, bead*)
The little _____ flew around the flower. (*be, bee*)
Grandpa found a _____ growing in the garden. (*beat, beet*)
The sailboat moved on the _____. (*see, sea*)
I asked Mom for a _____ of pie. (*piece, peace*)
The _____ were carrying a big box. (*men, mean*)

12 **CHALLENGE** Challenge your student to write a poem or a set of simple rhyming sentences using some of the words he or she learned today. Encourage him or her to draw pictures to accompany his or her writing.

13 **DISTRIBUTE** Distribute Student Learning Page 12.A. Read the directions together before your student begins. Give guidance as necessary as he or she completes the page.

Branching Out

FOR FURTHER READING

Clifford the Big Red Dog Phonics Fun (Scholastic Trade, 2002).

Sheep in a Jeep, by Margot Apple (Houghton Mifflin Company, 1999).

The War Between the Vowels and the Consonants, by Priscilla Turner (Farrar, Straus, and Giroux, 1999).

Wool Gathering: A Sheep Family Reunion, by Lisa Wheeler (Atheneum, 2001).

TEACHING TIP

When you are reading a sentence to your student that includes words with vowel pairs, omit those words from the sentence. Then invite your student to complete the sentence with the correct word. Reading and hearing words in context will help your student learn how to spell and use words with vowel pairs.

CHECKING IN

To assess your student's understanding of the lesson, say the following words and have your student write them: *speed, meal, green, brief, lean,* and *field.* Then have your student pronounce the words and underline the vowel pairs that represent the long /ē/ sound.

Build Words with
ee, *ea*, and *ie*

Read the story. Complete each word. Write the
letter pairs *ee*, *ea*, or *ie* on each line to make
the word.

1. I saw a little, white sh_____p playing in

    a f___ie___ld.

2. It danced on grass that was soft and

    gr_____n.

3. Then the sheep sat on a s_____t beneath

    a tr_____.

4. Surprise! It pulled a big, round p_____ch

    off the tree!

5. "Yummy," said the sheep. "What a fine

    m___ee___l!"

6. Do you bel_____ve my story?

What's Next? You Decide!

Now it's your turn to choose what to do next in the lesson. Read the activities and decide which one you want to do—you may want to try them both!

Play a Flashlight Game

MATERIALS

❑ 3 sheets cardboard
❑ 1 flashlight

STEPS

❑ Write the vowel pair *ee* in big letters on one sheet of cardboard.
❑ Write the vowel pairs *ea* and *ie* on the other two sheets of cardboard.
❑ Line up the three sheets of cardboard on the floor.
❑ Turn off the lights.
❑ Shine the flashlight on a card. The other player says a word with those letters in it.
❑ The player who says the most words wins!

Make Word Puzzles

MATERIALS

❑ 6 index cards
❑ markers or crayons
❑ 1 pair scissors

STEPS

Make word puzzles with *ee, ea,* and *ie.*
❑ Write a word on each index card.
❑ Color the cards with markers or crayons.
❑ Cut each word apart in a zigzag way.
❑ Mix up the pieces.
❑ Try to fit the words back together!

Discovering Poetry

*The poet is not unlike the painter, except
the poet creates images with words!*

OBJECTIVE	BACKGROUND	MATERIALS
To have your student identify, read, and write poetry	Poetry is considered the most expressive form of writing. Poems often describe strong feelings and include vivid words that help readers create images in their minds. Poems are usually organized into lines called stanzas. Poems may have words that rhyme or they may not. In this lesson, your student will learn some of the characteristics of poetry. Your student will also write his or her own poem.	<ul><li>Student Learning Pages 13.A–13.B</li><li>1 Dr. Seuss book, such as *Green Eggs and Ham, Hop on Pop,* or *The Cat in the Hat* (or any rhyming poem or tale)</li><li>1 sheet drawing paper</li><li>markers or crayons</li></ul>

Let's Begin

1 **INTRODUCE** Begin this lesson by reading out loud a Dr. Seuss book to your student. If you don't have a Dr. Seuss book, read a rhyming poem or tale to your student. Ask your student how what you've just read is different from other books he or she has read. [student may say that the words are silly or that the words sound the same, or rhyme]

2 **DISTRIBUTE** Tell your student that he or she is going to read a poem in this lesson. Explain that poems usually have words that help readers see pictures in their minds. Then distribute Student Learning Page 13.A.

3 **EXPLAIN** Tell your student that some poems have rhyming words and some poems don't. Share that the poem he or she is going to read has words that rhyme. Be sure your student understands that most rhyming words have the same ending sounds, such as *run/fun, cat/hat, can/fan,* and *race/face.* Ask your student to share examples of words that rhyme.

4 **GUIDE** Have your student hold up his or her pointing finger. Tell your student that this finger is his or her reading finger. To help your student match sounds to printed words, have him or her point to each word using the reading finger. Point out the title of the poem. Then ask your student to put his or her reading finger on the first word of the title.

PROMOTING LITERACY

LESSON 1.13

5 **READ** Read the poem three different ways. Invite your student to move his or her reading finger along the words as you read out loud. Next, have your student do the same thing as you both read the poem together. Finally, have your student read the poem out loud by himself or herself. Actively assist your student while he or she is reading. Remember that having a relaxed and positive approach is a key factor in helping your student become a confident reader.

6 **EXPLORE** Invite your student to explore how words in the poem describe things. Ask, *What pictures did you see in your mind from the words in the poem?* Invite your student to draw some of his or her images using markers or crayons on a sheet of drawing paper.

TAKE A BREAK

Tell your student that many poems are sung as songs. Join hands and sing "Ring Around the Rosey" while moving in a circle.

7 **IDENTIFY** Have your student identify rhyming words in the poem. [possible answers: *snow/go/slow/know; said/sled/Fred/head*] Have your student underline rhyming words that are part of the same word family. Remind your student that words in the same word family have the same letter parts. Then ask your student to tell you which vowel sounds he or she hears in the rhyming words. [long *o*, short *e*, short *a*, short *i*]

8 **WRITE** Invite your student to write his or her own rhyming poem. Tell your student that his or her poem should be four lines long. Give your student time to write the poem. When your student is done, have him or her read the poem to you.

9 **EXPAND** Suggest to your student that he or she write longer (or shorter) poems about his or her favorite animal, favorite food, favorite things to do on a rainy day, or about anything he or she likes. Be sure to allow enough time for self-expression of his or her ideas. Encourage your student to get creative and silly. Remember not to be critical or judgmental about his or her ideas, which can diminish your student's enthusiasm for learning!

FOR FURTHER READING

A Child's Book of Poems, by Gyo Fujikawa, ill. (Michael Friedman Publishing Group, 2002).

The Complete Tales and Poems of Winnie the Pooh: The 75th Anniversary of Winnie the Pooh, by A. Milne and Ernest H. Shepard, ill. (Penguin Putnam Books for Young Readers, 2001).

Writing Poetry with Children, by Jo Ellen Moore and Marilyn Evans, eds. (Evan-Moor Educational Publishers, 1999).

Branching Out

TEACHING TIP

Make reading and writing a natural part of your student's day by having regular at-home story times, taking trips to the library, reading words out loud, listening to story tapes, and writing notes.

CHECKING IN

To assess your student's understanding of the lesson, ask him or her to tell you how a poem is different from other types of writing, such as a story.

Enjoy a Poem

Fred's Sled*
by Kenn Nesbitt

"Snow! Snow!"
Fred said.
"Let's go!
Let's sled!"

"Go slow,"
Mom said.
"I know,"
said Fred.

Fred ran
in shed.
Had plan.
Grabbed sled.

Up hill
went Fred.
Down hill
Fred sped.

*This is an excerpt taken from the complete poem.

What's Next? You Decide!

Now it's your turn to choose what to do next in the lesson. Read the activities and decide which one you want to do—you may want to try them both!

Make a Rhyme Book

MATERIALS

- ❏ construction paper
- ❏ markers or crayons
- ❏ 1 length ribbon

STEPS

- ❏ Write each line of a poem you wrote on a sheet of paper.
- ❏ Draw and color a picture for each line.
- ❏ Write the poem's title on another sheet of paper.
- ❏ Make a hole in the top left corner of each sheet of paper.
- ❏ Put a ribbon through the holes and tie the pages together.

Act Out a Poem

MATERIALS

- ❏ 1 poem

STEPS

- ❏ Find a poem you like.
- ❏ Read the poem together with an adult.
- ❏ Act out different lines of the poem.
- ❏ Don't say the words!
- ❏ Ask the adult to guess which lines you're acting out.
- ❏ Now ask the adult to act out a line in the poem.
- ❏ Guess which line he or she is acting out.
- ❏ Now do it again with another poem.

Enjoying Fiction

Now is the perfect time to promote a love of reading in your student!

OBJECTIVE	BACKGROUND	MATERIALS
To help your student read and enjoy a fiction story	After spending a lot of time learning phonics, your student may be feeling the desire to read independently. It's important to help your student approach this goal with a friendly and fun attitude. As your student reads, encourage him or her to enjoy the story as well as understand the words. In this lesson, your student will read a fiction story and summarize the story's most important ideas.	<ul><li>Student Learning Pages 14.A–14.C</li><li>1 sheet paper</li><li>markers or crayons</li></ul>

Let's Begin

1 **INTRODUCE** Explain to your student that in this lesson he or she will be reading a story. Guide your student as necessary, remembering to help him or her with unfamiliar words in a noncritical, nonjudgmental manner. Then distribute Student Learning Page 14.A. Read the title out loud to your student. Invite him or her to repeat it after you. Then ask your student to begin reading out loud with you. Tell your student that many of the words have vowel sounds that he or she has learned in past lessons. Invite your student to sound out the letters of the words as he or she reads. Also encourage your student to look for familiar words so as to increase his or her confidence.

2 **EXPLAIN** Tell your student that stories have a beginning, a middle, and an end. Ask your student to think about what happens at the beginning, middle, and end of his or her day. Point out that stories work the same way. Ask your student to point to the beginning of *Bat's Surprise* and explain what happened. [Bat wants help to make something of his own] Repeat this exercise with the middle and end of the story. [Bat asks everyone to help him in the middle, but no one will; at the end, Bat surprises everyone by making something of his own]

3 **IDENTIFY** Explain that many stories demonstrate how things happen. For example, something a person does can make something else happen. To help your student understand cause-and-effect relationships, ask questions about details in the story, such as *Why did Bat ask for help?* [he wanted to make

+

ENRICH THE EXPERIENCE

Remember to make reading a frequent part of your student's life. Plan library trips, encourage him or her to listen to stories on audio recordings, read familiar words on signs and in magazines, and have a regular story time.

something] *Why did Bat make something on his own?* [no one would help him]

4 **COMPARE AND CONTRAST** Ask questions that help your student compare and contrast. Identifying how things are similar and different will help your student understand story details. Ask, *How is Bat like the others in the story?* [he wants to make something] *How is he different?* [he never made anything before] *How are the others in the story the same?* [they all make something] *How are they different?* [they all go to different places to make something]

5 **SUMMARIZE** Explain to your student that a summary tells the most important parts of a story. Point out that a summary usually tells about the animals and people in the story. Then it tells the problem in the story and how it's solved. Ask your student to summarize *Bat's Surprise* in his or her own words. Then have him or her write a few simple sentences describing the story.

6 **DISCUSS** Write each of the following words on a sheet of paper: *said, help, hello, the, day, have,* and *what.* Point to each word as you read it, and invite your student to repeat it after you. Explain that each of these words occurs more than once within the story. Ask your student to review the story and underline each of the words. Then invite him or her to use each word in a sentence.

7 **PRACTICE** Distribute Student Learning Page 14.B. Invite your student to review the story's sequence of events visually. Have your student draw a picture for the beginning, middle, and end of the story.

Branching Out

TEACHING TIP

It's important that your student view reading as an enjoyable experience. If he or she becomes frustrated with sounding out words, help your student blend letter sounds. If possible provide audio recordings of your student's favorite stories to help him or her connect sounds to letters.

CHECKING IN

To assess your student's understanding of the lesson, find another fiction story at his or her reading level. Read it with your student. Then invite him or her to identify what happened at the beginning, middle, and end of the story.

Read a Story

Bat's Surprise

by Kelli C. Foster and Gina C. Erickson

"How can I make something of my own?" said Bat.

"I need help. I must get help."

"Hello, Pug. Hello, bugs. Can you help me?"

"No," said Pug. "You must make something of your own."

The bug club ran to the old red rug to make something.

(CONTINUED)

And Bat sat.

"Hello, Lop. Hello, Pop. Can you help me?"

"No," said Pop and Lop. "We must make something of our own."

Pop and Lop went to the shop to make something.

And Bat sat and sat.

"Hello, Ned, Ted, and Jed. Can you help me?"

"No, Bat," they said. "You must make something of your own."

Ned, Ted, and Jed ran to the shed to make something.

And Bat sat and sat and sat.

(CONTINUED)

Yes, all day long Bat sat. Trish, Pat, Ed, and Rat all saw Bat.

They would not help him. They all ran to make something of their own.

Swish, slop, trim, chug, drop, plop, splat, tug.

Day in and day out Bat sat.

"Hello, Bat. The day is here. Come see what we have made."

"Yes," said Bat. "Let's see what *we* all have made."

Lop, Pop . . .

Nat, Ned . . .

Pug, Trish . . .

Pat, Ed . . .

(CONTINUED) ▶

The fat Rat, Jed, Ted . . .

Slim Jim and what?

Surprise! Bat made something . . .

"Bat, how did you make something of your own?"

"We saw you sit day in and day out."

"I had help from all of you."

Draw the Story

Draw pictures showing what happens in *Bat's Surprise.*

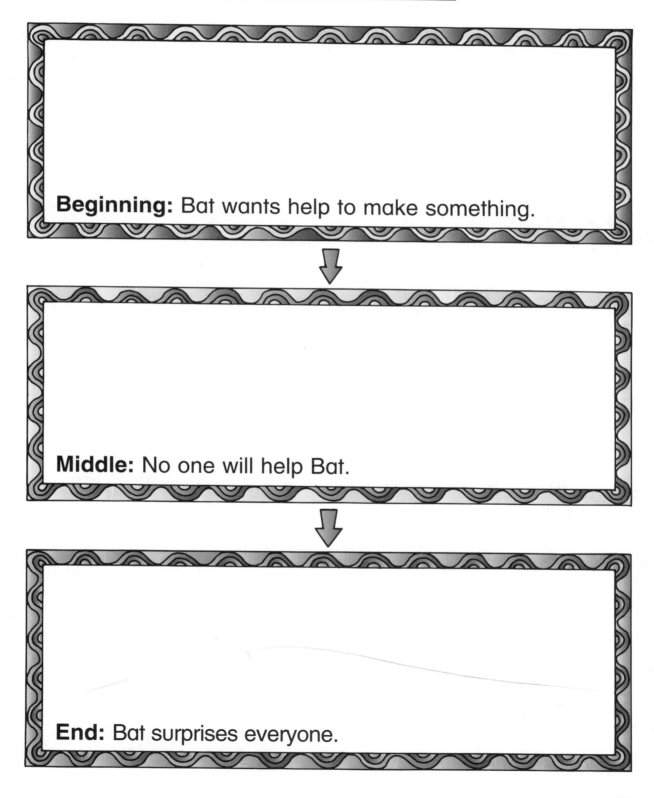

Beginning: Bat wants help to make something.

Middle: No one will help Bat.

End: Bat surprises everyone.

What's Next? You Decide!

Now it's your turn to choose what to do next in the lesson. Read the activities and decide which one you want to do—you may want to try them both!

Tell a Story

❑ MATERIALS

- ❑ 1 audiocassette recorder (optional)
- ❑ 1 audiocassette tape (optional)

❑ STEPS

- ❑ Practice telling a favorite story out loud.
- ❑ Then share your story with family and friends using an audiocassette recorder.
- ❑ Ask an adult to help you record your story if you'd like.
- ❑ Now ask your family and friends to tell you some stories.

Make a Book Cover

Bat's Surprise

❑ MATERIALS

- ❑ 1 folder
- ❑ markers or crayons

❑ STEPS

Make a book cover for *Bat's Surprise.*

- ❑ Write the story title on the front of the folder.
- ❑ Draw a picture for the story, too.
- ❑ On the back of the folder, write why you like the story.
- ❑ Put the pages of *Bat's Surprise* in the folder with other stories you like.

Reading Tall Tales

Stretch your imagination—read a tall tale!

OBJECTIVE	BACKGROUND	MATERIALS
To have your student use various reading strategies to understand a tall tale	Tall tales are stories that aren't true. Tall tales usually feature main characters who have exaggerated or superhuman qualities. These characters often have a specific task or goal in the story. Most tall tales include problems that are solved in an unrealistic way. In this lesson, your student will practice using different reading strategies. He or she will also learn about the characteristics of tall tales.	■ Student Learning Pages 15.A–15.C

VOCABULARY

TALL TALE a fictional story that has a main character with exaggerated abilities

STEED a horse

PRISTINE original; clean

TUMBLEWEED a plant that breaks off and is blown by the wind

BULLDOGGED thrown

BUCKAROOS cowboys

REQUEST something that is asked for

Let's Begin

1 **INTRODUCE** Begin by writing the following words from this lesson's story on a sheet of paper: *best, West, Pecos Bill, Tess, twister,* and *mess.* Since they appear in the story frequently, work with your student to make sure he or she is familiar with these words before focusing on the selection. Tape the sheet of paper on a wall where your student can see it. Ask your student to point to each word and repeat it after you. Next, ask your student to read the words by himself or herself. Be sure your student is comfortable pronouncing the short /ĕ/ and short /ĭ/ sounds in the words. As a review, invite your student to tell which words rhyme or are part of the same word family. [*best/West* and *Tess/mess*]

2 **DISTRIBUTE** Tell your student that he or she is going to read a type of story called a **tall tale.** Explain that tall tales are made up. Also point out that the most important person in a tall tale is usually able to do things that people can't do in real life. Explain that exaggeration in a fictional tale is for entertainment

and is not considered a lie as it would be in real life. Then distribute Student Learning Page 15.A. Review the boldfaced terms with your student before beginning. Have him or her say each word. Remember to help your student with unfamiliar words in a noncritical, nonjudgmental manner.

3   **READ**   Read the story as your student reads along with you. Assist your student with any words he or she doesn't know by explaining their meanings and helping him or her sound them out. Provide encouragement and praise as your student reads. If he or she becomes frustrated while reading the story, consider reading it dramatically or singing part of it to foster a fun, relaxed approach. Remember to take as much time as needed with the lesson. As your student shows interest in tall tales, you may wish to complete the lesson in one or two sittings, or you may prefer to read more tales and return back to the lesson's activities over the course of a week or so.

4   **SEQUENCE**   Distribute Student Learning Page 15.B. Read the directions with your student. Then read out loud each sentence before your student begins. Be sure your student understands how to put the events of the story in order.

5   **REVEAL**   Reveal to your student that the tall tale he or she read includes compound words. Explain that a compound word is a word made by joining together two smaller words, such as *cowboy*. Say aloud other compound words that your student would be familiar with, such as *cupcake, butterfly, popcorn, football,* and *campground*. Write them down for your student to see. Then say them aloud with your student as you point to the words. Have your student think of other compound words. Encourage him or her to look around the house for hints (such as *bathtub* or *mailbox*). Then point out the compound words in the story. Encourage him or her to choose a favorite book and tell you which words are compound words.

6   **SUMMARIZE**   Remind your student that a summary tells the most important parts of a story. Invite your student to use the completed Student Learning Page 15.B to summarize the story in his or her own words.

Branching Out

TEACHING TIP

Help your student appreciate the oral tradition of tall tales. Read out loud another tall tale during an at-home story time.

CHECKING IN

To assess your student's understanding of the lesson, ask your student to suppose he or she is Pecos Bill and act out the story. Remind your student of any events he or she leaves out of the demonstration.

? DID YOU KNOW?

Settlers who lived in the American wilderness first shared tall tales. People gathered to tell each other stories as a means of entertainment after a long, hard day of work.

FOR FURTHER READING

The Complete Book of Reading: Grades 1 and 2 (American Education Publishing, 2001).

Jack and the Beanstalk, by Albert Lorenz (Harry N. Abrams, 2002).

Discover a Tall Tale

Pecos Bill Cleans Up the West

Now, everyone knows Pecos Bill was the best,
The neatest cowboy in all the West.

One day, Bill was riding the range on Tess,
The fastest and smartest **steed** in the West,
When he saw a most unwelcome guest.

It was a twister,
Picking up litter and dust and trash,
And plumb making a mess
Of the entire West.

(CONTINUED)

Pecos Bill was the best,
The best in the West.

Bill said to Tess, "I must confess,
If there's one thing I detest, it's a mess!"

Tess knew that meant Bill wouldn't rest
'Til he'd put that twister under arrest,
Or tamed that blustery, gusty pest
That was messin' up the **pristine** West.

Pecos Bill was the best,
The best in the West.

Bill started to ride, astride his steed,
Through the dust and the tumbling **tumbleweed,**
Swinging his lasso over his head,
On his quest to stop that twister dead.

Tess sprang with the springiest spring
That was ever sprung.
Bill flung his lasso with the flingiest fling
That was ever flung.

(CONTINUED)

And Bill whooped, "Whoa!"
To that whirling wind, until
It stopped, like a **bulldogged** steer, stock still.

Pecos Bill was the best,
The best in the West.

And with old Tess holdin' that twister steady,
Bill jumped on its back, and he got himself ready,
And then old Pecos Bill was sent on
The wildest ride that anyone ever went on!

(CONTINUED)

Well, **buckaroos,** you can guess the rest of it.
That twister knew Bill had got the best of it.
And so, at Pecos Bill's **request,**
It cleaned up the mess it had made of the West.

Pecos Bill was the best,
The best in the West.

And easy as you please, that tame twister
Started dumping every last little bit of litter
Into trash cans, not forgetting
To separate out all the recyclables.

Pecos Bill was the best,
The best in the West.

Write Story Events in Order

The sentences tell what happens in "Pecos Bill Cleans Up the West." They aren't in the correct order, however. Write the sentences in the correct order on the lines.

Pecos Bill makes the twister clean up the litter.

A twister makes a mess of the West.

Pecos Bill rides Tess.

Pecos Bill puts his lasso around the twister.

1. _____

_____

_____

2. _____

_____

_____

3. _____

_____

_____

4. _____

_____

_____

What's Next? You Decide!

Now it's your turn to choose what to do next in the lesson. Read the activities and decide which one you want to do—you may want to try them both!

Tell Tall Tales

MATERIALS

- ❑ 1 brown paper bag
- ❑ 12 index cards

STEPS

Make up your own tall tales!

- ❑ Think of 12 different words.
- ❑ Write each word on one index card.
- ❑ The words should name people, places, animals, and things.
- ❑ Put the index cards in the brown paper bag.
- ❑ Pull out three cards from the bag.
- ❑ Make up a tall tale that has the three words.
- ❑ Make the tall tale as silly as you want!

Tell About Pecos Bill

MATERIALS

- ❑ 1 sheet construction paper
- ❑ markers or crayons

STEPS

Write another story about Pecos Bill.

- ❑ Think of the other people or things that are in your story.
- ❑ What does Pecos Bill do in the story?
- ❑ Write four sentences.
- ❑ Draw a picture for your story.
- ❑ Share your Pecos Bill story with family and friends!

Comprehending Words with *s* Blends

Study s *blend words to get a scope of spelling that sticks!*

OBJECTIVE	BACKGROUND	MATERIALS
To help your student recognize words with *s* blends and build words that begin with them	Many words have consonant blends—consonants that are used together to make a "blended" sound when they are pronounced. In this lesson, your student will learn to identify words with *s* blends. He or she will also build words that begin with *sc, sk, sl, sm, sn, sp, st, sw, scr,* and *str*.	■ Student Learning Pages 16.A–16.B ■ several magazines ■ 1 children's dictionary ■ 8 index cards ■ markers or crayons

Let's Begin

1 **INTRODUCE** Tell your student that many words begin with the letter *s* and another consonant. Remind your student that a consonant is any letter that isn't a vowel. Write the word *sky* on a sheet of paper. Ask your student to name the two consonants at the beginning of *sky*. Then sound out each letter in the word: /s/ /k/ /ī/. Invite your student to say the word *sky* after you. Then ask your student which sound the letters *s* and *k* make. [/sk/] Help your student isolate the sound of the *sk* blend by stretching the individual sounds of the two consonants: /s/ /s/ /s/ /k/ /k/ /k/. Invite your student to repeat the blended sound.

2 **EXPLAIN** Write the word *scarf* on a sheet of paper. Say the words *scarf* and *sky* out loud. Ask, *Do the words* scarf *and* sky *begin with the same sound?* [yes] Then show your student the sheet of paper with *scarf* and *sky*. Ask, *Do both words begin with the same letters?* [no] Explain that many words that begin with the letters *sc* also have the /sk/ sound. Now say more sight words that have the letters *sc*, such as *scale, score,* and *scare*. Hold the /sk/ sound as you say each word. Then ask your student to say each word after you. Then identify the /skr/ sound and say the words *scrap* and *scrape*. Write these sight words on the sheet of paper and show your student how they begin with the letters *scr*.

3 **SORT** Draw a large three-column chart on a sheet of paper. Label the columns with these headings: "sl," "sm," and "sn." Show your student each heading and tell him or her that many

TAKE A BREAK

Let your student be the guide as to how fast or slow to go through the lesson. You may wish to complete it in an hour, or you may prefer to take breaks and return to it periodically.

words begin with these letters. Write each of the following words in the correct column: *sled, small,* and *snow.* Say each word out loud while stretching the initial blend sounds: *ssslll, sssmmm,* and *sssnnn.* Invite your student to say each word on his or her own. Next, say the sight word *smile* out loud. Ask your student to point to the word in the chart that begins with the same sound. Then write the word *smile* in the correct column. Repeat this exercise with the words *slow* and *smart.* Then continue with a different set of *s* blends.

4 **EXPLAIN** Tell your student that just as some words begin with the letters *sk, sp,* and *st,* they can end with those letters, too. Write the words *mask, clasp,* and *list* on a sheet of paper. Say each word out loud while stretching the final *s* blend sounds, such as *lĭsssttt.* Invite your student to sound out the letters in each word after you. Repeat this exercise with other final *s* blend words, such as *mist, fast, wasp, grasp, desk,* and *task.*

5 **REVIEW** Be sure to review with your student commonly used sight words that have *s* blends, along with the phonics instruction, which can boost your student's reading skills. Encourage your student to write simple sentences using *s* blend words that he or she learned in the lesson.

6 **BUILD** Distribute Student Learning Page 16.A. Explain the directions to your student. Invite him or her to build *s* blend words. Read clues that your student might not understand out loud. Guide your student through each item as needed.

Branching Out

TEACHING TIP

Be sure your student understands the difference between silent letters and blended letters. Explain that each letter in a blend still has a sound even though it's mixed with the sound of another consonant. You may want to show your student the dictionary pronunciation of a word with a silent letter and a word with an *s* blend.

CHECKING IN

Write each of these *s* blends on separate index cards: *sc, sk, sl, sm, sn, sp, st,* and *sw.* Then slowly call out words with each of these blends. After you say each word, have your student point to the index card that shows the correct *s* blend. You may want to have your student choose from three index cards at a time to simplify the activity.

FOR FURTHER READING

Letters and Sounds, by Rosemary Wells (Puffin Books, 2001).

Space Race, by Judith Bauer Stamper and Jerry Zimmerman, ill; phonics activities by Wiley Blevins (Scholastic, 1998).

Wow! I'm Reading!, by Jill Frankel Hauser (Williamson Publishing, 2000).

Build *s* Blend Words

Write letters in the boxes to make words.
Use the clues.

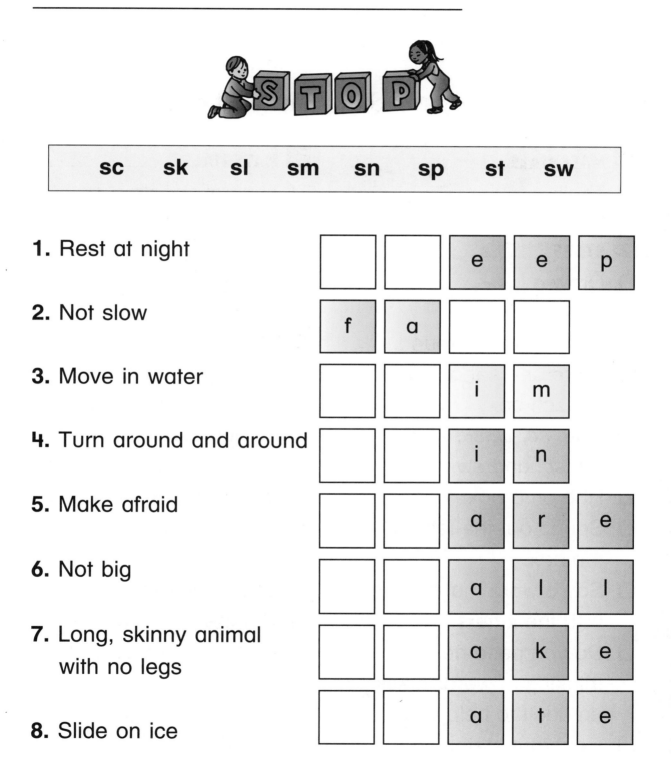

sc	sk	sl	sm	sn	sp	st	sw

1. Rest at night

		e	e	p

2. Not slow

f	a		

3. Move in water

		i	m

4. Turn around and around

		i	n

5. Make afraid

		a	r	e

6. Not big

		a	l	l

7. Long, skinny animal with no legs

		a	k	e

8. Slide on ice

		a	t	e

What's Next? You Decide!

Now it's your turn to choose what to do next in the lesson. Read the activities and decide which one you want to do—you may want to try them both!

Play *s* Blend Hopscotch

a **MATERIALS**

❑ chalk

a **STEPS**

❑ Draw a hopscotch board on the ground.

❑ Write one set of letters in each box.

❑ Use: *sc, sl, sk, st, sm, sn, sp,* and *sw.*

❑ Hop on a box.

❑ Sound out the letters in the box.

❑ Say a word that begins with the letters.

❑ Do you need help thinking of words? Ask an adult to help you.

❑ Repeat the steps for all the boxes.

	sw	
sn		sp
	sm	
sk		st
	sl	
	sc	

Make an *s* Blend Catalog

a **MATERIALS**

❑ several sheets construction paper

❑ markers or crayons

❑ 1 stapler

a **STEPS**

Suppose you have a store that only sells things with *s* blend names.

❑ Draw pictures of things in your store. Write the name of each thing.

❑ Use a separate sheet of paper for each picture.

❑ Put the pages of your catalog together. Make a cover, too.

❑ Staple the pages together. Ask an adult to help you.

Using Words with *r* Blends

Without r *blends, some wods just don't wok!*

OBJECTIVE	BACKGROUND	MATERIALS
To help your student recognize words with *r* blends and build words that begin with them	Initial consonant blends are two or more consonants at the beginning of a word, such as in *bread* and *track*. Their sounds are blended when the word is pronounced. Many of these words have an initial consonant blended with *r*. In this lesson, your student will learn to identify words with *r* blends. He or she will also build words that begin with *br, cr, dr, fr, gr, pr,* and *tr*.	■ Student Learning Pages 17.A–17.B ■ 1 copy T Chart, page 355 ■ 8 index cards

VOCABULARY
BLENDED mixed

Let's Begin

1 **INTRODUCE** Begin the lesson by helping your student focus on the /r/ sound. Say the word *tap* slowly so your student can hear the separate sounds. Ask, *What sounds do you hear in the word* tap? [/t/ /ă/ /p/] Then say the word *trap* slowly. Ask, *What sounds do you hear in the word* trap? [/t/ /r/ /ă/ /p/] *What is the difference between the two words?* [the word *trap* has an /r/ sound in it] Have your student repeat the word *trap*. Point out that the *t* and *r* are **blended** together. This means they make a sound that's different from the sound of *t* by itself or *r* by itself. Repeat the same question-and-answer pattern with these word pairs: *fog/frog, tip/trip,* and *fee/free*. Challenge your student to say what words are formed when *r* is added to these words: *tick* and *tail*.

2 **EXPLAIN** Tell your student that many words begin with a consonant blended with *r*. Say these words slowly, emphasizing the consonant and /r/ sounds: *bridge, crop, drink, front, great, print,* and *track*. Have your student repeat the word and then say just the initial consonant plus /r/ sound. Next, write the words. Have your student underline the consonant + *r* blend in each word. As you continue through the lesson, remember to incorporate commonly used *r* blend sight words with the phonics instruction. Combining both methods can boost reading abilities.

3 **EXPLAIN** Write these *r* blends in a list for your student: *br, cr, dr, fr, gr, pr,* and *tr*. Explain to your student that many *r* blend

TAKE A BREAK

Teach your student some tongue twisters with *r* blends. For example, have your student say, *Friendly Frank freezes fruit on Friday.* Or he or she can say, *Brother brushes brown bricks.* Encourage your student to make up his or her own tongue twisters!

words begin with these letters. Then write each of these words next to the *r* blend it matches: *brick, crow, drag, frost, grape, press,* and *truck.* Have your student sound out each consonant + *r* blend and then say the word that begins with that blend.

4 **PRACTICE** Prepare a copy of the T Chart found on page 355. List the words in the columns shown below. Then give the copy to your student. Tell him or her to draw a line from each word in the first column to the word in the second column that has the same *r* blend. Have your student underline the letter patterns that match in each pair. Then distribute Student Learning Page 17.A. Explain the directions before your student begins.

brave	crown
creek	true
drop	drum
friend	bread
green	fruit
proud	present
track	grade

5 **EXPLORE** Tell your student that sometimes two or more words have the same letters except for the beginning consonant + *r* blends. An example is *free* and *tree.* Then prepare eight index cards. Write a word part on each card: *br, cr, dr, tr, own, ain, ag,* and *ead.* Help your student move the cards around to make words. Then have him or her select a few words and write simple sentences using the words.

Branching Out

FOR FURTHER READING

It Grows in Spring: Learning the GR Sound, by Autumn Leigh (PowerKids Press, 2002).

Phonics Practice Readers: Series B, Set 3: Blends (Modern Curriculum Press, 2001).

Ready, Set, Read!, by Jean Feldman (Crystal Springs Books, 1999).

TEACHING TIP

Your student should be stretching out words as he or she pronounces sounds and blends. If your student has trouble saying words slowly enough, try this: Say the word slowly yourself and have your student say it fast. Then reverse roles—he or she says the word slowly and you say it fast. Remember to guide him or her in a noncritical, nonjudgmental manner.

CHECKING IN

To assess your student's understanding of the lesson, say the following words one at a time: *trap, free, bridge, crib, drop, greet,* and *print.* Have him or her write the consonant + *r* blend that begins each word. Then have him or her use each blend to write a new word.

Write *r* Blend Words

Unscramble the letters to make *r* blend words.
Write the words on the lines.

1. i t r u f

2. u k t c r

3. m u r d

4. w c o r

Crow

5. r o c n w

6. g r o f

What's Next? You Decide!

Now it's your turn to choose what to do next in the lesson. Read the activities and decide which one you want to do—you may want to try them both!

Play Clues in a Hat

It has leaves.

MATERIALS

❑ 1 pair scissors
❑ 1 hat

STEPS

❑ Cut strips of paper.
❑ Write a clue for an *r* blend word on each strip.
❑ Fold the strips and put them in a hat.
❑ A player takes a clue and says the answer.
❑ Here's one to start.
   Clue: *It has leaves.*
   Answer: *tree*

Make a Menu

MATERIALS

❑ 1 sheet construction paper
❑ markers or crayons

STEPS

Make a menu. Pretend your restaurant only has *r* blend foods!

❑ Write a list of foods that start with *r* blends.
❑ Put these words on your menu: *bread, cream, fruit, grains,* and *grapes.*
❑ Add more foods that start with *r* blends.
❑ Draw pictures of the foods.
❑ Color your menu.

Identifying Words with *l* Blends

Learning words with l *blends will help you name
things such as . . . well,* l *blends!*

OBJECTIVE	BACKGROUND	MATERIALS
To help your student identify words with *l* blends and build words that begin with them	Your student has learned that many words have consonants that make blended sounds. Words with *l* blends include a consonant followed by the letter *l*, such as in the word *flag*. In this lesson, your student will learn to identify words with *l* blends. He or she will also build words that begin with *bl, cl, fl, gl, pl,* and *sl*.	■ Student Learning Pages 18.A–18.B ■ sticky notes

Let's Begin

1 **INTRODUCE** Begin the lesson by inviting your student to complete this sentence: *The sky is . . .* [blue] Ask your student to write the word *blue* on a sheet of paper. Correct or confirm the spelling of the word and then say it out loud. Sound out each letter in the word: /b/ /l/ /o͞o/. Have your student repeat the word after you. Be sure he or she makes the *l* blend sound in the word: /bl/. Then ask your student to tell you which letters make the /bl/ sound at the beginning of *blue*. [*b* and *l*] As you go through this lesson, remember to incorporate commonly used *l* blend sight words in addition to *l* blend phonics concepts.

2 **EXPLAIN** Tell your student that many words begin with a consonant and the letter *l*. Remind your student that the word *blue* is one example. Then write the word *clap* on a sheet of paper. Ask your student to name the two consonants at the beginning of the word. Sound out the letters of the word while stretching the sound of the *l* blend letters: /c/ /c/ /c/ /l/ /l/ /l/ /ă/ /p/. Invite your student to say the word *clap* on his or her own. Repeat this exercise for the word *fly*. Ask your student to identify the two letters at the beginning of the word. Then sound out each letter while emphasizing the initial *l* blend. Ask your student to say the word *fly*. Finally, have your student repeat these sentences after you: *The clown claps. The flag flies.* Be sure he or she enunciates each sound that makes up the *l* blend sound, and remember to help your student with unfamiliar words in a noncritical, nonjudgmental manner.

3 **BUILD** Use sticky notes to help your student build words that begin with the *l* blends *bl, cl,* and *fl*. Write each of these letters on a separate sticky note: *b, c, f, l, o, c,* and *k*. Arrange five of the sticky notes on a sheet of paper to form the word *block*. Remove the consonant *b* and leave the letters *l, o, c,* and *k*. Ask your student if he or she can add another consonant on a sticky note to form a new word. [*clock* or *flock*] Write more letters on sticky notes and repeat this exercise with other *l* blend sight words, such as *blue/clue, blow/flow, clap/flap, blame/flame,* and so on.

4 **EXPAND** Teach your student words with the *l* blends *gl, pl,* and *sl*. Write these sight words on a sheet of paper: *glad, place,* and *slip*. Slowly say each word while stressing the initial *l* blend sounds. Then ask your student to repeat each word after you. Then say these words one at a time: *pull, glow, plot, sail, girl,* and *slow*. After you pronounce each word, say, *Does this word begin with a consonant and an* l? Have him or her identify the first two letters in each *l* blend word and then say each *l* blend word on his or her own.

5 **BUILD** Revisit the word-building exercise from Step 3. This time help your student build *l* blend words with six *l* blends, *bl, cl, fl, gl, pl,* and *sl*. Use the sticky notes from Step 3 and add notes for the letters *g, p,* and *s*. Then write the letters *o* and *w* on separate sticky notes. Arrange the notes to form the word *blow*. Invite your student to replace the initial *b* with other consonants on the sticky notes. Challenge your student to build and say as many *l* blend words as possible. Then have your student write simple rhyming sentences using *l* blend words.

6 **PRACTICE** Distribute Student Learning Page 18.A. Help your student read the directions.

Branching Out

FOR FURTHER READING

Reading Success Mini-Books: Initial Consonants, by Mary Beth Spann (Scholastic, 1999).

Vowels and Consonants: 1st Grade, by Audrey Carangelo and Duendes Del Sur, ill. (Cartwheel Books, 2001).

TEACHING TIP

You might want to review vowel sounds as you help your student sound out letters in *l* blend words. For example, ask your student to identify the sound of a vowel that follows an *l* blend. Then have him or her tell which vowel makes the sound. Integrating knowledge of sounds associated with all letters is the key factor that will enable your student to read and write.

CHECKING IN

Write these words: *blue, clap, flat, glad, plan,* and *slow*. Then say the different *l* blend words out loud. After you say each word, ask your student which word on the sheet of paper begins with the same sound.

Build *l* Blend Words

Name the pictures. Write letters on the lines to make words. Then say the words.

bl	cl	fl	gl	pl	sl

1.

___ ___ **i d e**

2.

___ ___ **a n k e t**

3.

___ ___ **a g**

4.

___ ___ **o b e**

5.

___ ___ **a n t**

6.

___ ___ **o w n**

What's Next? You Decide!

Now it's your turn to choose what to do next in the lesson. Read the activities and decide which one you want to do—you may want to try them both!

Act Out *l* Blend Words

MATERIALS

❑ 12 index cards

STEPS

❑ Write one *l* blend word on 12 different index cards. Write words that name something or show action.
❑ Ask a partner to choose a card and act out the word.
❑ Guess the word on the card.
❑ Now it's your turn. Choose a card. Act out the word.
❑ Have your partner guess the word.

Play an *l* Blend Picture Game

MATERIALS

❑ construction paper
❑ markers or crayons

STEPS

❑ Draw a picture to show an *l* blend word.
❑ Show other players your picture. Ask them to guess the word.
❑ The first person to guess the word gets a point.
❑ Take turns drawing.
❑ The person with the most points after four turns wins!

Exploring Consonant Combinations

Blending consonants can produce a myriad of sounds.

OBJECTIVE	BACKGROUND	MATERIALS
To help your student recognize the sounds of initial and final digraphs and build words with them	Many English words begin or end with digraphs. A digraph is a pair of consonants that form one sound. For example, the *sh* in *ship* forms the sound /sh/. In this lesson, your student will learn to recognize the sounds of initial and final digraphs as well as associate those sounds with letters. He or she will also practice building words with initial and final digraphs.	■ Student Learning Pages 19.A–19.B ■ 15 index cards ■ alphabet flash cards or alphabet blocks (optional)

Let's Begin

1 **INTRODUCE** Say the word *shape* slowly so your student can hear the separate sounds. Ask, *What sounds do you hear in the word* shape? [/sh/ /ā/ /p/] Have your student repeat the word several times. Ask, *What sound do you hear in the beginning of* shape? [/sh/] Have your student repeat the sound several times: /sh/, /sh/, /sh/. Then say the word *chin*. Ask, *What sounds do you hear in* chin? [/ch/ /ĭ/ /n/] Have your student repeat the word and then repeat the beginning sound several times: /ch/, /ch/, /ch/. Now say the word *thank* and help your student isolate and repeat the sound /th/. Challenge your student to say other words that begin with /sh/, /ch/, and /th/. Throughout the lesson be sure to incorporate commonly used digraph sight words in addition to the phonics concepts. Combining both can boost your student's ability to read.

2 **EXPLAIN** Tell your student that many English words begin with the sounds /sh/, /ch/, and /th/. These sounds are written as two consonants side by side: *sh, ch,* and *th*. The two consonants join to make one new sound. Write *sh, ch,* and *th* on a sheet of paper. Have your student refer to the paper while you say the following words. Say each word slowly, emphasizing the initial sound: *sheep, child, thin, shut, chain,* and *thick*. After you say each word, ask your student to point to the written letters that represent the beginning sound of the word. Then write the words. Finally, have your student underline the letters that combine to make the beginning sound in each word.

Let your student be the guide as to how long to spend on each step. You may wish to complete this lesson all in one sitting, or you may prefer to return to it over the course of a period of time.

3   **PRACTICE** To help your student recognize the letters that represent the sounds /sh/, /ch/, and /th/, prepare a three-column chart. Write these sight words as headings for the columns: *ship*, *chin*, and *thick*. Then give your student this list of words: *she*, *chips*, *thorn*, *shelf*, *chop*, and *thumb*. Have your student say each listed word out loud and decide if it has the same beginning sound as *ship*, *chin*, or *thick*. Tell your student to write each word below the word in the chart that has the same beginning sound. Then have your student choose three of the words and write three sentences using the words.

4   **EXPLAIN** Say the words *whale* and *phone*. Ask, *What sounds do you hear in these words?* [/hw/ /ā/ /l/, /f/ /ō/ /n/] Have your student repeat the initial sounds several times: /hw/, /hw/, /hw/, /f/, /f/, /f/. Explain that these two sounds can be written as *wh* and *ph*. Then write the words *wheel*, *white*, *photo*, and *phone*. Say the words slowly, emphasizing the initial sound. Tell your student to repeat the words and then say just the initial sounds. Have him or her underline the letters that combine to make the beginning sound in each word.

5   **PRACTICE** To help your student associate the /hw/ and /f/ sounds with words, play a game. Say this list of words: *check*, *shell*, *wheat*, *phone*, *chain*, *thump*, *phrase*, *shelf*, *whip*, and *thorn*. Tell your student to listen carefully as you say the words. Whenever your student hears a word that begins with the /hw/ or /f/ sound, he or she should stand up and repeat the word. If it's appropriate, you might ask your student to spell the *wh* and *ph* words, too. Be sure to direct him or her to sit down again before you say the next word.

6   **EXPAND** Remind your student that many words begin with *sh*, *ch*, *th*, *wh*, and *ph*. Play a game with your student to help him or her practice recognizing some of these words. Draw a large tic-tac-toe game on a sheet of paper. In the corner of each of the nine squares, write these digraphs: *sh*, *ch*, *th*, *wh*, *ph*, *sh*, *ch*, *th*, and *wh*.

DID YOU KNOW?

The letters *ch* have three different sounds in English. In addition to the /ch/ sound in *chin* and *chop*, *ch* can be pronounced with a /k/ sound, as in *chorus* and *chord*. It can also be pronounced with a /sh/ sound, as in *chef* and *chiffon*. For a beginning reader, it's less confusing to teach only the first sound, /ch/.

sh	ch	th
wh	ph	sh
ch	th	wh

Prepare 15 index cards. Write one of these words on each card: *sheet*, *she*, *shape*, *chin*, *chips*, *chop*, *thumb*, *thick*, *think*, *why*, *white*, *where*, *phone*, *photo*, and *phrase*. Shuffle the cards. Have your student draw a card. He or she should say the word on the card and write the word in a square that matches its beginning sound. Then you draw a card and follow the same pattern. Take turns until all the tic-tac-toe squares are filled. Then have your student choose rhyming words and write simple rhyming sentences.

7 **REVIEW** Help your student build words with initial digraphs. Distribute these alphabet flash cards or alphabet blocks to your student: *s, c, t, w, p, h, o, i,* and *e.* If you don't have alphabet flash cards or blocks, write the letters on index cards. Next, say the word *shop.* Have your student repeat the word several times. Ask, *What's the first sound?* [/sh/] *What letters represent that sound?* [*s* and *h*] Tell your student to find the *s* and the *h.* Ask, *What's the next sound?* [/ŏ/] Have him or her find the *o* and put it to the right of the *s* and the *h.* Ask, *What's the last sound?* [/p/] Your student should put the *p* next to the *o.* Have him or her spell the word and say it out loud. In the same manner, guide your student in building some or all of the following words: *chew, chop, she, ship, the, whip,* and *white.*

8 **DISCUSS** Say the word *fish* slowly so your student can hear the separate sounds. Ask, *What sounds do you hear in the word* fish? [/f/ /ĭ/ /sh/] Have your student repeat the word. Ask, *What sound do you hear at the end of* fish? [/sh/] Have him or her repeat the /sh/ sound several times. Then say the word *rich.* Ask, *What sounds do you hear in* rich? [/r/ /ĭ/ /ch/] Have your student repeat the word and say the /ch/ ending sound several times. Now say the word *path* and help your student isolate and repeat the /th/ sound. Challenge your student to say other words that end with /sh/, /ch/, and /th/.

9 **PRACTICE** Help your student recognize words with final digraphs. Write these letter combinations at the top of a sheet of paper: *sh, th, ch,* and *tch.* Then write the clues listed below. Also, write the answer word with the letters missing as shown. Have your student fill in one of the letter combinations to complete each word. Then have him or her pronounce each word.

TAKE A BREAK

Scan a few pages from a book or the newspaper comics with your student. Have him or her point out digraphs at the beginning of words. Then reread the same pages and encourage your student to find digraphs at the end of words.

Clues	Answers
kind of fruit	pea_____
place for walking	pa_____
tells time	wa_____
belongs on a dog	lea_____
direction	nor_____
to come out of an egg	ha_____
part of a tree	bran_____
hurry	ru_____

Exploring Consonant Combinations **87**

10 **CHALLENGE** Tell your student that many words end with *sh* and *th*. They stand for the sounds /sh/ and /th/, just as they do when they are at the beginning of words. Write these examples for your student: *fresh, brush, tooth,* and *bath.* Say the words slowly, emphasizing the final digraphs. Invite your student to repeat the words after you. Then tell your student that the /ch/ sound can be found at the end of words, too. However, it can be spelled two ways. It can be spelled *ch,* as it is in the words *beach* and *peach.* It can also be spelled *tch,* as it is in the words *match* and *patch,* but the *t* is silent. Both spellings are pronounced /ch/. Have your student list other words that rhyme with *match* and *patch* and end with the letters *tch.* [*batch, catch, hatch, latch,* and so on]

11 **REVIEW AND DISTRIBUTE** Remind your student that *sh, ch, th, wh,* and *ph* are common letter combinations that begin words. Also remind him or her that *sh, th, ch,* and *tch* are common letter combinations that end words. Ask your student to name some words that begin and end with these letters. Then distribute Student Learning Page 19.A. Read the directions together before your student begins. Provide guidance as necessary as your student completes the page.

Branching Out

TEACHING TIP

As your student begins to read independently, he or she will run across unfamiliar words. Suggest that he or she follow these steps to figure them out. First, tell your student to look at the letters from left to right and say the sound for each letter. Second, tell your student to look for word parts he or she knows and blend the sounds. Finally, suggest that your student ask himself or herself the questions, Do I know this word? Does the word make sense in the sentence?

CHECKING IN

To assess your student's understanding of the lesson, say the following words one at a time: *sheep, chin, thin, wheat,* and *phone.* Have him or her write the letters that represent the beginning sound of each word. Now say these words one at a time: *brush, rich, patch,* and *bath.* Have your student write the letters that represent the ending sound of each word. Then ask your student to say a new word using each beginning or ending sound he or she wrote.

FOR FURTHER READING

Farfallina and Marcel, by Holly Keller (Greenwillow, 2002).

Giggle, Giggle, Quack, by Doreen Cronin (Simon and Schuster, 2002).

Henry Builds a Cabin, by D. B. Johnson (Houghton Mifflin, 2002).

Hondo and Fabian, by Peter McCarty (Henry Holt and Company, 2002).

Use Consonant Combinations

Circle the word that names the picture. Write the word on the line.

1. shovel   shelf

2. chat   child

3. health   hatch

4. tooth   thick

5. wheel   whale

6. brush   batch

What's Next? You Decide!

Now it's your turn to choose what to do next in the lesson. Read the activities and decide which one you want to do—you may want to try them both!

Make a Card Game

shell   whale

MATERIALS

❑ 12 index cards
❑ markers or crayons

STEPS

❑ Write a different word on six index cards. Use words with *sh, ch, th, wh,* and *ph*.
❑ Draw a picture of each word on each card.
❑ Color the pictures with markers or crayons.
❑ Put the cards facedown on a table.
❑ Players take turns matching a word with its picture!

Write a Picture Story

MATERIALS

❑ 4 sheets construction paper
❑ markers or crayons
❑ 1 hole puncher
❑ 1 length ribbon

STEPS

❑ Think of a story that has some *sh, ch,* and *wh* words in it.
❑ Write the story. Make it four pages long.
❑ Draw pictures to show what happens.
❑ Make a hole in the top left corner of each page.
❑ Put a ribbon through the holes and tie the pages together.

Reading Nonfiction

Discover the wonders of our world through nonfiction.

OBJECTIVE	BACKGROUND	MATERIALS
To help your student read and analyze nonfiction writing	Nonfiction writing tells about real people, places, things, or events. Nonfiction writing often focuses on topics such as animals, countries, people, and plants. Many nonfiction articles also include new vocabulary related to a particular topic. In this lesson, your student will read and analyze a nonfiction article.	■ Student Learning Pages 20.A–20.C ■ 1 copy Web, page 356 ■ markers or crayons

VOCABULARY

FLUKES the end of a whale's tail

KRILL tiny, shrimplike crustaceans that are about as long as a person's thumb

CRUSTACEANS animals that live in water and have hard shells

EXTINCT a species that has died out

NONFICTION a type of writing that tells about real people, places, things, or events

Let's Begin

1 **PREVIEW** Read the literature excerpt before beginning the lesson. This reading selection may be challenging to some new readers, so you may wish to identify difficult or hard-to-pronounce words ahead of time. Be sure to help your student with unfamiliar terms in a noncritical and nonjudgmental manner. Remember to let your student guide you as to how fast or slow to proceed through the lesson. You may wish to enjoy this lesson all in one sitting, or you may prefer to go back to it over a period of time as your student shows interest in reading about whales, animals, or anything else! Let your student be the guide.

2 **INTRODUCE** Distribute Student Learning Page 20.A. Ask your student to scan the selection and look for words that are in darker letters. Point to each boldface word and pronounce it for your student—**flukes, krill, crustaceans,** and **extinct.** Ask your student to repeat each word after you.

3 **EXPLAIN** Tell your student that he or she is going to read a type of writing called **nonfiction.** This type of writing tells about real people, places, things, or events. Explain that the topic tells what a nonfiction article is about. Tell your student that the topic of the nonfiction selection he or she is about to read is

whales. Invite your student to share what he or she already knows about whales.

4   **READ**   Read *Blue Whales* aloud to your student while he or she follows along. Then encourage your student to read if you feel he or she is ready for this selection. As your student reads, help your student identify familiar words. If your student doesn't know a word, help him or her pronounce it so that reading out loud remains enjoyable. Calmly reread difficult parts of the selection and allow your student more time to read out loud. Be sure to also explain the meanings of the vocabulary words or other unfamiliar terms in simple terms. When it seems that your student is comfortable reading, invite him or her to make inferences. Tell your student that he or she can use the words in *Blue Whales* to guess what might happen next.

5   **CATEGORIZE**   Tell your student that *Blue Whales* can be broken down into four parts. Each part explains something different about blue whales. Help your student identify the four categories of information that the selection explains about the animal. [blowing and diving; what blue whales eat; the blue whale's body; the number of blue whales today]

6   **SUMMARIZE MAIN IDEAS**   Tell your student that main ideas tell the most important things that happen in a story or article. Distribute a copy of the Web found on page 356. Write "Whales" in the center. Have your student write the most important things that he or she learned about whales in the surrounding ovals. Your student may write that other animals can hear the whale sound from thousands of miles away, that blue whales are big, or that blue whales eat a lot. Ask your student to use what he or she wrote to retell the most important parts of *Blue Whales* in his or her own words.

7   **EVALUATE**   Invite your student to share what he or she liked about *Blue Whales*. Also have your student tell what he or she didn't like about the selection. Encourage your student to explain his or her opinions. Then distribute Student Learning Page 20.B.

Branching Out

TEACHING TIP

Read out loud a fable with talking animals. Ask your student to tell how *Blue Whales* is different from the fable.

CHECKING IN

To assess your student's understanding of the lesson, ask him or her to explain what nonfiction tells about. Then ask your student to describe what a blue whale is like in his or her own words.

ENRICH THE EXPERIENCE

Check out a book about whales from your local library. You might want to have your student read *DK Readers: Journey of a Humpback Whale* by Caryn Jenner. This book allows your student to progress through stories that are written at four different reading levels.

FOR FURTHER READING

Rainbow Fish and the Big Blue Whale, by Marcus Pfister (North South Books, 1998).

Theodore and the Whale, by Mary Man-Kong and Bernat Serrat, ill. (Random House, 1999).

Explore Nonfiction

Blue Whales

by Victor Gentle and Janet Perry

When a blue whale blows, it makes a noise loud enough to be heard a mile away—over howling winds, crashing waves, and roaring boat engines. When a blue whale rumbles underwater, other whales can hear the sound for thousands of miles.

When a blue whale dives, its back seems to go on and on. You could easily read this page, draw a picture, or finish your math homework while you waited for it to plunge into the sea and wave bye-bye with **flukes** as wide as a bus is long.

While a blue whale feeds, it gulps tons of tiny animals and many swimming pools full of water—in every mouthful! Blue whales are BIG!

If you were as big as 30 Indian elephants, how much food would you need? *A lot!* A fully grown blue whale eats

(CONTINUED)

during about eight months of the year. For four of those months it gobbles up about 8,000 pounds (3,600 kg) of food a day. In human food, that would be 14,000 carrots, 1,200 bowls of thick soup, and 4 whole cows (bones and all) every day for four whole months!

Blue whales are the biggest animals on Earth, and yet, they eat the smallest animals in the sea—**krill.** Krill are tiny, shrimplike **crustaceans** that are about as long as a person's thumb—1 to 2.5 inches (2.5 to 6.4 centimeters). A bucket of krill-filled ocean water would hold over 100 of the little beasties.

How can an animal as long as seven or eight jeeps and as heavy as a herd of cattle swim faster than a champion human swimmer?

A blue whale's long, slender body is shaped like a speedboat. Its head has a ridge from the blowholes to the snout that helps the whale slice through the water. Because most of its muscle is in its tail,

(CONTINUED)

Blue whales are Earth's largest animal. They can grow to be more than 100 feet long.

a blue whale surges through the water with each stroke of its powerful flukes.

A blue whale also has a lot of blubber, or fat. Blubber keeps the blue whale warm and helps it store food. It helps the whale float, too. Otherwise, the whale would have to use some of its precious energy to keep from sinking.

(CONTINUED)

At one time, being speedy and huge kept blue whales safe from whalers.

In 1864, there were hundreds of thousands of blue whales. By 1964, there were fewer than 10,000. In 100 years, one blue whale's lifetime, blues were almost **extinct.**

Sixty years ago, we finally heard blue whales. At 180 decibels, they are as loud as an airplane, but the sound is so low that you can only feel it. As blues call to and answer each other across wide seas, we just feel thunder in our chests, around our hearts.

Describe an Animal

Choose an animal you like. Answer each question.
Then draw a picture to show the answers.

Name of animal: _____

1. What does it look like?

_____

_____

2. Where does it live?

_____

_____

3. What does it eat?

_____

_____

What's Next? You Decide!

Now it's your turn to choose what to do next in the lesson. Read the activities and decide which one you want to do—you may want to try them both!

Watch for Whales

MATERIALS

❏ 1 small piece paper
❏ 1 baseball cap
❏ tape
❏ 2 chairs

STEPS

❏ Write "Whale Guide" on the small piece of paper and tape it to the cap.
❏ Put two chairs in front of each other. Imagine the chairs are a boat.
❏ Ask a friend or family member to sit in the boat.
❏ Suppose you are in the ocean looking for whales.
❏ Tell what you know about whales.

Make a Whale Postcard

MATERIALS

❏ 1 large index card
❏ markers or crayons
❏ postage stamps

STEPS

❏ Draw a picture of a blue whale. Use the blank side of the index card.
❏ Turn the index card over. Write something about the blue whale.
❏ Write your friend's name and address on the postcard.
❏ Ask an adult to help you put a stamp on the postcard.
❏ Send the postcard to your friend.

Writing Sentences

Writing gives voice and structure to our emotions, ideas, and knowledge.

OBJECTIVE	BACKGROUND	MATERIALS
To help your student write sentences about a topic	Your student has been working hard to read words written by others. Now it's time for him or her to put ideas into words by writing sentences. In this lesson, your student will learn to write complete sentences about a particular topic.	■ Student Learning Pages 21.A–21.B ■ several sheets construction paper ■ 1 copy Web, page 356 ■ several copies Writing Lines, page 357

Let's Begin

1 **EXPLAIN** Tell your student that he or she will learn to write sentences in this lesson. Explain that learning how to write is important as well as fun! Writing helps us share our thoughts and feelings with others. Then talk to your student about sentences. Tell your student that every sentence has two parts, a naming part and an action part. The naming part answers the question, *Who?* or *What?* The action part answers the question, *What happened?* Write the following sentences on a sheet of paper:

Jill sang a song. The cat slept all day.

Point out the naming part in each sentence. [Jill, the cat] Then point out the action part [sang, slept]. Invite your student to tell you three things that happened yesterday. Encourage your student to say sentences with a naming part and an action part.

2 **RECORD** As your student tells about three things that happened yesterday, write down the sentences he or she says on construction paper. Invite your student to circle the naming part in each of the sentences you wrote down. Then ask your student to underline the action part in each of the three sentences.

3 **PRACTICE** Distribute Student Learning Page 21.A. Invite your student to fill in the blank parts of the sentences using his or her imagination. Help your student spell words as needed.

4 **DISTRIBUTE** Distribute a copy of the Web found on page 356. Use the Web to help your student write a few sentences about a topic. Invite your student to think of someone he or she knows well. Write this person's name in the center of the Web. Ask

DID YOU KNOW?

When your student begins writing, he or she will often ask you to how to spell words. Instead of providing the letters, ask your student to think about the sounds he or she hears in the word. As your student keeps writing, he or she will learn and remember more sounds.

your student to describe the person to you. As he or she relates the description, help your student write the person's qualities in the outer circles of the Web (one word per circle). Invite your student to review the Web and read each word out loud.

5 **WRITE** Help your student use the Web to write three simple sentences about the person. Distribute several copies of the Writing Lines found on page 357. Choose one of the words in the outer ovals and model for your student how to write a sentence describing the person. Then help him or her choose one of the words in an outer circle of the Web and write a simple sentence using the Writing Lines. Encourage him or her to write two more simple sentences. Then have him or her read them aloud to you.

6 **EXPAND** Invite your student to think of his or her pet or a favorite animal. Ask him or her to describe it to you, such as what it looks like, what it eats, what it does, and what it means to your student. Then have him or her write a few simple sentences about it on the Writing Lines. Encourage your student to take his or her time thinking about what to write. When your student is finished writing, have him or her review his or her sentences to make sure they are complete. If your student is having trouble, you may wish to return to the first part of the lesson for review, or you may prefer to take a break and return to the lesson later. Let your student guide you to a comfortable learning pace.

A BRIGHT IDEA

Instill an interest in writing by asking your student to write a letter to a friend or family member. It's best if he or she writes to someone who will write back. Help your student write the letter and address the envelope. Put it in the mail and wait for a response!

Branching Out

TEACHING TIP

If your student is having trouble writing, make it more appealing to him or her. Provide fun stationery, pens, markers, stickers, or anything else you can think of to make writing more engaging.

CHECKING IN

To assess your student's understanding of the lesson, invite him or her to write three sentences about a favorite food. Then ask your student to point out the naming part and action part of each sentence.

FOR FURTHER READING

Gifted and Talented Writing Grade 1, by Tracy Masonis (McGraw-Hill Companies, 2002).

Odd Jobs (*Road to Writing, First Journals, Mile 4*), by Sarah Albee (Golden Books Publishing, 2002).

Write Sentences

Write the action part of the sentences.

1. The elephant _____.

2. My friends and I _____.

3. Sam and his cousin _____.

Write the naming part of the sentences.

4. _____ stayed up late last night.

5. _____ ate pizza for lunch.

6. _____ barked loudly at the boys.

What's Next? You Decide!

Now it's your turn to choose what to do next in the lesson. Read the activities and decide which one you want to do—you may want to try them both!

Write About a Picture

MATERIALS

❑ 1 photo or a picture from a magazine

STEPS

❑ Find a picture you like.

❑ The picture can be a photo of your family or friends.

❑ The picture can also be from a magazine.

❑ Write a story about what is happening in the picture.

❑ Make sure your sentences have a naming part and an action part.

❑ Share your story with your family and friends.

Create Silly Sentences

MATERIALS

❑ 5 long strips paper

❑ 1 pair scissors

❑ 1 sheet construction paper

❑ markers or crayons

STEPS

❑ Write five sentences on strips of paper.

❑ Cut apart the naming part and the action part of each sentence.

❑ Mix up the sentence pieces and put different naming and action parts together.

❑ Make silly sentences!

In Your Community

To reinforce the skills and concepts taught in this section,
try one or more of these activities!

Take an Alphabet Walk

Take a walk with your student around your community. Ask your student to find things as you walk whose names begin with specific letters of the alphabet. You can give your student any letters of the alphabet, from *A* to *Z*. You can also adjust the activity from initial letters in words to initial consonant or vowel sounds, words with specific long or short vowel sounds, or any specific combination of consonant sounds. Use the activity to solve problems your student may have with specific letters or to reinforce your student's understanding of the alphabet.

Explore a Nonfiction Topic

If your student enjoys nonfiction, find a nonfiction book about a person, place, or thing in your town. Read the book with your student and then explore your community for ways he or she can learn more about the subject. For example, if you read a nonfiction work about an important historical figure from your town, you might find related information or artifacts at a museum. You can also visit a building or other site where an important historical event happened. Use your imagination as you explore possibilities with your student.

Write a Poem

Invite your student to talk about some of his or her favorite places in your community, such as a park or a playground. Tell your student to choose one of those places. Then take your student on a field trip to the location. Walk or drive around the place and ask your student what things make it special or fun to visit. Then have your student write a poem with simple rhymes. Remind your student to use the qualities or descriptions he or she mentioned during your discussion.

Write a Guide Book

Talk to your student about which places or things in your community make it a special town to visit. Then have your student create a guidebook for travelers highlighting the places or things that can be seen in your community. Go to each place and ask your student to draw a picture of an object or scene and write one word that stands for the chosen spot. When your student has finished, staple the sheets together with a cover he or she designed. If possible, arrange to take a copy of the guidebook to your local chamber of commerce, community center, or other community interest group for public display.

Book Shopping

If your student has read and enjoyed books by a particular author or about a favorite topic, expand your student's library and nurture his or her enthusiasm for reading by shopping for books. There are many ways to find books at a reasonable price. Many used bookstores have great children's book sections that list prices at a fraction of the cost of new books. Libraries often have book sales where books can be purchased even more cheaply. Another good way to find inexpensive books is to attend garage sales or flea markets. Classified ads in newspapers often include information about items that will be sold, and books are frequently mentioned.

We Have Learned

Use this checklist to summarize what you and your student have accomplished in the Promoting Literacy section.

❏ **Grammar and Phonemic Awareness: Short Vowels**
❏ short *a, e, i, o,* and *u* words
❏ short *a, e, i, o,* and *u* word families

❏ **Grammar and Phonemic Awareness: Long Vowels**
❏ long *a, e, i, o,* and *u* words with consonant-vowel-consonant-*e* spelling pattern
❏ long *a, e, i, o,* and *u* word families

❏ **Grammar and Phonemic Awareness: Consonant Combinations**
❏ words with *s* blends (*sc, sk, sl, sm, sn, sp, st, sw*)
❏ words with *r* blends (*br, cr, dr, fr, gr, pr, tr*)
❏ words with *l* blends (*bl, cl, fl, gl, pl, sl*)
❏ words with initial digraphs (*sh, ch, th, wh, ph*)
❏ words with final digraphs (*sh, ch, th*)

❏ **Grammar and Phonemic Awareness: Vowel Patterns**
❏ long /ā/ sound with *ay* and *ai*
❏ words with *ay* and *ai*
❏ long /ē/ sound with *ee, ea, ie*
❏ words with *ee, ea, ie*

❏ **Fiction**
❏ reading and analyzing fiction
❏ understanding characteristics and elements of fiction

❏ **Tall Tales**
❏ reading and analyzing tall tales
❏ understanding characteristics and elements of tall tales

❏ **Poetry**
❏ reading and analyzing poetry
❏ understanding characteristics and elements of poetry

❏ **Nonfiction**
❏ reading and analyzing nonfiction
❏ understanding characteristics and elements of nonfiction
❏ writing sentences on a topic

We have also learned:

_____

_____

_____

_____

_____

_____

Math

Math

Key Topics

Exploring Numbers and Patterns

Teachers have many tasks. The task that crosses all content areas is also the most important: The teacher teaches a student how to learn.

OBJECTIVE	BACKGROUND	MATERIALS
To help your student explore numbers and patterns	The basic understanding of numbers and patterns in numbers—equal, greater, and lesser amounts—is the foundation of math. It leads to an understanding of place value and provides the basis for all mathematical operations: addition, subtraction, multiplication, and division. In this lesson, your student will explore numbers and number patterns.	■ Student Learning Pages 1.A–1.D ■ 20 red checkers or counters ■ 20 black checkers or counters ■ 4 plastic sandwich bags ■ markers or crayons ■ 21 index cards, labeled with the digits 0–20 ■ 1 hat or shoebox ■ 9 paper strips

VOCABULARY
PATTERNS fixed orders of shapes or numbers

Let's Begin

MORE, LESS, AND THE SAME

1 **MODEL AND EXPLAIN** Use counters, such as black and red checkers, throughout the lesson. Begin by making a group of 8 red checkers and a group of 10 black checkers. Ask, *Which group has more?* [black] *Which has fewer?* [red] Remove 2 black checkers and ask your student to explain the relationship between the groups. [the number of checkers are now the same] As you work through this lesson, let your student be the guide as to how much time to spend on the concepts and skills. You may wish to complete the activities in two hours, or you may wish to review the concepts and skills throughout the day.

2 **DISCUSS** Continue to use different numbers of red and black checkers to reinforce the terms *same, fewer,* and *more.* Give your student 5 counters of each color and invite him or her to use the counters to demonstrate each term as you say it. Say, *Make two groups. The group of red counters will have more than the group of black counters.* Then check your student's work.

MATH

LESSON 2.1

MOST AND FEWEST

1 **CHALLENGE** Use all red and black counters and separate them into various groups. Have your student tell you which of the groups has the same, fewer, or more quantities. Introduce *fewest* and *most*. Have your student make two red groups and two black groups of counters. Say, *Make two groups of red counters. Make two groups of black counters. One group of red counters will have the most. One group of black counters will have the fewest.* Then check your student's work to make sure that one of the red groups has the most counters of the four groups and one group of black counters has the fewest of the four groups.

2 **TAKE TURNS** Now take turns with your student dividing the counters. Have him or her call out how the groups should be (certain groups having fewest, most, same, fewer, or more) and you divide the counters. Then have your student divide the groups as you call out the groups.

3 **DISTRIBUTE** Distribute Student Learning Page 1.A for practice learning same, fewer, fewest, more, and most.

PATTERNS WITH NUMBERS

1 **EXPLAIN** Continue to use different colored counters to model number patterns. Slide 5 red counters in front of your student. Say, *Here are 5 red counters.* Slide 5 black counters in front of your student, counting out the pieces as you do so. Say, *Here are 5 black counters.* Slide 5 more red counters and 5 more black counters, making sure they are in one line. Ask, *What is the number **pattern?*** [5 red, 5 black, 5 red, 5 black]

2 **EXPLORE** Continue with the same number pattern and remove 2 red counters from each red group and add 3 black counters to each black group. Then ask, *What is this number pattern?* [3 red, 8 black, 3 red, 8 black] Challenge your student and make up a series of patterns using all 20 red and all 20 black counters. Have your student identify each number pattern and then write the pattern in his or her notebook for additional reinforcement with numbers. Now distribute Student Learning Page 1.B for practice with number patterns.

3 **CHALLENGE** Explain that numbers have patterns. Reveal that one common number pattern is counting by 5's. Say, *5, 10, 15, 20, 25, 30, 35, 40.* Have your student create this number pattern with the counters. [student should separate the counters into 5's, alternating 5 red and 5 black counters using all 40] Observe as he or she creates this pattern. For additional reinforcement with numbers, have him or her say aloud the number pattern and then write the pattern in his or her notebook. Encourage him or her to continue counting up to 100 (and beyond!).

TAKE A BREAK

Combine additional reinforcement of the numbers from 1 to 10 with a snack. Use raisins, grapes, pieces of cereal, snack crackers, or other small treats as counters. Name a number and have your student count out the correct amount. Then repeat with a second number. Ask your student to identify which number is fewer. The reward for a correct answer is a snack!

MATH
LESSON
2.1

4 **REINFORCE** Share that another common number pattern is counting by 2's. Say, *2, 4, 6, 8, 10, 12, 14, 16, 18, 20.* Have your student create this number pattern with the counters. Observe as he or she creates this pattern. Then have him or her say this number pattern orally, counting as high as he or she can. Have him or her write the number pattern in his or her notebook.

5 **CONTINUE** Have him or her think of other number patterns, such as counting by 3's, 4's, or odd numbers, and have him or her make a pattern with the counters. Encourage him or her to say the pattern aloud to you orally, counting as high as he or she can. Then have him or her write the pattern in his or her notebook. Then distribute Student Learning Page 1.C for more practice.

NUMBER RELATIONSHIPS

1 **IDENTIFY** Use counters to review all of the one-digit numbers. Name numbers at random and have your student count out counters to match each number you name. End the activity by asking your student to count out 9 checkers. Then add 1 checker to the 9 checkers. Ask, *How many checkers are there now?* [10] Write the digits on a sheet of paper. To help your student understand this new, two-digit number, have him or her write the digits 0 to 9 in his or her notebook. Ask, *What is different about the number 10?* [it has 2 digits instead of 1]

A BRIGHT IDEA

Using counters can help your student understand the one-to-one relationship between the counters and numbers named.

2 **INTRODUCE** Use counters to introduce place values to your student. Have your student count out 10 counters. Help him or her put the counters in a plastic sandwich bag or other small container. Explain that your student now has 1 set of ten, or 1 ten, in the bag. Use additional counters to help your student understand the place values in the number 10. Count out 9 for yourself. Say, *I have 9 counters.* Ask, *Do I have more or fewer than your 1 ten?* [fewer] Invite your student to count out 10 more counters and place them in another plastic bag. Ask, *How many tens do you have now?* [2] Ask your student to use the counters to show 2 tens. [20] Then have him or her put 10 more counters in another bag and ask him or her how many tens he or she has. [3] Then have him or her put 10 more counters in another plastic bag and identify them as 4 tens.

3 **CHALLENGE** Using the 4 bags of tens, have your student remove 6 counters from one of the bags. Tell him or her that he or she now has 3 tens and 4 ones. Look at the bags with your student and show him or her how that is possible. Identify the number he or she has just created as 34. Then say, *Using the counters and your bags, make 21.* [student should make 2 bags with 10 each, and 1 bag with 1] Call out other numbers and have your student make them.

4 **REVIEW AND PLAY** Help your student make a chart like this in his or her notebook. This game can be played with one or two

Exploring Numbers and Patterns **109**

MATH

LESSON 2.1

people. Tell your student that he or she will play a game like Tic Tac Toe. On each strip of paper, write one of these coordinates: *A1, A2, A3, B1, B2, B3, C1, C2, C3.* Put the strips of paper into a hat or shoebox. Without looking, choose a strip of paper and call out the coordinate. Then have your student complete the task in that coordinate. If he or she completes it correctly, have him or her place a counter on that spot. If he or she doesn't, put the strip of paper back in the hat (your student will get a chance later in the game to do it correctly). If there are two people playing the game, the object is to have the first person get three in a row. If your student is the only one playing, the object of the game is to place counters on all of the spaces on the first try.

	A	B	C
1	Count by 3's	Show 1 Ten and 1 One	Show 2 Tens and 2 Ones
2	Make a Number Pattern	Count by 2's	Find a Number Pattern
3	Show 3 Tens and 6 Ones	Count by 5's	Make a Number Pattern Using 3's

FOR FURTHER READING

Counting Caterpillars and Other Math Poems, by Betsy Franco (Scholastic Trade, 1999).

Exploring Numbers, by Andrew King (Copper Beech Books, 1998).

My First Math Book, by David Clemson and Wendy Clemson (DK Publishing, 2001).

Branching Out

TEACHING TIP

Understanding numbers and their patterns can be aided with real-world applications. As you go through the day or week, point out any number patterns you see in your town, such as at the grocery store, or on television.

CHECKING IN

Hold up index cards with digits from 0 to 20. Have your student count out counters to show the digit you have displayed. Continue the assessment by using pairs of numbers. Ask your student to tell you if the numbers are the same or which is more.

Practice with More and Fewer

Write how many. Circle the set that is more.

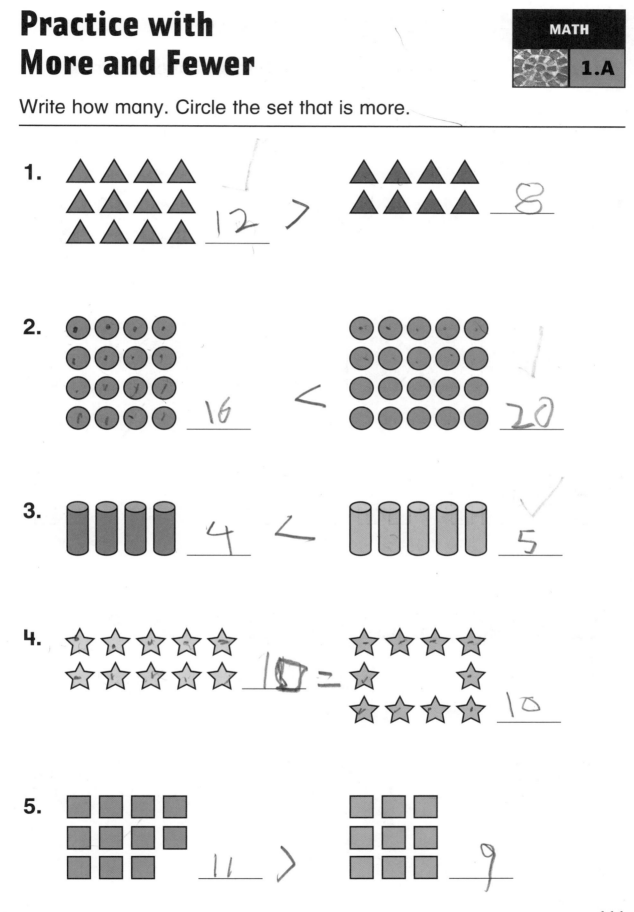

1. 12 > 8

2. 16 < 20

3. 4 < 5

4. 10 = 10

5. 11 > 9

Student Learning Page 1.A: Practice with More and Fewer   **111**

MATH 1.B

Explore Patterns

Finish the patterns. Circle what comes next.

Which comes next?

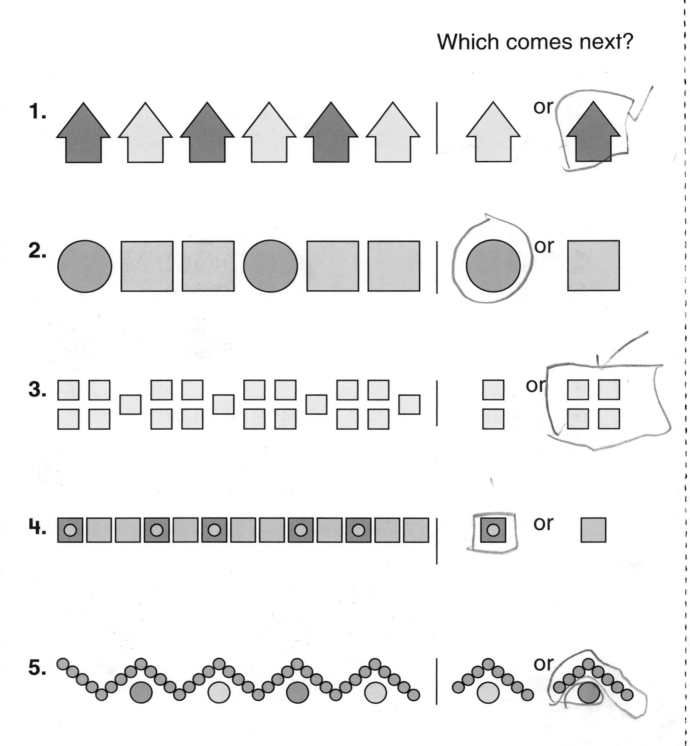

Show Numbers

Color the pictures to finish the patterns.

1.

2.

3.

4.

5.

MATH 1.D

What's Next? You Decide!

Now it's your turn to choose what to do next in the lesson. Read the activities and decide which one you want to do—you may want to try them both!

Choose Your Cards

MATERIALS

- ❏ 10 index cards
- ❏ markers or crayons

STEPS

- ❏ Write the numbers 1, 2, 3, 4, 5, 6, 7, 8, 9, and 10 on the cards.
- ❏ Mix up the cards and place them in a pile with the numbers facedown.
- ❏ The first player chooses a card and turns it over to show the number.
- ❏ The second player chooses a card. Then he or she turns it over to show the number.
- ❏ The player with the higher number wins both cards.
- ❏ When the pile is gone, the player with more cards wins.

Hunt for Numbers

MATERIALS

- ❏ markers or crayons

STEPS

- ❏ Look around your house.
- ❏ Find all these things: 7 books, 3 windows, 4 chairs, 10 buttons, 9 crayons, 5 shoes, and 1 table.
- ❏ When you find something, draw a picture of it in your notebook. Write the number next to your picture.

Understanding Numbers to 100

Let your student know that he or she can always count on you.

OBJECTIVE	BACKGROUND	MATERIALS
To have your student explore tens and ones, and identify and compare numbers to 100	Understanding numbers is the foundation your student will learn to add, subtract, multiply, and divide on. What your student learns about number values and patterns at this young age will even aid in complex concepts taught in algebra and statistics. In this lesson, your student will explore tens and ones. He or she will also explore comparing numbers to 100.	■ Student Learning Pages 2.A–2.C ■ 1 copy T Chart, page 355 ■ 100 counters ■ 1 sheet graph paper

Let's Begin

1 **EXPLORE** Explain to your student that we use place value to determine how large or small a number is. Understanding how tens and ones are combined to form numbers will help your student understand number values. Give your student 14 counters, and ask him or her to count them out loud. Ask your student to make groups of 10 with the counters. Ask, *How many groups of 10 did you make?* [1] *How many counters are left over?* [4] Label the columns of a copy of the T Chart found on page 355 as "Tens" and "Ones." Write a 1 in the tens column and a 4 in the ones column. Have your student place the group of 10 counters under the 1 and the 4 leftover counters under the 4. Have your student say, *1 ten and 4 ones is 14.* Invite him or her to continue the activity with various numbers to 50.

2 **EXPAND** Have your student count out 5 tens and 6 ones using counters. Ask, *How much is 5 tens?* [50] *How much is 6 ones?* [6] *So, how much is 50 + 6?* [56] Help your student understand that 56, 5 tens 6 ones, and 50 + 6 are all ways of writing the same number. Continue the exercise with various numbers to 99.

3 **EXPLAIN** Which pair of shoes is least expensive? Will 25 napkins be enough for 18 guests? Comparing numbers is a skill your student will use every day.

A BRIGHT IDEA

There are a variety of things you can use for counters, such as beans, buttons, and toothpicks. Varying the types of counters will keep young students interested.

Ask your student, *Which number is larger, 13 or 11?* [13] *How could you use counters to prove to me that 13 is larger than 11?* Help your student show both numbers using counters. Help him or her understand that both numbers have 1 ten, but that 13 has more ones than 11, so 13 is larger. Use the same exercise to find which number is smaller, 23 or 14.

4 **MODEL** Write the following numbers on a sheet of paper: 32, 11, and 26. Ask your student, *Which number is the largest?* [32] *Which number is the smallest?* [11] If your student has difficulty identifying the largest or smallest number, help him or her use counters to find the answer. Ask, *What's the order of the numbers from smallest to largest?* [11, 26, 32] Have your student practice ordering groups of three and four numbers.

ENRICH THE EXPERIENCE

Head to http://www.funbrain.com for fun math activities and games.

5 **REVIEW PATTERNS** Build upon the number patterns learned in Lesson 2.1, place 16 counters in groups of 2 on a sheet of paper. Have your student count each counter as you write the even number under each group. Then point out that the counters are in groups of 2. Point to each number you wrote as you count by 2's. Ask, *How many counters do we have?* [16]

6 **ILLUSTRATE** Divide graph paper into 11 by 10 grids. Help your student write the numbers from 1 to 110 consecutively in the boxes. (Numbering the graph paper beyond 100 will show your student how the patterns begin repeating with three-digit numbers.) Color the 1 box yellow as you say, *one.* Have your student color the box for 2 blue as he or she says, *two.* Continue taking turns counting and coloring the odd-numbered boxes yellow and the even-numbered boxes blue. Then have your student point to each blue box as he or she counts by 2's. Make two more grids and repeat the activity for counting by 5's and 10's. Point out the number patterns in each grid. Then distribute Student Learning Pages 2.A and 2.B.

Branching Out

TEACHING TIP

When comparing numbers, use the words *greater* and *less* as well as *largest* and *smallest.* This will help introduce to your student the mathematical terms he or she will learn later.

FOR FURTHER READING

Amanda Bean's Amazing Dream, by Marilyn Burns (Scholastic Trade, 1998).

Exploring the Numbers 1 to 100, by Mary Beth Spann (Cartwheel Books, 1999).

CHECKING IN

Give your student four numbers to order from least to greatest. Then ask your student to write each of the numbers in three different ways.

Practice Tens and Ones

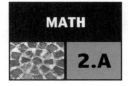
Circle sets of 10. Write the number.

1.

_____4_____ tens = __46__

2.

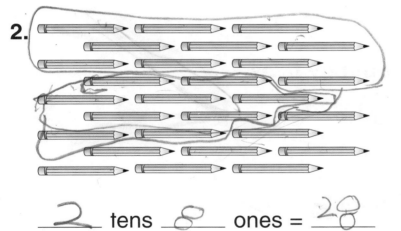

_____2_____ tens __8__ ones = __28__

Draw 21 circles. Circle the sets of 10.

3. ⊙⊙⊙⊙⊙⊙⊙⊙⊙⊙⊙
⊙⊙⊙⊙⊙⊙⊙⊙⊙⊙ ⊙

_21_ TENS _1_ ONES = 21

Write the numbers.

4. 7 tens 2 ones = __72__   **5.** 3 tens 9 ones = __39__

Compare Numbers

Circle the largest number.

1. (32) 18 27

2. 67 74 (96)

Circle the smallest number.

3. 83 (29) 31

4. 26 27 (25)

Count the nickels. Count by fives.

5.

___5___ ___10___ ___15___ ___20___ ___25___ ___30___ ___35___

Finish the pattern. Count by tens.

6. 10, 20, 30, ___40___, ___50___, ___60___, ___70___

Finish the pattern. Count by twos.

7. ___2___, 4, 6, 8, 10, ___12___, ___14___, ___16___

Finish the pattern. Count by odd numbers.

8. 1, 3, 5, 7, ___9___, ___11___, ___13___, ___15___

What's Next? You Decide!

MATH

2.C

Now it's your turn to choose what to do next in the lesson. Read the activities and decide which one you want to do—you may want to try them all!

Build Numbers

MATERIALS

- ❑ 1 spinner
- ❑ place-value blocks

STEPS

Use a spinner to build numbers.

- ❑ Spin the spinner. Make that number of tens with the place-value blocks.
- ❑ Spin the spinner again. Make that number of ones with the place-value blocks.
- ❑ How many blocks do you have? Write the number in your notebook.
- ❑ Play the game again.
- ❑ Is your new number larger or smaller than the first number?

Play Cards

MATERIALS

- ❑ 50 index cards

STEPS

- ❑ Write a different number on each card from 1 to 50.
- ❑ Mix up the cards.
- ❑ Close your eyes and take three cards.
- ❑ Put the cards in order from the smallest to the largest number.
- ❑ Now close your eyes and take four cards.
- ❑ Put the numbers in order from smallest to largest.

(CONTINUED)

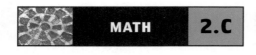

Make a Chart

MATERIALS

- ❑ several small counters to glue on paper, such as beans, cereal, or macaroni
- ❑ 1 posterboard
- ❑ glue

STEPS

Make a chart for counting by twos. Ask an adult to help you find counters.

- ❑ Glue counters on the paper in groups of two.
- ❑ Count by twos. Write the number under each group of counters as you count.
- ❑ Use your chart to practice counting by twos.
- ❑ Make more charts for counting by threes, fours, and fives.

Hunt for Patterns

STEPS

Find things in your home with number patterns.

- ❑ Chairs have four legs. How many chairs are in your home?
- ❑ Count the total number of legs.

- ❑ Many clocks have two hands. How many clocks are in your home?
- ❑ Count the total number of hands.
- ❑ Count other patterns in your home.
- ❑ Then, if you'd like, draw the patterns you found.

Understanding Addition

Add to your math knowledge: Learn addition!

OBJECTIVE	BACKGROUND	MATERIALS
To introduce your student to addition and the various ways to add	Mastering addition is essential to mathematical progress. In this lesson, your student will learn helpful strategies to add whole numbers from zero to 18.	■ Student Learning Pages 3.A–3.B ■ 18 two-sided counters ■ black, red, yellow, orange, blue, and brown crayons

Let's Begin

ADDITION

1 **DISPLAY** Explain to your student that addition is about finding the total amount of different groups or parts. Ask him or her to make a pile of 2 counters and a pile of 1 counter. Each pile should be a different color. Have your student count the number in each pile. Ask, *How many counters are there of each color?* Then ask, *How many counters are there in all?* [3] Note that as you work through the lesson's addition concepts, you may wish to take breaks throughout and cover the skills and exercises over the course of a few days. Or you may prefer to take an hour or so and move right through it. Let your student be the guide.

2 **REVIEW** Have your student write 2 + 1 = 3 in his or her notebook. Use the counter piles to explain the addition sentence. Say, *2 plus 1 equals 3*. Have your student read the addition sentence out loud.

3 **EXPAND** Explain that the same addition sentence can be written horizontally and vertically. Move the counters so that one pile is above the other pile. Then write 2 + 1 vertically on the paper, including the equation bar. Explain to your student how to add the top number to the bottom number. Then model how to write the answer beneath the equation bar. Ask, *How many counters are there in all?* [3] Have your student write the answer.

4 **ASK** Direct your student to make a pile of 3 counters and a pile of 1 counter. Help your student write a horizontal and vertical addition sentence for the piles in his or her notebook.

!

A BRIGHT IDEA

Have your student add groups of objects in the room. Present word problems such as the following: *There are 4 pictures in the bedroom. There are 3 pictures in the living room. How many pictures are there in both rooms?* [7]

ADDITION STRATEGIES

1 **MODEL** Counting on is one way to solve addition problems. A number line can help your student count on. Model how to solve 3 + 2 by counting on the number line below (start at 3 and count on 2 spaces to get 5). Point at each number with your finger as you model counting on. Then have your student count on the number line to solve 9 + 9. [18] Encourage your student to use his or her finger as a guide. Then challenge your student to think of other ways he or she could count on.

2 **EXPAND** Explain to your student that a number added to zero equals itself. Tell him or her that adding zero to a number doesn't change the number. Have your student count on to solve 6 + 0. [6] Then give your student other problems to write and solve in his or her notebook.

+

ENRICH THE EXPERIENCE

For games and activities on adding and subtracting, go to http://www.aaamath.com.

3 **INTRODUCE** If your student had trouble with the problems in Step 2, you may wish to introduce this addition strategy: making a 10. Give your student 11 counters. Have him or her make a pile of 9 and a pile of 2. Then ask, *What is 9 + 2?* [11] Model forming a 10 using the counters. Ask, *What is 10 + 1?* [11] *What is similar about the two addition problems?* [they both have the same answer] Ask your student to find another addition problem that has 11 as the answer. [8 + 3]

4 **PRACTICE** Hand 15 counters to your student. Then present this problem: 9 + 6. Have your student demonstrate making a 10. [student should take 1 from the pile of 6 and add it to the pile of 9] Ask, *What is another way to show 15?* [student should make piles of 9 and 6 or 8 and 7] Then have your student complete Student Learning Page 3.A.

Branching Out

TEACHING TIP

Creating picture stories is a fun way to solve addition sentences. Give your student this problem: 2 + 5. Have him or her make up a picture story to accompany the problem and then draw pictures to solve it.

FOR FURTHER READING

The Hershey's Kisses Addition Book, by Jerry Pallotta (Cartwheel Books, 2001).

I Can Add, by Anna Nilsen (Larousse Kingfisher Chambers, 2000).

CHECKING IN

To assess your student's understanding of the lesson, give him or her several problems that can be solved in a variety of ways, such as making a 10, using doubles, or counting on. Observe your student's addition techniques. Make sure your student adds and subtracts from the appropriate addends when making a 10.

Practice Addition

Look at the pictures. Write the addition sentence.

1.

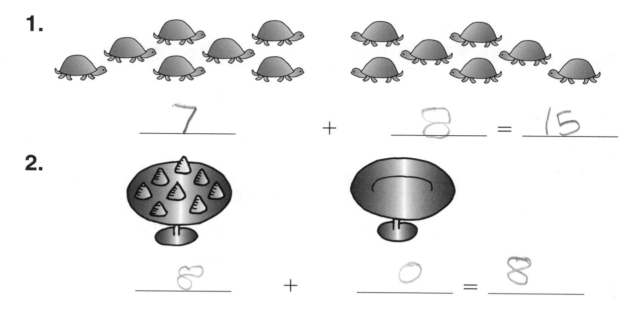

_____7_____ + _____8_____ = _____15_____

2.

_____8_____ + _____0_____ = _____8_____

Add. Then read the colors in each section and color the butterfly.

3.

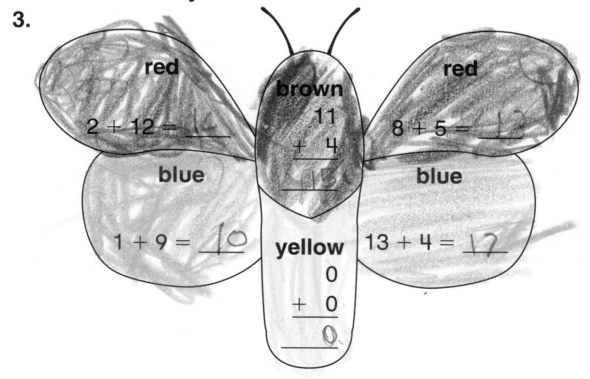

red

2 + 12 = _____

blue

1 + 9 = _10_

brown

$$\begin{array}{r} 11 \\ +\ 4 \\ \hline \end{array}$$

red

8 + 5 = _____

blue

13 + 4 = _17_

yellow

$$\begin{array}{r} 0 \\ +\ 0 \\ \hline 0 \end{array}$$

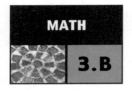

MATH

3.B

What's Next? You Decide!

Now it's your turn to choose what to do next in the lesson. Read the activities and decide which one you want to do—you may want to try them both!

Make a Math Storybook

MATERIALS

- ❑ 19 index cards labeled 0–18
- ❑ 1 binder
- ❑ markers or crayons

STEPS

- ❑ Lay the index cards facedown. Choose two cards.
- ❑ Write and solve an addition sentence using the numbers.
- ❑ Draw a picture story for the sentence.
- ❑ Choose more cards to make picture stories.
- ❑ Put the stories in the binder.
- ❑ Read your storybook to your family.

Hop to It!

MATERIALS

- ❑ sidewalk chalk

STEPS

- ❑ Draw a chain of 19 squares on a sidewalk or driveway. Each square should be big enough for you to stand in.
- ❑ Label the squares with the numbers 0 to 18.
- ❑ Have an adult read each story. Hop to the sum.
  - There are 3 black dogs and 8 yellow dogs. How many dogs are there?
  - Jo has 9 pears and 0 plums. How many pieces of fruit does Jo have?

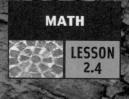

MATH

LESSON 2.4

Adding Two-Digit Numbers

The more energy a teacher applies to teaching, the greater the enthusiasm of a student.

OBJECTIVE	BACKGROUND	MATERIALS
To help your student add two-digit numbers	For many students, the quantum leap in understanding the operation of addition occurs when they learn how to add two-digit numbers. The discovery of the mechanics of regrouping when adding two-digit numbers aids in adding even larger numbers. In this lesson, your student will explore ways to add two-digit numbers.	<ul><li>Student Learning Pages 4.A–4.B</li><li>100 counters</li><li>10 plastic sandwich bags or other small containers</li><li>2 small paper bags</li><li>3 dimes and 15 pennies</li></ul>

VOCABULARY
REGROUPING combining ones into tens; exchanging 10 ones for 1 ten

Let's Begin

ADDITION WITH TENS

1   **REVIEW** Use counters, such as beans, to review counting on with ones to form tens. Have your student count out 10 beans and put them in a plastic sandwich bag. Ask, *What does 10 ones make?* [1 ten] Then say, *Let's make 9 tens.* [student should count out 10 beans nine times to fill nine sandwich bags] *Each bag of beans is 1 ten. Can you add 3 tens together? What is the sum?* [30] Continue to count on with ones and tens to review. If appropriate have your student count on by ones to 10 and then backward from 10 to 1. Then have him or her count on by tens to 100.

2   **RECOGNIZE** As you work through this lesson, you may find that you need to review the simple, single-digit addition concepts taught in Lesson 2.3. Let your student guide you as to how fast or slow to progress through this lesson. If you find that your student struggles with two-digit addition, take a break and try a different approach. You may find that your student prefers to hold and manipulate counters. You may recognize that he or she works best when writing numbers in his or her notebook. Or perhaps he or she prefers to see the numbers written, or pictures of objects. Remember to make learning fun!

3   **MODEL AND ADD** Have your student label two paper bags "Tens" and "Ones." Have him or her put the 9 bags of beans

A BRIGHT IDEA

Some students will be very comfortable with the pattern of adding tens, especially when they are using a 100 table. Draw a 100 table as a grid of 100 squares (10 rows of 10 cells). The first row has the numbers 1 to 10 across. The 10 rows (from top to bottom) begin with 1, 11, 21, 31, 41, 51, 61, 71, 81, and 91. Challenge your student by encouraging him or her to find sums mentally. Also encourage him or her to look for other patterns (diagonal or vertical) on a 100 table and to color the patterns he or she finds.

FOR FURTHER READING

Math Made Easy: A First-Grade Workbook, by Sue Phillips and Sean McArdle (Dorling Kindersley, 2001).

My First Math Book, by David Clemson and Wendy Clemson (DK Publishing, 2001).

Write-and-Read Math Story Books (*Grades K–2*), by Betsy Franco (Scholastic Paperbacks, 1999).

into the Tens sack and put 9 individual beans into the Ones sack. Make three columns in your student's notebook and label the columns "My First Number," "My Second Number," and "The Sum." Have your student choose some tens and ones and write his or her first number (for example, 3 tens and 4 ones; 34). Then have him or her choose only tens and write the second number (for example, 2 tens; 20). Ask, *What is the sum of your first and second numbers?* [54] Have your student write the sum. Direct him or her to repeat the activity a few times for practice.

TWO-DIGIT ADDITION

1 **DEMONSTRATE AND EXPLAIN** Draw or use place-value blocks as shown below or continue to use sandwich bags and beans to introduce the idea of **regrouping** to your student. Ask, *To add 23 and 9, are there more than 9 ones?* [yes] Then say, *When there are more than 9 ones, we can regroup 10 of the ones into 1 ten.* Have your student circle 10 place-value blocks or put 10 beans into a sandwich bag. Ask, *How many tens do we have now?* [3] *How many ones are left?* [2] *What is the sum?* [32] Have your student use the blocks or beans to add 37 + 5, 14 + 8, and 42 + 7. Be sure your student understands that no regrouping is needed for 42 + 7.

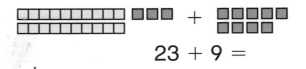

$$23 + 9 =$$

2 **DISTRIBUTE** Have your student complete Student Learning Page 4.A for more practice.

Branching Out

TEACHING TIP

The basic concepts a student needs to add two-digit numbers are those of place value and tens. Be careful to note if your student counts a ten as a one or writes numbers of tens in regrouping activities as single digits.

CHECKING IN

Invite your student to tell a math story that requires adding two-digit numbers. Have him or her use tens (bags of counters) and ones (individual counters) to show his or her math story. Ask your student to explain if regrouping is needed and when.

Practice with Addition

(handwritten: 56 / +09 / 65)

Circle the ones to regroup. Solve.

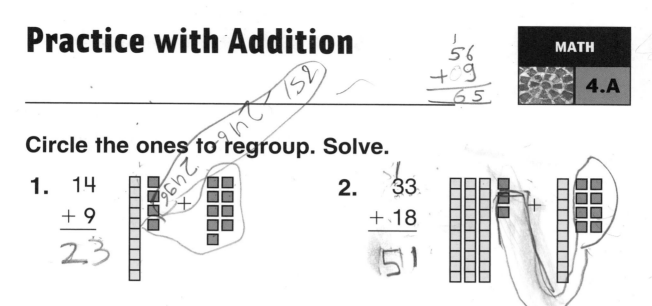

1. 14
    + 9
    23

2. 33
    + 18
    51

Use counters to help solve. The first one is done for you.

	Show This Many	Add This Many	Do You Need to Regroup?		Solve
	15	3	yes	no	15 + 3 = 18
3.	56	9	yes	no	56 + 9 = 65
4.	74	8	yes	no	74 + 8 = 82

Use counters to help solve. Write the number sentence with the answer.

5. There are 23 children on the Ferris wheel. Then 8 more children get on. How many children are on it now?

_23_ + _8_ = _31_ chidren

6. Sara has 32 plants. Adam has 14 plants. How many plants do they have in total?

_32_ + _14_ = _____

(handwritten right margin: 23 / + 8 / 32 ... + 14)

What's Next? You Decide!

Now it's your turn to choose what to do next in the lesson. Read the activities and decide which one you want to do—you may want to try them both!

Add Fast!

MATERIALS

❑ 2 sets of 13 index cards labeled with the numbers 0–12

STEPS

❑ Keep one set of cards. Give the other set to another player.

❑ Mix up the cards. Put the cards in a pile with the numbers down.

❑ Each player turns over a card at the same time.

❑ The player who says the sum of the two cards first wins both cards.

❑ The player with the most cards wins.

Find the Biggest Sum

MATERIALS

❑ 1 pencil
❑ 1 paper clip

STEPS

❑ Make a spinner with eight spaces and mark the spaces 1 through 8.

❑ Hold the paper clip at the center of the spinner with the pencil and spin the paper clip with your finger twice.

❑ The two digits make your first number.

❑ Spin two more times to make a second number.

❑ Add the two numbers.

❑ Spin again to find another sum. Continue adding to 100.

Understanding Subtraction

Lessen your student's fear of math: Make subtraction fun!

OBJECTIVE	BACKGROUND	MATERIALS
To help your student explore subtraction and subtraction methods	A student who understands subtraction recognizes parts and wholes, which is necessary for upcoming work with division, fractions, and basic geometry. In this lesson, your student will use various strategies to subtract whole numbers.	■ Student Learning Pages 5.A–5.B ■ 4 equal squares of paper ■ 8 connecting cubes ■ 18 counters

Let's Begin

INTRODUCTION TO SUBTRACTION

1 **INTRODUCE** Use the 4 paper squares to make a single large square. Show this model to your student. Explain to him or her that you will use it to explain subtraction. Say, *I have 4 pieces of cake. I eat 1 piece.* Remove 1 square. Then ask, *How many pieces do I have left?* [3]

2 **CONNECT** Write 4 − 1 = 3 on a sheet of paper. Write it both horizontally and vertically. Show the subtraction sentences to your student. Tell him or her that both sentences mean the same thing. Explain to your student that the numbers relate to the cake problem. Say that both sentences represent the amount of cake left over. Then have your student read the sentences out loud.

3 **ASK** Give your student a new cake problem. Say, *There are 4 pieces of cake. Cindy eats 2 pieces of cake. How many pieces of cake should you remove?* [2] *How many pieces are left?* [2] Allow your student to use the paper squares to model the problem. Have him or her write the subtraction sentence for this problem both horizontally and vertically. [4 − 2 = 2]

4 **EXTEND** Explain to your student that a number minus zero always equals itself. Demonstrate this with the squares. Show your student that if you have 4 paper squares and subtract zero, you still have 4 squares. Then ask, *What is 9 – 0?* [9] *How do you know?* [student should demonstrate an understanding of subtracting zero]

ENRICH THE EXPERIENCE

Demonstrate to your student the importance of order in subtraction. Have him or her connect 5 of the connecting cubes. Ask him or her to subtract 3. Then reverse the steps. Discuss why your student can't take 5 away from 3.

SUBTRACTION STRATEGIES

1   **MODEL**   Model counting back with counters. Say, *I had 18 counters. You took 2 of them. This leaves me with 16 counters.* As you speak, demonstrate your words with the counters. This will help your student relate the words with the actions. Write 18 − 2 = _____ in your student's notebook. Have him or her fill in the answer. Then have your student count back to solve 15 − 3 = _____. [12]

Reverse the roles of the subtraction activity in Step 1. Ask your student to think of a subtraction problem and model it by counting back with counters. Make sure he or she demonstrates his or her words with the counters.

2   **EXPLORE**   Challenge your student to count back using a number line. Have him or her use the number line in Lesson 2.3 or draw one for your student. Have him or her solve the problems 6 − 0 = _____ and 8 − 7 = _____. [6, 1]

3   **DEMONSTRATE**   Using pictures is a fun way to count back. Draw 6 yellow balloons and 4 red balloons. Ask, *How many yellow balloons are there?* [6] *How many red balloons are there?* [4] *How many balloons are there in all?* [10] Then say, *All of the red balloons pop.* Cross out each red balloon. *How many balloons are left?* [6] Help your student write a subtraction sentence for the problem. [10 − 4 = 6] Have your student draw balloons or other pictures to solve 9 − 2 = _____ and 17 − 14 = _____. [7, 3] Observe that he or she crosses out the correct number of pictures.

4   **DISTRIBUTE**   Have your student complete Student Learning Page 5.A for more practice with subtraction.

5   **ASSIST**   If your student chooses the bowling activity on Student Learning Page 5.B, set up the cups in the following manner.

Branching Out

Monster Musical Chairs: Level 1—Subtracting One (Mathstart), by Stuart J. Murphy (HarperTrophy, 2000).

Subtraction Fun (Yellow Umbrella Books: Math), by Betsy Franco (Pebble Books, 2002).

TEACHING TIP

While this lesson may not take long to cover, take whatever time necessary to make sure your student has a complete understanding of the material in each step before moving on to the next step.

CHECKING IN

To assess your student's understanding of the lesson, provide your student with a group of subtraction problems. Include both vertical and horizontal subtraction sentences. Observe as he or she uses counters and makes a 10 to solve them.

Practice Subtraction

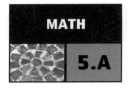

Help Tommy get the ball. Solve the subtraction problems.

1.

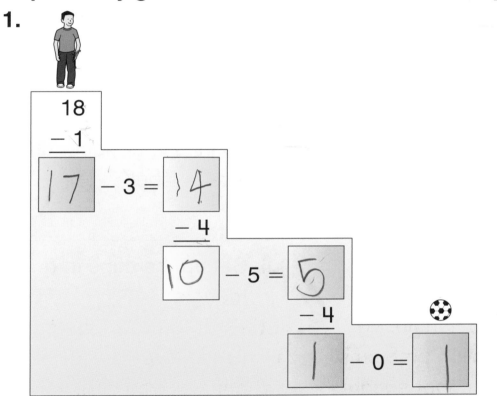

$$18 - 1$$

$$17 - 3 = 14$$

$$- 4$$

$$10 - 5 = 5$$

$$- 4$$

$$1 - 0 = 1$$

Cross out the correct number of pictures. Then solve.

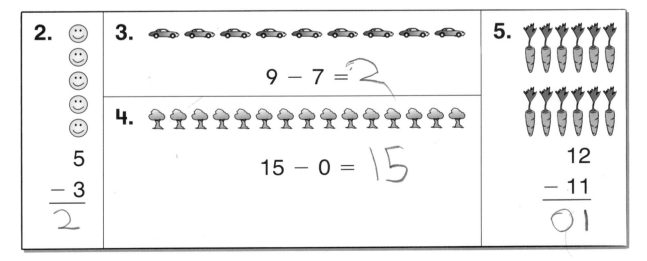

2.

$$\begin{array}{r} 5 \\ -3 \\ \hline 2 \end{array}$$

3.

$$9 - 7 = 2$$

4.

$$15 - 0 = 15$$

5.

$$\begin{array}{r} 12 \\ -11 \\ \hline 01 \end{array}$$

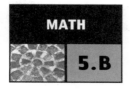

What's Next? You Decide!

Now it's your turn to choose what to do next in the lesson. Read the activities and decide which one you want to do—you may want to try them both!

Beat the Clock!

MATERIALS

❑ 1 stopwatch
❑ 19 squares of paper labeled 0–18
❑ 1 paper bag

STEPS

You have two minutes to solve subtraction problems.

❑ Place the paper squares in the bag.
❑ Ask an adult to time you.
❑ Choose two squares.
❑ Write a subtraction problem on paper. Put the larger number first!
❑ Solve the problem.
❑ Continue until time runs out. How many problems did you solve?

Bowl and Subtract

MATERIALS

❑ 15 plastic or paper cups
❑ 1 tennis ball

STEPS

❑ Set up the cups in a triangle.
❑ Roll the ball at the cups. Knock over as many cups as you can.
❑ How many cups are left over? Write a subtraction problem. The answer is your score.
❑ Set all of the cups up again. Let another person roll.
❑ The lowest score wins.

Exploring Two-Digit Subtraction

If caring is subtracted from teaching, there's nothing left over.

OBJECTIVE	BACKGROUND	MATERIALS
To explore a variety of ways to subtract and to introduce two-digit subtraction	How much is left? How much time do we have left? How much money do we have left? How many pieces of dessert are left? We ask these questions every day. Subtraction is the tool we use to answer them. Your student also uses subtraction on a daily basis. In this lesson, your student will learn to subtract two-digit numbers.	■ Student Learning Pages 6.A–6.B ■ 20 counters ■ place-value blocks ■ masking tape or chalk ■ 1 copy T Chart, page 355

Let's Begin

COUNTING BACK

1 **REVIEW** Before beginning this lesson, you may find it helpful to review simple subtraction with your student in Lesson 2.5. Throughout this lesson, remember to let your student guide you as to how long to spend covering each section. You may find it helpful to cover the material over the course of a few days and keep coming back to it and exploring the activities.

2 **TEACH** Counting back is one strategy for solving subtraction problems. Have your student solve $9 - 3 =$ _____. [6] Ask, *What did you think about to find the answer?* Discuss your student's strategy. Draw a number line from zero to 20 on a sheet of paper. Say, *Sometimes when I subtract, I count back to find the answer.* Put your finger on the number line at 9. Show your student how to count back 3. Say, *I start at 9. Then I hop back 3 . . . 8, 7, 6.* Use the number line to continue the activity with several subtraction sentences. Ask your student to explain how to solve $14 - 5 =$ _____ by counting back. [count back 5 from 14 to find 9]

3 **PRACTICE** Make a giant number line from 1 to 20 by applying tape to the floor or by using chalk to draw one on the sidewalk. Show your student how to solve $11 - 3 =$ _____ by standing on the 11 and then hopping (or stepping) back 3. Have your student use the number line to practice solving subtraction problems.

SUBTRACTION WITH TENS

1 **MODEL** Explain that visualizing numbers in groups of 10 is another strategy for solving subtraction problems. Have your student solve 13 − 5. [8] Ask, *What did you think about to find the answer?* Discuss your student's strategy. Say, *Sometimes when I subtract, I think about how many tens and ones are in the number I started with.* Show your student how to arrange 13 counters or place-value blocks to show 1 ten and 3 ones. Then model taking 5 away, beginning with the 3 ones. Take the 2 remaining ones away from the 1 ten. As you practice subtracting with this method, stress the order of removing the ones first and then taking away from a whole group of ten. Continue the activity by having your student model other subtraction problems.

2 **EXPLAIN** Ask, *Why do you think we always remove the ones first?* Help your student understand that removing the ones first leaves 1 ten, which can help solve the problem. Think out loud as you model how to solve 16 − 7. Say, *I've arranged 16 counters as 1 ten and 6 ones. Now I have to take away 7. When I remove the 6 ones, I have 1 ten left. I know that 6 + 1 is 7, so I need to take away 1. I know that if I take 1 away from the ten, I will have 9 left.* Give your student more problems to solve.

TWO-DIGIT SUBTRACTION

1 **EXPLAIN** Label the columns on a copy of the T Chart found on page 355 as "Tens" and "Ones." Place 4 tens and 6 ones blocks on the chart. Ask, *How many blocks do you see?* [46] *How many will we have left if we take 25 away?* [21] Show your student how to take 25 blocks from 46. Stress the importance of taking the 5 ones away first and then the 2 tens. Show your student how to write 46 − 25 vertically. Then have your student subtract 37 − 19 using counters or place-value blocks.

2 **DISTRIBUTE** Have your student complete Student Learning Page 6.A for more practice with two-digit subtraction.

Branching Out

TEACHING TIP

Interlocking toy blocks can be used as place-value blocks. Beans, macaroni, marbles, or paper clips can be used as counters.

CHECKING IN

To assess your student's understanding of the lesson, have your student solve 12 − 3, 32 − 11, and 43 − 27. Ask him or her to explain the strategies he or she used to solve the problems.

DID YOU KNOW?

As your student practices manipulating the counters using this method, he or she will begin to form mental pictures that will become the basis for mental math.

FOR FURTHER READING

Math Made Easy: First Grade Workbook, by Sue Phillips and Sean McArdle (Dorling Kindersley, 2001).

Subtraction Action, by Loreen Leedy (Holiday House, 2000).

Subtract Two-Digit Numbers

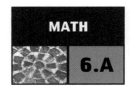

Solve the problems. Use the number line to count back.

0 1 2 3 4 5 6 7 8 9 10 11 12 13 14 15 16 17 18 19 20

1. $17 - 3 =$ _____

3. $13 - 1 =$ _____

2. $20 - 4 =$ _____

4. $12 - 9 =$ _____

Think about tens and ones. Cross out to subtract.

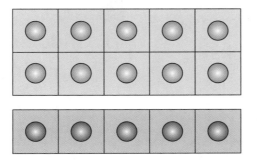

5. $15 - 8 =$ _____

6. $7 - 2 =$ _____

Subtract. Use counters to help.

7. $\begin{array}{r} 29 \\ -\ 16 \\ \hline \end{array}$

8. $\begin{array}{r} 52 \\ -\ 27 \\ \hline \end{array}$

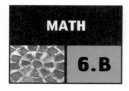

What's Next? You Decide!

Now it's your turn to choose what to do next in the lesson. Read the activities and decide which one you want to do—you may want to try them both!

Play Subtraction Tic-Tac-Toe

STEPS

❏ Draw a tic-tac-toe grid. Have an adult help you.

❏ Write a subtraction problem in each square.

❏ The first player picks a box and solves the problem.

❏ If the solution is correct, the player marks an X in the box.

❏ The second player chooses a box and solves the problem.

❏ If the solution is correct, the player marks an O in the box.

❏ Play the game until someone gets 3 boxes in a row.

Write Math Stories

MATERIALS

❏ 10 index cards labeled 0–9

❏ markers or crayons

STEPS

❏ Choose a card for the number of tens. Choose a card for the number of ones.

❏ Choose two cards again to make a second number.

❏ Write a subtraction problem with your numbers.

❏ Write or draw a story about your numbers.

❏ Choose more numbers and make up more stories.

Investigating Fractions

An educator is one half teacher and one half student.

OBJECTIVE	BACKGROUND	MATERIALS
To teach your student to identify equal parts of wholes and groups and to associate fractions with those parts	Working with fractions will help your student see the connections between parts and wholes or groups. In this lesson, your student will explore equal parts, fractions of a whole, and fractions of a group.	■ Student Learning Pages 7.A–7.B ■ 1 pair scissors ■ 1 unpeeled orange ■ markers or crayons ■ 2 copies T Chart, page 355 ■ 8 two-sided counters

VOCABULARY
FRACTION the relationship of some equal parts to the total number of equal parts

Let's Begin

INTRODUCING FRACTIONS

1 **CONNECT** Throughout this lesson, be sure to incorporate as many visuals as needed. You may find that your student understands fractions best when he or she is able to connect it to something hands-on.

2 **PACE** Be sure to pace yourself during this lesson. Fractions can sometimes be difficult to grasp, so you may prefer to take a break between each section. You may find that your student is ready to return to the next section in an hour or two, or perhaps the next day. Let your student be the guide!

EQUAL PARTS

1 **EXPLORE** Draw a square on a sheet of paper. Draw a vertical line through it to make 2 equal parts. Show the drawing to your student. Explain to him or her that the square has 2 equal parts, or pieces, that are exactly the same size and shape. Say, *Suppose this square is a sandwich. If you and I each took 1 part, would we get the same amount of sandwich?* [yes] *Why?* [because both parts are the same size and shape]

2 **EXPAND** Now draw a new square with a horizontal line through it to make 2 equal parts. Show the drawing to your

A BRIGHT IDEA

Have your student use scissors to cut each square into equal parts. Then ask him or her to form a whole from the equal parts. This will help your student see the relationship between equal parts and wholes.

DID YOU KNOW?

Remind your student that when a group of people share something, each person receives an equal amount of that thing. Quiz your student's understanding of this concept by presenting scenarios involving different numbers of people.

student. Ask, *Does this square also have 2 equal parts?* [yes] *How do you know?* [both parts are the same size and shape] Then divide a square into 2 unequal parts. Have your student tell you whether or not the square shows equal parts. [no] Ask, *How can you tell?* [not the same size and shape]

3 **APPLY** Tell your student that there are different ways to divide shapes into equal parts. Draw a square on a sheet of paper and show it to him or her. Ask, *In what ways can you divide the square into 2 equal parts?* [by drawing a diagonal line, horizontal line, or vertical line]

4 **EXPLAIN** Explain to your student that shapes can have more than 2 equal parts. Draw three more squares on the paper. Divide one into 3 equal parts, another into 4 equal parts, and the third one into 6 equal parts. Ask, *Do these squares have equal parts?* [yes] *How many equal parts does each square have?* [3, 4, 6]

5 **EXTEND** Draw two circles. Have your student divide them into 2 and 4 equal parts.

HALVES

1 **REVIEW** Hold up an orange for your student to see. Say, *Suppose you and I want to share this orange. How many equal parts should I cut it into?* [2]

2 **EXPLAIN** Slice the orange into 2 equal parts. Give 1 part to your student. Explain to him or her that each equal part of the orange is called a half. Then tell him or her that 2 halves make a whole. To model this, ask your student to put the orange halves together to form a whole.

3 **DEVELOP** Draw an X on the skin of 1 orange half. Then write $\frac{1}{2}$ on a sheet of paper. Explain to your student that this symbol is a **fraction** called one half. Tell him or her that the 1 represents the equal part of the orange with the X. The 2 represents the total number of equal parts of the orange. Continue to model the concept of fractions with your student, making sure to help your student in a noncritical and nonjudgmental manner. Then, on a sheet of paper, draw a heart divided equally in half. Ask, *Does the heart have equal parts?* [yes] *How many?* [2]

4 **ASK** Ask your student to color one half of the heart. Then ask, *What fraction shows the colored half of the heart?* [$\frac{1}{2}$] Have him or her write it next to the heart.

THIRDS AND FOURTHS

1 **MODEL** Show your student the triangle on the next page. Ask, *How many equal parts does the triangle have?* [3] Then explain that each equal part of the triangle is called one third and that 3 thirds make up a whole. Point to the fraction $\frac{1}{3}$ and tell your student what it represents. Ask, *How many thirds does the triangle have?* [3]

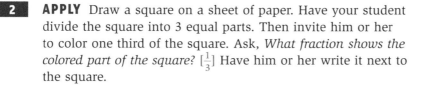

$$\frac{1 \text{ (shaded part)}}{3 \text{ (equal parts)}} = \text{one third}$$

2   **APPLY** Draw a square on a sheet of paper. Have your student divide the square into 3 equal parts. Then invite him or her to color one third of the square. Ask, *What fraction shows the colored part of the square?* [$\frac{1}{3}$] Have him or her write it next to the square.

3   **DEVELOP** Introduce fourths to your student. Draw a rectangle and divide it into 4 equal parts. Show the drawing to your student. Explain to him or her that each part is one fourth of the rectangle. Then explain the fraction $\frac{1}{4}$. Draw a circle on a sheet of paper and show it to your student. Say, *Four people want to share this pie. How would you divide it so that each person gets an equal amount?* [divide it into 4 equal parts] Have your student divide the circle and point to the amount of pie that each person will receive. Ask, *What fraction of the pie will each person get?* [$\frac{1}{4}$] Then direct your student to color one fourth of the circle and have him or her write the fraction next to it.

4   **EXPLAIN** Explain to your student that there are different ways to show one half, one third, and one fourth. Draw two circles divided into 4 equal parts. In one circle, have your student color the top 2 parts. In the other, instruct him or her to color the top-left and bottom-right parts. Tell your student that one half of each circle is colored. Have him or her draw four more circles. Challenge your student to show one half in four other ways. He or she should color the bottom 2 parts, right 2 parts, left 2 parts, and the opposite diagonal parts. Repeat the activity for one third and one fourth, using circles or squares. Have your student explain how he or she colors the parts.

FRACTIONS OF A GROUP

1   **EXPLAIN** Tell your student that he or she has learned about fractions of wholes. Then explain that fractions can also name parts of groups. Show your student 4 two-sided counters. Ask, *How many counters are in this group?* [4]

2   **DEMONSTRATE** Explain that each counter is 1 part of a group of 4. Then have your student turn over 1 of the counters so that it shows a different color (such as red) than the others. Ask, *How many parts of the group are red?* [1 part]

3   **REVIEW** Review what the top and bottom numbers of a fraction represent. Then ask, *Does this group of counters show the fraction $\frac{1}{4}$ or $\frac{1}{3}$?* [$\frac{1}{4}$] Help your student explain the numbers in the fraction. [1 is the number of equal parts related to the total number of equal parts] Then have him or her use the two-sided counters to show $\frac{1}{3}$ and $\frac{1}{2}$.

GET ORGANIZED

Help your student remember halves, thirds, and fourths. Make a copy of the T Chart found on page 355. Write "one half," "one third," and "one fourth" on the left side. Then direct your student to write the correct numerical fraction on the right side.

4   **EXPLAIN** Explain that your student can form equal sets to find fractions of a group. Display the picture below to your student, covering the bottom sentence. Explain that all of the flowers together are a group. Ask, *How many flowers are in the group?* [6] Then point to each set. Ask, *How many yellow flowers are there?* [3] *Pink?* [3] Explain that each color represents an equal set. Explain that equal sets contain the same number of items. Then ask, *How many equal sets are there?* [2] *How many flowers are in each equal set?* [3]

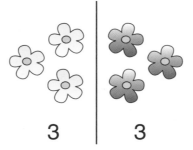

3   3

One half of 6 is 3.

5   **DEMONSTRATE** Explain that your student must make 2 equal sets to find the number of flowers in one half of the group. Point to the set of yellow flowers. Lead your student to complete the last sentence. Say, *There are 3 yellow flowers. One half of the 6 flowers are yellow. This tells you that one half of 6 is* _____. [3]

6   **DISTRIBUTE** Give Student Learning Page 7.A to your student and have him or her complete it for additional practice with fractions.

Branching Out

FOR FURTHER READING

Can You Eat a Fraction?, by Elizabeth D. Jaffe (Pebble Books, 2002).

Clean-Sweep Campers (*Math Matters*), by Lucille Recht Penner (Kane Press, 2000).

The Hershey's Milk Chocolate Bar Fractions Book, by Jerry Pallotta (Cartwheel Books, 1999).

TEACHING TIP

Help your student remember the number of equal sets he or she must make to find a certain fraction in a group by relating the number of equal sets to the name of the fraction. For example, relate the number 2 to the word *half:* Two halves make up a whole. Then give your student a copy of the T Chart found on page 355. Label the headings "Name of Fraction" and "Number of Equal Sets." Have your student complete the chart.

CHECKING IN

To assess your student's understanding of the lesson, have him or her practice forming equal parts of a whole and equal sets of a group. Observe to ensure your student's comprehension. Make sure he or she understands halves, thirds, and fourths.

Explore Fractions

Help Jennifer share her lunch.

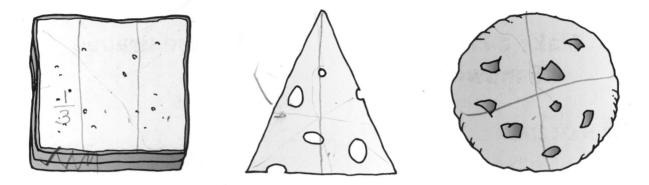

1. Divide the sandwich into 3 equal parts. Divide the piece of cheese into 2 equal parts. Divide the cookie into 4 equal parts.

2. Color $\frac{1}{3}$ of the sandwich blue. Color $\frac{1}{2}$ of the cheese yellow. Color $\frac{1}{4}$ of the cookie red.

Make equal sets. Color one set blue. Color the other set green. Then finish the sentence.

3.

One half of 8 is _____.

What's Next? You Decide!

Now it's your turn to choose what to do next in the lesson. Read the activities and decide which one you want to do—you may want to try them both!

Make a Fraction Sandwich

MATERIALS

- ❏ 1 slice bread
- ❏ peanut butter
- ❏ honey
- ❏ 1 banana

STEPS

Have an adult help you with this activity.

- ❏ Fold the slice of bread in half.
- ❏ Spread peanut butter on one half of the bread.
- ❏ Spread honey on the other half of the bread.
- ❏ Cut the banana into fourths. Put the pieces on one half of the bread.
- ❏ Enjoy your sandwich!

Eat the Grapes

MATERIALS

- ❏ 2 red grapes
- ❏ 6 green grapes
- ❏ 3 index cards labeled $\frac{1}{2}, \frac{1}{3}, \frac{1}{4}$

STEPS

- ❏ Place all of the grapes on a table. Make 4 equal sets.
- ❏ What part of the grapes is red? Hold up the correct index card.
- ❏ Eat 2 green grapes.
- ❏ Now what part of the grapes is red? Hold up the correct index card.
- ❏ Eat 2 more green grapes.
- ❏ What part is red? Hold up the correct card.

Working with Money

MATH

LESSON
2.8

You can't put a price on your student's education.
Knowledge is priceless.

OBJECTIVE	BACKGROUND	MATERIALS
To teach your student to identify pennies, nickels, dimes, and quarters and to count and compare coin combinations	It doesn't take a child long to realize that money is an important factor in life. As adults, we know that there's rarely anything in life that's free. Even a quiet walk in the park often requires us to buy fuel for the car that gets us there. No matter what your student's future holds, he or she will have to deal with money many times. In this lesson, your student will explore coins and their values and count and compare coin combinations.	■ Student Learning Pages 8.A–8.B ■ real or play coins (pennies, nickels, dimes, quarters) ■ several old magazines and catalogs

Let's Begin

COINS

1 **COLLECT** Gather together several pennies, nickels, dimes, and quarters. You will use these throughout the lesson. Give your student ample opportunity to hold and work with the coins.

2 **PACE** Be sure to pace yourself during this lesson. Your student will probably already be familiar with money in some way; nonetheless, let your student be the guide as to how much time to spend working with each set of coins. This lesson has been divided into four sections: pennies, nickels, dimes, and quarters. You may prefer to take a break between each section—you can return to the next section in an hour or two, or the next day. Let your student guide you as to his or her interests and limits in learning.

PENNIES

1 **EXPLORE** Pennies are easy to count for your student because he or she is already used to counting by ones. Show your student one of each coin: a penny, nickel, dime, and quarter. Ask him or her to pick out the penny. Give clues to help him or her if necessary. Ask your student to describe the penny. [round, brownish color, a man's face on one side and a building on the other side, and so on] Tell your student that the man on the

MATH

LESSON 2.8

coin is President Abraham Lincoln and that the building is the Lincoln Memorial, which is in Washington, D.C. Ask, *Do you know how much a penny is worth?* [1 cent]

2 **EXPLAIN AND COUNT** If your student doesn't know the value of a penny, explain its worth to him or her. Then give him or her four pennies. Have your student count the pennies. Show him or her how to write "4¢" on a sheet of paper. Reveal the symbols used when writing amounts of money: the dollar sign ($) and the cent sign (¢). Then have your student practice counting various numbers of pennies.

3 **ENGAGE** Cut a variety of pictures of items from old magazines and catalogs. Label each item with a price of 1 to 15 cents to create a store for your student to shop in. The prices don't need to be accurate, because the goal is for your student to make the connection between the prices and the pennies. You may wish to have your student help find the pictures. Have him or her choose an item and count out the correct number of pennies needed to buy it. Give your student a certain number of pennies, such as seven, and ask, *What can you buy with your money? Do you have enough money to buy the ice skates? What are some items that are too expensive to buy with 7 cents?*

4 **EXPAND** Choose two items, such as an item for three cents and an item for nine cents. Ask your student to count out the number of pennies needed to pay for both items. Ask, *How did you know those items would cost 12 cents?* Give your student a certain number of pennies, such as 14. Ask questions such as, *Can you buy the drum and the hat with 14 cents? What two things could you buy?*

NICKELS

1 **EXPLORE** One nickel is worth five pennies. Show your student one of each coin: a penny, nickel, dime, and quarter. Ask him or her to pick out the nickel. Give clues to help him or her if necessary. Ask your student to describe the nickel. [round, silver, bigger than a penny, thicker than a penny, a man's face on one side and a building on the other, and so on] Tell your student that the man is President Thomas Jefferson and that the building is called Monticello, which is where Jefferson lived. Ask, *Do your know how much a nickel is worth?* [5 cents]

2 **EXPLAIN** If your student doesn't know the value of a nickel, explain that one nickel is the same as five pennies. Practice counting by fives with your student. Then model how to count the value of different groups of nickels. Touch each nickel as you count by fives. Help your student count by fives to find the values. Ask, *How much is a nickel worth?* [5 cents]

3 **EXPAND** Give your student one nickel and three pennies. Model how to count the coins. Point to each coin as you say, *five, six,* *seven, eight cents.* Help your student count nickel and penny combinations, first using one nickel and then increasing the number of nickels as your student's ability increases. Ask your student to explain how to count nickels and pennies. [count the nickels by fives and then count by ones to add the pennies] Give your student 10 pennies. Show him or her how to trade the pennies for nickels. [five pennies for each nickel] Have your student practice trading pennies for nickels using different numbers of pennies.

4 **PRACTICE** Cut more pictures of items from old magazines and catalogs and price them from 15 to 20 cents. Again, the prices don't need to be accurate. Add the items to the store you used during the penny activity. Have your student purchase items from your store using nickels and pennies as a form of payment. Give your student a certain amount of nickels and pennies. Ask questions such as, *Do you have enough to buy the necklace? Which items can you buy with your money?*

DIMES

1 **EXPLORE** Explain to your student that dimes are worth 10 cents. Tell him or her that ten pennies, two nickels, or one nickel and five pennies are all equal to one dime. Show your student one of each coin: a penny, nickel, dime, and quarter. Ask him or her to pick out the dime. Then have your student describe the dime. [round, silver, smallest, thinnest, rough edge, a man's face on one side and some branches and a torch on the other, and so on]

2 **CONNECT** Tell your student that the man on the dime is President Franklin D. Roosevelt. Explain that the pictures on the other side stand for important feelings about our country. Ask, *How much is a dime worth?* [10 cents] Model how to find the value of a group of dimes by counting by tens. Then have your student practice counting various numbers of dimes. Instruct him or her to count by tens to find the values, helping if necessary.

3 **PRACTICE** Cut more pictures of items from old magazines and catalogs and price them from 20 to 99 cents. Add the items to the store. Have your student count out the correct value in coins to buy items that he or she chooses. Then give your student certain amounts of change and have him or her choose which items he or she can afford to buy with the coins. Ask questions such as, *How many dimes would you need to buy the beach bag? If you had seven nickels, could you buy the radio?*

4 **COMPARE** Give your student two sets of coins, one with a value of 35 cents and one with a value of 27 cents. Ask him or her to count each set. Ask your student to choose the set that has the greater value. If he or she has trouble, explain that 35 cents is worth more money than 27 cents. Continue the activity, asking your student to identify both greater and lesser amounts.

DID YOU KNOW?

The torch on the back of the dime signifies liberty. The oak branch to the right stands for strength and independence. The olive branch on the left symbolizes peace.

QUARTERS

1 **EXPLORE** The quarter is the largest coin your student will count at this level. Show your student one of each coin: a penny, nickel, dime, and quarter. Ask him or her to pick out the quarter. Have your student describe the quarter to you. [round, silver, biggest coin, a man's face on one side and a bird on the other, rough edge, and so on] Tell your student that the man is President George Washington and that the bird is the American bald eagle. Ask, *Do your know how much a quarter is worth?* [25 cents] Have your student use pennies, nickels, and dimes to make 25 cents. Challenge him or her to find at least four ways to make 25 cents. You may wish to help him or her make a chart showing different ways to make 25 cents.

2 **EXPAND** Students at this level usually have no trouble remembering that four quarters equal $1.00 and that two quarters equal 50 cents, but don't rush the process. Some students have trouble counting on from 25 cents and 75 cents. Start slow, adding pennies to one quarter, then pennies and nickels, and so on. Practice counting combinations of pennies, nickels, dimes, and quarters. Model how to arrange the coins from greatest to least value [quarters, dimes, nickels, pennies] and to begin counting with the largest coin. Continue counting amounts to $1.00. Ask, *How many quarters do I need to make $1.00?* [4] *How many dimes, nickels, and pennies do I need?* [10, 20, 100]

3 **PRACTICE** Add more items to the store with prices up to $1.00. Have your student practice counting money by buying more products. Ask questions such as, *Which costs more, the kite or the newspaper? Do you have enough money to buy the coat? If I give you another dime will you have enough?* Then ask, *Do you think it would be a good idea to only have pennies to pay for things?* [no] *Why or why not?*

4 **DISTRIBUTE** Give Student Learning Page 8.A to your student and have him or her complete it for more practice using money.

DID YOU KNOW?

All of the bills and coins in the United States have portraits of people who are no longer living. It's against the law to mint currency with portraits of living people.

Branching Out

FOR FURTHER READING

The Coin Counting Book, by Rozanne Lanczak Williams (Charlesbridge Publishing, 2001).

A Dollar for Penny, by Julie Glass (Random House, 2000).

TEACHING TIP

Give your student a multitude of ways to practice using money. Play restaurant, hair salon, or act out any other event that will allow your student to count coins.

CHECKING IN

Give your student an amount of coins to 99 cents. Ask him or her to count the money. Then have your student take a certain amount of money from the coins. Ask your child to identify each coin.

Count Money

Count the money.

1.

Draw coins to make 36 cents.

2.

Circle the group that is worth more.

3.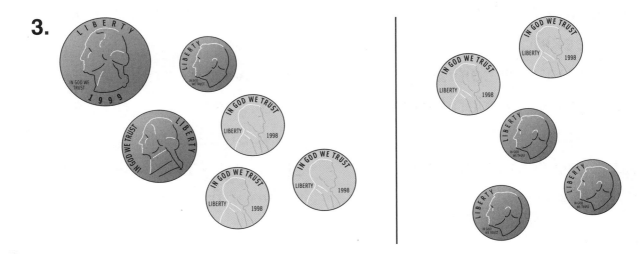

What's Next? You Decide!

Now it's your turn to choose what to do next in the lesson. Read the activities and decide which one you want to do—you may want to try them both!

Play a Coin Game

MATERIALS

❑ 6 pennies, 6 nickels, 6 dimes, and 6 quarters
❑ 1 bag
❑ 1 die

STEPS

Play this game with a friend.

❑ Put the coins in the bag.
❑ Roll the die.
❑ Take that number of coins from the bag. No peeking!
❑ Count the coins.
❑ Now your friend takes a turn.
❑ Who has more money?

Make a Poster

MATERIALS

❑ 1 posterboard
❑ markers or crayons

STEPS

❑ Draw two circles for pennies on the posterboard.
❑ Show what the front of a penny looks like.
❑ Show what the back of a penny looks like.
❑ Write how much a penny is worth.
❑ Now show nickels, dimes, and quarters on your poster.
❑ Hang your poster where your friends and family can see it.

Examining Measurement

The enthusiasm that you show for learning is contagious!

OBJECTIVE	BACKGROUND	MATERIALS
To teach your student fundamental customary and metric units of length, height, weight, and capacity	On top of forming the foundation of geometry and the sciences, mastering the basic concepts of measurements is an important life skill. The differences between the customary and metric systems of measurement aren't as confusing to students who learn both systems at the same time. In this lesson, your student will learn basic measurements for length, height, weight, and capacity.	<ul><li>Student Learning Pages 9.A–9.B</li><li>2 sheets construction paper</li><li>1 pair scissors</li><li>markers or crayons</li><li>1 ruler marked with inches and centimeters</li><li>1 object that weighs a pound, such as a bag of dried beans</li><li>common household items to measure and weigh, such as paper clips, a stapler, books, pencils, pens, crayons, a drinking glass, and so on</li><li>1 bathroom scale</li><li>1 small balance scale (or 1 wire clothing hanger, 2 containers, and paper clips to make one)</li><li>3 measuring cups (1 cup, 1 pint, and 1 quart)</li><li>1 quart rice</li><li>1 tall, clear glass jar</li><li>1 permanent marker</li><li>1 paper cup</li></ul>

VOCABULARY

LENGTH how long something is

HEIGHT how tall something is

INCH a basic unit of length in the customary system

CENTIMETER a basic unit of length in the metric system

POUND a basic unit of weight in the customary system

CUP a basic unit of capacity in the customary system

PINT a customary unit of capacity equal to 2 cups

QUART a customary unit of capacity equal to 2 pints or 4 cups

Let's Begin

LENGTH AND HEIGHT

1 **PREVIEW** Explore this lesson with your student at a comfortable pace. You may wish to take breaks between learning each type of measurement, or you may prefer to cover the lesson over the

MATH

LESSON 2.9

course of a few days or longer as your student shows interest. Let your student guide you.

2 | **EXPLAIN** Introduce the concepts of **length** and **height** as measurements for finding how long or tall things are. Help your student understand the difference between the measurements by showing him or her an object, such as a window. Ask, *Is the window longer than it is tall?* [answers will vary] *How about this door?* [taller] Have your student name something that's longer than it is tall. Then have him or her name something that's taller than it is long.

3 | **COMPARE** To reinforce the difference between length and height, ask your student to say which measurement would be used to measure different items. Then ask your student if he or she would use length or height to measure different parts of his or her body. Ask, *Would you measure the length or the height of your foot?* [length] *What about your arm?* [length] *What about the distance from the ground to the top of your head?* [height]

4 | **MEASURE** Continue emphasizing length and height by having your student trace his or her hand on a sheet of construction paper. Then help him or her use scissors to cut out the tracing. Invite your student to use the cutout to measure nearby objects, such as the height of a chair, in "hands."

INCHES AND CENTIMETERS

1 | **EXPLAIN** Display the ruler to your student. Introduce the terms **inch** and **centimeter** by showing him or her the different markings. Explain that centimeters and inches are both ways to measure length and height. Inches are part of the customary system of measurement, and centimeters are part of the metric system. Say, *In the United States we usually use inches, but people in other countries usually use centimeters. Scientists also usually use the metric system.* Have your student compare the marks on the ruler. Ask, *What differences do you notice?* [centimeters are shorter than inches] Invite your student to measure the length and width of his or her hand using both systems of measurement.

2 | **COMPARE** Guide your student to recognize that centimeters and inches are useful for measuring smaller objects. Help your student measure a variety of familiar objects in both inches and centimeters. Ask him or her to compare the lengths.

3 | **DRAW** To help your student use both inches and centimeters, have him or her make bookmarks. Assist your student as he or she cuts two strips from construction paper, one 6 inches long and one 15 centimeters long. Have your student draw lines to mark one strip with inches and the other with centimeters. Invite him or her to use markers or crayons to decorate the bookmarks. When each bookmark is complete, ask your student

A BRIGHT IDEA

If your student is confusing inches and centimeters, use two different rulers or measuring sticks and work with the measurements separately.

to write his or her name on the back. Then allow him or her to use the bookmarks or to give them away as gifts.

WEIGHT IN POUNDS

1 **EXPLAIN** Talk about weight with your student. Tell him or her that weight is how heavy something is. Explain that a **pound** is a customary unit used to measure how heavy things are. Give him or her a 1 pound weight, such as a bag of dried beans. Say, *This weighs 1 pound.* Then ask, *Does it weigh more or less than you do?* Use a bathroom scale to determine your student's weight. Say, *You weigh much more than 1 pound.* Use other common household items, such as toys or books, to help your student classify weights as heavier than, lighter than, and about equal to 1 pound.

2 **COMPARE** To explore the concept of weight measurements and comparisons further, use a small balance scale. If you need to you can build a scale using a wire clothing hanger and two containers, such as paper cups, of equal weight. Use paper clips to attach the cups to each end of the hanger. Hold the hook of the hanger to balance it. Have your student compare weights by placing items in the cups. Ask, *Is the stapler heavier than a pencil?* [yes] *Do a crayon and a pencil weigh about the same?* [yes] Expand by comparing objects to the 1 pound weight. Help your student use the balance scale to determine which items weigh less than and more than a pound. Guide him or her to make lists of items that are more than and less than a pound.

CUPS, PINTS, AND QUARTS

1 **INTRODUCE** Place a 1 cup, 1 pint, and 1 quart measuring cup on the table. Write the words **cup, pint,** and **quart** on a sheet of paper next to each measure. Explain to your student that these are the names of different measurements used to find out how much of something a container holds. Point to the word *cup* and pronounce it with your student. Help your student use the measuring cup to measure 1 cup of water. Ask him or her to say, *I have 1 cup of water.*

2 **COUNT** Repeat the activity with the pint and quart measures. Then reinforce the different measures with your student. Ask, *Which measure is the largest?* [quart] *Which is the smallest?* [cup] Then have your student use the 1 cup measure to fill the 1 pint measure. Ask, *How many cups are in a pint?* [2] Then guide him or her to use the 1 pint measure to fill the 1 quart measure. Ask, *How many pints are in a quart?* [2] Finally, ask your student to fill the 1 quart measure using the 1 cup measure. Ask, *How many cups are in a quart?* [4]

3 **MODEL** Have your student pour 1 cup of rice into a tall, clear glass jar. Use a permanent marker to indicate the level of the rice. Ask, *How much rice is in the jar?* [1 cup] Write "cup" next

MATH
LESSON 2.9

TAKE A BREAK

To help explore units of capacity, bake some cookies together or mix up a fruit-drink recipe. Have your student measure the ingredients, comparing the sizes of the bowls and measuring cups that are used.

to the line on the jar. Invite your student to add another cup of rice. Again draw a line on the jar to show the level. Ask, *How many cups of rice have we added to the jar?* [2 cups] *What is another name for the amount of rice in the jar?* [1 pint] Write "pint" next to the line. Have your student add 2 more cups of rice. Mark the jar with another line. Then ask, *How many cups are in the jar now?* [4] *How many pints are in the jar?* [2] *How should I label the highest line?* [quart]

4 **REVIEW** Give your student a paper cup. *How many times do you think a quart will fill this cup?* After he or she gives an estimate, help your student test the estimate by pouring water from the 1 quart measure into the cup. Extend the activity by asking your student to identify other containers of liquid as being more or less than a cup, pint, or quart. Ask, *Is a juice box more than or less than a quart?* [less] *A bottle of milk?* [more or less, depending on the size] *A can of soda?* [less] *Is a spoonful of water more than or less than a cup?* [less]

Branching Out

TEACHING TIP

Many students will quickly comprehend the different units of measurement presented in this lesson and their uses. Knowing how many centimeters are in an inch is not important for your student at this point. Concentrate on helping your student understand the difference between length and height and using the inch and centimeter measurements. It's more important for your student to understand that a cup is less than a pint, and a pint less than a quart, than to be able to quickly convert quarts into cups or pints.

CHECKING IN

To assess your student's understanding of the lesson, play a game with him or her. Use a group of items with different lengths. Direct your student to choose two items. Then ask him or her to tell you which item is longer. Next, use groups of items with different weights and capacities. Ask your student to choose two items and explain which is heavier or holds more water.

FOR FURTHER READING

Me and the Measure of Things, by Joan Sweeney and Annette Cable, ill. (Bantam Doubleday Dell Books for Young Readers, 2002).

Teaching Math with Favorite Picture Books, by Judy Hechtman, Deborah Ellermeyer, and Sandy Ford Grove (Scholastic, 1999).

Measure the Objects

How many inches long is the paintbrush?

1. _____ inches

How many centimeters long is the crayon?

2. _____ centimeters

Circle the things that weigh more than 1 pound. Draw an X on the things that weigh less than 1 pound.

3.

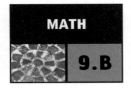

What's Next? You Decide!

Now it's your turn to choose what to do next in the lesson. Read the activities and decide which one you want to do—you may want to try them both!

Play Longer and Shorter

MATERIALS

❑ 1 inch ruler
❑ 1 centimeter ruler
❑ 1 die

STEPS

❑ Roll the die. Draw a line on a sheet of paper for the number of inches shown on the die.

❑ Have a friend roll the die and draw a line on a sheet of paper.

❑ Roll the die again. This time, use the centimeter ruler to add to your line.

❑ Have your friend take a turn with the centimeter ruler.

❑ See who can draw a line across the paper first.

Make Sand Castles

MATERIALS

❑ 1 one-cup measure
❑ sand (at a playground or a beach)

STEPS

❑ Measure 10 cups of sand into a pile.

❑ Use the cup measure to add water to make a sand castle.

❑ How many cups of water did you use to make a castle?

❑ Now measure 20 cups of sand into a pile.

❑ Add more cups of water to make another castle.

❑ How many cups of water did you need to add?

Comprehending Time

It's about time!

OBJECTIVE	BACKGROUND	MATERIALS
To teach your student to read the time, use a calendar, and identify the seasons of the year	Knowing how to tell time and read a calendar are crucial everyday skills. People need to know these things in order to schedule activities and be on time. In this lesson, your student will learn to read the time on the hour and half hour. He or she will also learn to use a calendar and to organize months by the seasons.	■ Student Learning Pages 10.A–10.B ■ 1 analog clock ■ 1 digital clock ■ 1 current-year calendar ■ 3 index cards

Let's Begin

TIME: READING AND WRITING

1 **PRESENT** Tell your student that he or she needs to know the time so that he or she can do things on time. Set both an analog clock and a digital clock to 2:00. Explain to your student that both types of clocks show the time. Say, *Both clocks show that it's 2 o'clock.* Have your student repeat the time aloud to you. Then show your student that 2:00 could be written as *2:00* or *2 o'clock*.

2 **ASK** Set both clocks to 3:00. Ask your student to say aloud the time. Then help your student practice identifying other times on the hour, such as 4:00, 6:00, and 8:00. Ask him or her to say each time. Then have your student select times for you to say aloud.

3 **EXPLAIN** Say, *We use hours and minutes to tell time.* Point to and name the minute and hour hands on the analog clock. Explain to your student that the short hand is the hour hand. It points to the hour. Then say that the long hand is the minute hand. It tells how many minutes past the hour it is. Say that when the minute hand points to 12, it's zero minutes past the hour. Set the clock to 7:00. Then say, *The clock shows 7:00. What number is the hour hand pointing to?* [7] *The minute hand?* [12]

4 **DEVELOP** Set the clock to 6:00. Read the time to your student. Ask, *What number is each hand pointing to?* [minute: 12; hour: 6] Now set the clock to 4:00. Say, *The minute hand points to 12. The hour hand points to 4. What time is it? How do you know?* [student should display an understanding of the hour and minute hands]

MATH
LESSON 2.10

A BRIGHT IDEA

If your student doesn't already have a wrist-watch, you might wish to consider purchasing one for him or her to wear.

ENRICH THE EXPERIENCE

Teach your student this rhyme to help him or her remember the number of days in each month:
Thirty days has September,
April, June, and November.
All the rest have 31,
Except February, which has 28
And sometimes 29.

5 **EXPLAIN** Set the clock to 2:30. Read the time out loud. Point out that the hour hand is between 2 and 3, so the time is after 2:00 but before 3:00. Explain to your student that when the minute hand is pointing to 6, the time will be 30 minutes past the hour. Set the clock to 4:30. Ask, *What number is the minute hand pointing to?* [6] *How many minutes does 6 show?* [30] *Which numbers is the hour hand between?* [4 and 5] *What time does the clock show?* [4:30]

6 **MODEL** Set the clock to 12:30. Tell your student that there are two ways of saying this time. Say, *12:30 and 30 minutes after 12.* Then have him or her say the times with you and then say them aloud without your help. Then set the clock to 1:30. Say, *Tell what time the clock shows in two different ways.* [1:30 and 30 minutes after one]

CALENDARS

1 **EXPLAIN** Tell your student that calendars show the 12 months of the year. Explain to him or her the order of the months by paging through a calendar and reading out loud the name of each month in order. Have your student repeat after you. Allow him or her to look at the calendar. Then ask, *What is the first month?* [January] *Which month is August?* [eighth] *Which month is before July?* [June] *Which month comes after November?* [December] Continue to quiz your student on the months until he or she understands them all.

2 **DEVELOP** Say to your student that calendars also show the number of days in each month. Explain that each month has between 28 and 31 days. Tell him or her that each day of the month has a date, or number. Open the calendar to January. Move your finger across the calendar to show the progression of the numbers of the dates. Then point to January 1. Say that this is the first day of January. Then point to January 31. Explain that this is the last day of January. Ask, *How many days does January have?* [31]

3 **EXPAND** Have your student turn the calendar to February. Show him or her that this month's first day also begins with 1. Ask, *How many days does February have?* [28] Continue to introduce and explain the 12 months of the year. Ask your student to point to different dates for each month. Say, *Point to the 10th of this month.* Then ask, *How many days does September have?* [30]

4 **EXPLAIN** Explain to your student that there are weeks within each month. Then say that a week has seven days. Open the calendar to January. Point out the weeks and show your student the beginning and end of each week. Have him or her repeat after you. Tell your student that each month has four full weeks. Show this to him or her on the calendar. Then explain that a calendar lists the days of the week in order. Ask, *What is the first day of the week?* [Sunday] *What is the last day?* [Saturday] *What is the fourth day?* [Wednesday]

5 **DISCUSS** Have your student open the calendar to the current month. Move up and down the rows to show your student how to find the weeks. Model how to find the number of each day in the month. For example, point to the Tuesday column and follow it down to show your student the number of Tuesdays in the month. Then have your student demonstrate this technique. Say, *There are four/five Mondays in this month. How many Fridays are there?*

6 **CONNECT** Show your student how to put together the elements of a calendar. Point to today's date in the calendar. Read the date out loud, using an ordinal number. Have your student repeat after you. Then use your finger to show him or her how to find the day of the week for the date. Then say the entire date out loud. [For example, *Today is Monday, May 15th.*] Ask, *What is tomorrow's date?*

A BRIGHT IDEA

Review ordinal numbers with your student if necessary. Give him or her three index cards labeled "first," "second," and "third." Say, *Mary, Kim, and Sue have a race. Mary wins. Sue comes in after her. Kim finishes last.* Have your student hold up the correct card to describe each person's position in the race.

MONTHS AND SEASONS

1 **REVIEW** Review the seasons by asking your student what he or she already knows about each one. Make a four-column chart on a sheet of paper. Head the columns with the names of the seasons: autumn, winter, spring, and summer. Then ask your student questions, such as *Is this season hot? Cold? Rainy? What activities can you do during this season? What clothing do you wear during this season? Which season is your favorite? Why?* Write your student's answers in the proper columns.

2 **PRESENT** Display the chart on the next page to your student. Explain to him or her that different months are part of different seasons. Then help your student trace each month to the proper season. Guide him or her to understand that some months are part of two seasons. Explain that this is true because, for example, the beginning of September feels like summer and the end of September feels like autumn. Ask, *Which season is October in?* [autumn] *Which two seasons is March in?* [winter and spring]

3 **APPLY** Help your student apply his or her knowledge of months and seasons to dates he or she already knows. For example, ask, *What month is your birthday in? What season (or seasons) is your birthday month in?*

4 **DISTRIBUTE** Give your student a copy of Student Learning Page 10.A. Have him or her complete the page for more practice.

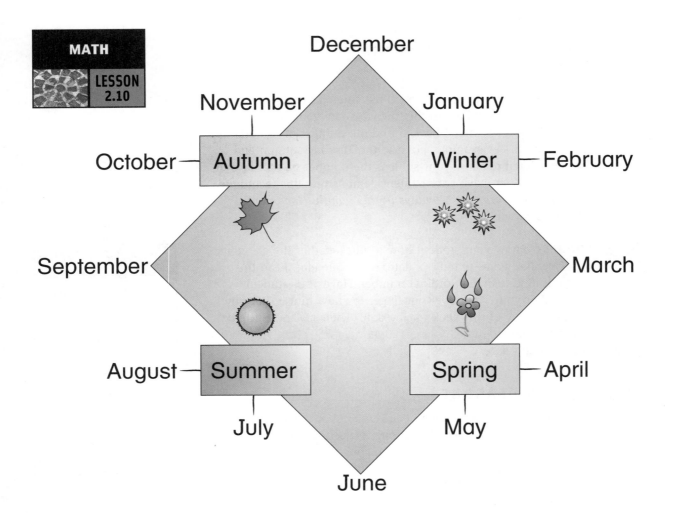

Branching Out

TEACHING TIP

Review with your student how to find the different things that a calendar shows. Model doing each of the things listed below. Then have your student perform each task.

- To find the name of a month, look at the top of the calendar page.
- To find a date, move across the calendar in numerical order.
- To find weeks, move up and down the columns.
- To find which day of the week a date is, move up to the top of the column.

CHECKING IN

To assess your student's understanding of the lesson, set the analog clock to 6:00. Say, *Mark says it's 12:30. Is he right?* [no] *What did he do wrong?* [he reversed the minute hand and the hour hand] Observe your student's technique to ensure that he or she understands the functions of the hour and minute hands. Then quiz him or her about months, dates, and seasons to assess his or her understanding of the concepts.

FOR FURTHER READING

It's About Time, Max! (*Math Matters AE Series*), by Kitty Richards (Kane Press, 2000).

Make Your Own Sticker Calendar, by Cathy Beylon (Dover Publications, 1999).

Math for All Seasons, by Greg Tang (Scholastic, 2002).

Practice with Time and Calendars

Help each person get to the game on time.
Draw lines to match the clocks and the games.

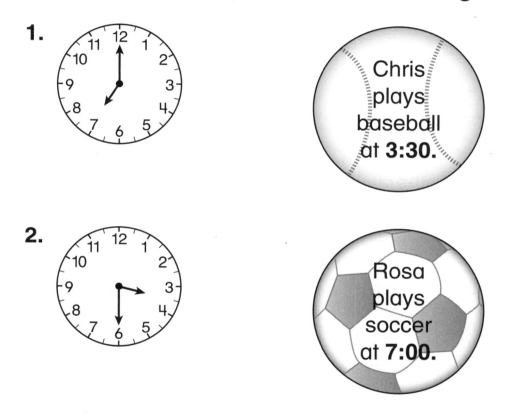

1.

Chris plays baseball at **3:30**.

2.

Rosa plays soccer at **7:00**.

Look at a current calendar. Then answer the questions.

3. What day of the week is June 4? _____

4. How many Sundays are in March? _____

What's Next? You Decide!

Now it's your turn to choose what to do next in the lesson. Read the activities and decide which one you want to do—you may want to try them both!

Make a Clock

MATERIALS

- ❑ 1 paper plate
- ❑ 1 pair scissors
- ❑ 2 pipe cleaners, one longer than the other

STEPS

- ❑ Write the numbers 1 to 12 around the edge of the paper plate.
- ❑ Make a very small hole in the center of the plate.
- ❑ Put the pipe cleaners in the hole. Bend the ends so that they will stay in place. These are the minute and hour hands.
- ❑ Use the clock to show 4:30, 1 o'clock, 30 after 7, and 9:00.

Stand in the Season

MATERIALS

- ❑ chalk

STEPS

You can also do this activity inside using sheets of paper.

- ❑ Draw one large square on a sidewalk.
- ❑ Make the square into four smaller squares. Make sure you can stand in the squares.
- ❑ Write the name of a season in each box.
- ❑ Stand in the correct box for January, August, September, and June.
- ❑ How did you stand in the two boxes for the two seasons of June and September?

Discovering Geometry

Just as shapes can be opened or closed, we can go through life with an open mind or a closed mind. Which shape are you in?

OBJECTIVE	BACKGROUND	MATERIALS
To identify and explore open and closed shapes, space shapes and plane shapes, and the different properties of shapes	Everything we see has shape. Some things, such as plates, balls, and books, are made of one shape. Other things, such as buildings, stove tops, and artwork, are made of a combination of shapes. Being able to identify shapes can help your student accurately describe things. In this lesson, your student will explore space and plane shapes and their attributes and will relate shapes to everyday items.	■ Student Learning Pages 11.A–11.C ■ 10 index cards ■ 1 large rubber band or 1 length yarn ■ dot paper ■ 2 copies T Chart, page 355 ■ several sheets construction paper ■ glue ■ 1 posterboard ■ 1 model each of a sphere, cube, rectangular prism, pyramid, cone, and cylinder

Let's Begin

OPEN AND CLOSED FIGURES

1 **TEACH** Tell your student that a closed figure is a shape whose sides meet, such as a circle, a square, and a star. Then say that an open figure has two ends that don't meet, such as a wavy line and the letter *C*. Show the figures below to your student. Use them to model and explain open and closed figures to him or her. Ask your student to identify each of the shapes as open or closed.

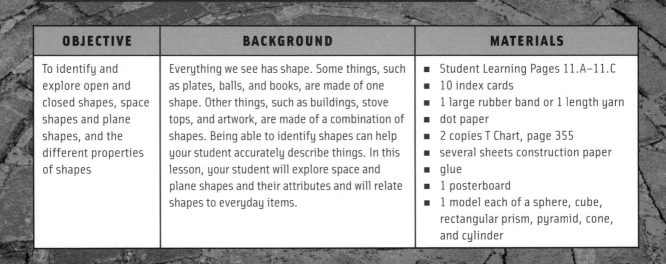

2 **PRACTICE** Use index cards to make several flashcards showing different open and closed figures. Quiz your student on which shapes are open and which are closed. Then have him or her sort the cards into a group of open figures and a group of closed figures. As you work through this lesson, remember to follow

MATH
LESSON
2.11

your student's guide as to how fast or slow to pace the lesson. You may wish to spend a few hours on this lesson, or you may prefer to return to it over the course of a few days.

3 **EXPAND** Draw various open shapes for your student. Point to one of the figures. Ask, *How could you turn this open figure into a closed figure?* Help your student understand that he or she can close the shape by drawing a line to join the two ends. Have your student draw lines to turn all the open shapes you drew into closed shapes.

4 **EXPLORE** Give your student a large rubber band or a length of yarn with the ends tied together. Model for your student how to position the rubber band to create various closed shapes. Then ask him or her to try. Have your student trace around each closed shape he or she makes. Ask, *Can you make an open figure with your rubber band?* [no, the ends of the band are already hooked together so all of the shapes made with it will be closed]

Hexagon

PLANE SHAPES

1 **REVIEW** Review plane shapes with your student. Explain that they are one-dimensional shapes, such as squares, circles, and triangles. Some of these terms and others in the lesson may be unfamiliar to your student. Remember to guide as necessary in a noncritical, nonjudgmental manner. Now draw a square, triangle, circle, and rectangle for your student. Ask, *Are these open or closed shapes?* [closed] Have your student name each shape, giving help where necessary. Ask, *What are some things that have a circle shape?* [plate, tire, button, and so on] Then ask your student to name things that have triangle, rectangle, and square shapes.

Pentagon

Rhombus

2 **OBSERVE** Ask your student, *What do you notice about the edges of these shapes?* Explain to him or her that the circle has round edges and that the square, rectangle, and triangle have straight edges. Ask, *How many edges does a square have?* [4] *A triangle?* [3] *A rectangle?* [4] Point to the corners. Tell your student that the places where the edges meet are called corners. Ask, *How many corners does each shape have?* [square and rectangle have 4; triangle has 3; circle has none] Then reveal that a square has four equal sides and that a rectangle has two sides that are longer.

Pentagon

Hexagon

3 **INTRODUCE** Introduce your student to some uncommon shapes. Draw and label the shapes below on a sheet of paper for your student. Ask, *Are these shapes open or closed?* [closed] Talk about each individual shape. Have your student count the sides and corners of each shape. Ask, *What do you notice about hexagons?* [hexagons are closed and have six sides] *What can you tell me about pentagons?* [pentagons are closed and have five sides] *What can you tell me about the rhombus?* [it's like a crooked square or a diamond]

4 **COMPARE** Add a circle, square, triangle, and rectangle to the drawings of the rhombus, hexagons, and pentagons. Tell your student that some shapes have parallel sides. Explain that parallel sides are like two roads built side by side. No matter how far the roads (or sides) go, they won't touch. Point out the two pairs of parallel sides in a square. Show where two sides of the triangle meet. Explain that the sides of a triangle aren't parallel. Help your student identify the shapes on your drawing that have parallel sides.

5 **CHALLENGE** Explain that a shape with four corners is called a quadrangle. Help your student identify the quadrangles in your drawing. Have your student use dot paper to create various quadrangles. Point to the corners of the square. Explain that each corner is an angle. Tell your student that there are different types of angles. Explain that the corners of a square are right angles. Help your student understand that when two sides meet in an L shape, the sides make a right angle. Have your student hunt for L shapes on the shape drawings and identify the right angles he or she sees.

6 **PRACTICE** Make two copies of the T Chart found on page 355. Draw six or seven plane shapes down one column of one T Chart. Draw the same shapes in a different order down the other side. Have your student draw lines to match the shapes. Then draw various plane shapes down one column of the other T Chart. Have your student copy each shape in the second column.

7 **EXPAND** Have your student help you draw and cut various shapes from construction paper of different colors. Invite him or her to use the shapes to make a picture. Help your student glue his or her picture onto a large posterboard. Assist your student in hanging his or her poster for friends and family to see.

SPACE SHAPES

1 **EXPLORE** Introduce space shapes to your student. Explain that space shapes are three-dimensional shapes. Space shapes are also called geometric shapes. Space shapes have a top, a bottom, and sides. Provide a model of each space shape below for your student. If you don't have models of the space shapes, you can make them out of clay or show the pictures to your student. Give him or her time to handle and observe the models. Ask your student to describe each shape to you. Name each space shape for him or her. Tell your student that the sides of space shapes are called faces. Help him or her count the faces of each space shape.

2 **COMPARE** Ask your student to pick up the cube. Ask, *How many faces does a cube have?* [6] *What plane shape is each of the cube's faces?* [square] *Can you find another space shape with six faces?* [rectangular prism] *What plane shapes are the faces of a rectangular prism?* [rectangle and possibly a square] Give help

MATH
LESSON 2.11

Cube

Sphere

Cylinder

Cone

Rectangular prism

Pyramid

,

TAKE A BREAK

Enjoy a geometric snack. Use sugar cones to make ice-cream treats. One cone + one sphere of ice cream = delicious!

when necessary as your student answers the questions. Then ask him or her to describe other space shapes. Encourage your student to talk about the plane shapes he or she sees on each of the space shapes. [possible answers: sphere: circle; pyramid: triangle, square; cylinder: circle; cone: circle]

3   **EXPAND**   Ask, *Which of these space shapes will roll?* [sphere, cylinder, cone] Allow your student time to experiment with each space shape. Ask, *Why do you think these shapes roll?* [some of the faces are curved or round] If necessary help your student recognize the curved faces. Ask, *Which of these shapes could be stacked?* [cube, rectangular prism, cylinder] Allow your student time to experiment with each shape. Ask, *Why do you think these shapes can be stacked?* [each has flat faces] If needed, help your student identify the flat faces.

Branching Out

TAKE A BREAK

It's not necessary to drill all of the new terms used in this lesson. For instance, it's not important at this level that your student remember the term *right angle.* However, it is important for your student to be aware that some shapes have angles. Allow him or her to explore the shapes at his or her own pace.

TEACHING TIP

Talk about and identify shapes throughout your entire day. This will help your student start thinking about how shapes are related to things. Encourage your student to use shapes to describe things in different rooms around the home. Ask him or her to describe things in the kitchen, his or her bedroom, and other rooms. To expand on this, quiz your student about shapes as you run errands or take trips.

CHECKING IN

To assess your student's understanding of the lesson, show your student a rectangular prism and a cylinder. Ask your student to describe the space shapes to you. Then send your student on a scavenger hunt to find more cylinders and rectangular prisms in your home. Allow time to observe the items he or she returns to you. Ask your student to describe why he or she knows the items are the correct space shapes.

FOR FURTHER READING

Cubes, Cones, Cylinders, and Spheres, by Tana Hoban (Greenwillow, 2000).

Sir Cumference and the First Round Table, by Cindy Neuschwander and Wayne Geehan, ill. (Charlesbridge Publishing, Inc., 1998).

Play with Plane Shapes

Count the plane shapes.

1.

_____ circles   _____ triangles

_____ squares   _____ rectangles

Draw a shape with five sides.

2.

Draw a shape with six sides.

3.

Look for Space Shapes

Find four objects that look like space shapes you learned about. Then draw each object in a box.

What's Next? You Decide!

Now it's your turn to choose what to do next in the lesson. Read the activities and decide which one you want to do—you may want to try them all!

MATH

11.C

Hunt for Shapes

MATERIALS

❏ 1 coloring book

❏ markers or crayons

STEPS

Find shapes in pictures!

❏ Choose a page in your coloring book.

❏ Look for shapes in the picture.

❏ Trace each shape with a different color marker or crayon. You could trace circles with red or triangles with blue.

❏ Count how many shapes you find.

❏ Now color the page.

❏ Play again with a new coloring book page.

Build a City

MATERIALS

❏ 1 package modeling clay

❏ 1 sheet cardboard

STEPS

Make space shapes from pieces of clay.

❏ Use the clay to make lots of different shapes.

❏ Then use the shapes to build a city on a sheet of cardboard.

❏ Make buildings, cars, and trees.

❏ How many of each shape did you use to build your city?

(CONTINUED)

Make a Design

MATERIALS

- ❏ 1 sheet cardboard
- ❏ 1 sheet drawing paper
- ❏ markers or crayons

STEPS

- ❏ Choose a plane shape.
- ❏ Draw your shape four times on the cardboard. Make each shape a different size.
- ❏ Cut out the four shapes.
- ❏ Trace your shapes many times on a sheet of drawing paper. Overlap some of the shapes.
- ❏ Keep tracing until you have made a fun design.
- ❏ Use markers or crayons to color your design.
- ❏ Share your design with a friend or family member.

Travel for Shapes

MATERIALS

- ❏ 1 posterboard
- ❏ markers or crayons

STEPS

- ❏ Ask an adult to take you for a drive or a walk.
- ❏ Look for signs as you travel.
- ❏ Draw each new sign you see in your notebook.
- ❏ When you get home, study all of your drawings.
- ❏ What kinds of shapes are the signs?
- ❏ What is the most common shape of traffic sign?
- ❏ Draw the signs on a posterboard and color them with markers or crayons.

Collecting Data

A teacher's success is not measured by how well a student performs on a test. Success is measured by how a student begins to love learning.

OBJECTIVE	BACKGROUND	MATERIALS
To teach your student to collect and use data to solve problems	Every day, your student gathers and analyzes data. Your student constantly sorts, classifies, analyzes, and orders information. Classifying some people as friends, others as acquaintances, and others as relatives is an example of collecting and analyzing data. In this lesson, your student will have many opportunities to use real-world examples to explore basic concepts of data collection, including surveys. He or she will also learn the foundation for problem-solving using data that he or she can apply to life situations.	■ Student Learning Pages 12.A–12.B ■ assorted pencils, crayons, and markers ■ 1 set silverware: spoons, forks, and knives ■ 1 die ■ 1 copy T Chart, page 355 ■ 20 counters: 10 of one color, 10 of another color ■ 1 box or bag

VOCABULARY

DATA a group of information

TALLY a table or chart used to count and compare numbers of items

GRAPH a table or chart that shows data

Let's Begin

DATA COLLECTION AND ORGANIZATION

1 **EXPLAIN** Begin by asking your student to take out pencils, crayons, and markers that he or she uses to draw and color with. Help your student sort the items into three rows, one for pencils, one for crayons, and one for markers. Explain that the rows of objects are **data.** Say, *Data are important information that can help us solve a problem. When we count the things you use to draw and color with, we are collecting data.* Then ask, *From the data we have collected, what do you have the most of? Crayons, pencils, or markers?*

2 **TALLY** Ask, *What are we trying to find?* [which object there is the most of] Then say, *We need to look at our data to answer the question. One way we can show the data is to make a **tally**.* Explain to your student that a tally chart is a table used to list and count data. Draw a three-column tally chart on a sheet of paper with the headings "Things We Use to Draw," "Tally," and "Total."

MATH

LESSON 2.12

(See the sample below.) Help your student decide what labels should be used in the first column. ["Crayons," "Pencils," and "Markers"] Then model for him or her how to use tally marks to fill in the chart, which can make it easier to count. Count the objects together as your student makes tally marks. Then have him or her write the total number in the Total column.

Things We Use to Draw	Tally	Total
Crayons		
Pencils		
Markers		

A BRIGHT IDEA

To help your student understand the concept of collecting data, take him or her on a trip to a pet store. Assist your student in creating a tally chart that lists three or four different types of pets, such as dogs, cats, birds, and rabbits. Then have him or her use the tally chart to make a quick count of the pets at the pet store.

3 **DISCUSS** Ask your student, *Does the tally chart show us the same result as when we lined up the pencils, crayons, and markers? How might the tally chart be a better way of collecting data?* [we can see the numbers easily]

4 **EXTEND** To reinforce the benefits of using a tally chart instead of lining up objects, give your student the following problem. Say, *Let's pretend that we want to have a group of people over for dinner, but we don't know if we have enough silverware for all the guests. Each guest will need a knife, a fork, and a spoon. What is the greatest number of guests we can have?* Place a pile of silverware on the table. Make sure that there are unequal numbers of knives, forks, and spoons. Say, *The pile of silverware is our data.* Invite your student to sort the knives, forks, and spoons. Then have him or her create a tally chart to find out how many complete sets you have. Ask, *How many guests can we invite?*

DATA IN GRAPHS

1 **INTRODUCE** Make a copy of the T Chart found on page 355. Label the two columns "Boys" and "Girls." Beneath the column headings, help your student write the names of his or her friends and relatives who are children. Ask, *If all these people were here, how could we find out if there are more boys or girls in the group?* [everyone could line up] Then say, *Another way to find out is to make a **graph**.* Explain to your student that a graph is a way of showing data so that someone can see the information very easily.

2 **DISCUSS** Discuss the T Chart you used in the last step. Then use chart paper to make a bar graph of the data. Explain the labels and bars to your student. Then say, *Use the graph to tell me if there are more boys or girls.* [correct your student's answer as needed] Ask, *Do you need to count the people to know if there* *are more boys or girls listed?* [no, the length of the bars shows the answer without counting]

3 **MODEL** Ask your student to guess what kind of pet is the most popular among the people he or she knows. Ask, *How many people have a dog? A cat? A fish? A bird? A hamster?* Help your student decide which pets to include, limiting the selections to three or four. Explain that to find out which pet is the most popular, your student can collect the data in a tally. Help him or her create a tally chart for the pets he or she has named to answer the question.

4 **GRAPH** Say, *Now that we have collected the data, let's put it in a graph.* Help your student turn the tally chart for the pet survey into a pictograph. Direct him or her to draw three or four rows on a sheet of paper, one for each pet in the survey. Divide the rows into cells large enough to contain a small drawing each. Then have him or her draw pictures of each kind of pet. Say, *Draw one picture of a dog for each dog you have thought of. Draw one cat for each person you know who has a cat.* Continue until the pictograph is complete. Ask, *Which pet is the most popular? Do we need to count the pets to know?* [no] Guide your student to see that the rows of drawings make it easy to read the data very quickly.

5 **EXPAND** Use the tally chart to show bar graphs to your student. Draw a grid on a sheet of paper and label it "Favorite Pets." Have your student draw each pet in his or her survey in the left-hand column of the grid and number the remaining cells from 1 to 10. Explain that it's usually easier to make a bar graph than to draw a picture of each item in a survey. Invite your student to color in cells for each pet to form a bar graph. Guide him or her to make the bars the correct length according to the tally chart. Ask, *Is the data in the bar graph the same as the drawings you made?* [yes] *How is the bar graph like the pictograph?* [both show how many] *How does the bar graph show us which pet is the most popular?* [that pet has the longest bar]

BAR GRAPHS IN PROBLEMS

1 **MODEL** Write this problem on a sheet of paper: *Ten children saw a movie. Two more children liked the movie than didn't like the movie. How many children liked the movie?* [6] Then draw a bar graph with two bars labeled "Liked the Movie" and "Did Not Like the Movie" and cells numbered 1 to 6 in the rows. Shade six cells next to "Liked the Movie" and four cells next to "Did Not Like the Movie." Ask, *Can you tell me now how many children liked the movie?* [yes, 6]

2 **DISCUSS** Use the bar graph to discuss with your student how a bar graph can help him or her quickly solve a problem. Ask, *What does a bar graph help us do very quickly?* [compare

TAKE A BREAK

To reinforce the idea of using data to make bar graphs, use favorite snacks, such as pieces of cereal, peanuts, or raisins, to illustrate the concept. Based on your student's preference, line up two or more different types of snacks on a grid. As your student eats the pieces, have him or her color in the squares to form a bar graph. Once the snack has been completed, have your student review the bar graph to find out which type of food he or she ate the most of.

different amounts] Explain that this is very useful when more than two things are being compared. On paper, draw a bar chart for rainfall in four different months. Label the columns "Month" and "Inches of Rain." Under Month list *March, April, May,* and *June.* Then fill in cells to indicate 3 inches in March, 4 inches in April, 3 inches in May, and 2 inches in June. Ask your student to tell you in which month the most rain fell. [April] Ask, *In which month did the least rain fall?* [June] *How do you know?* [by the length of the bars]

3 **REVIEW** Continue the discussion to emphasize·using the bar graph to solve problems. Guide your student to use the bars to find the numbers before adding or subtracting. Ask, *How many more inches of rain fell in April than in June?* [2] *Which two months had the same amount of rain?* [March and May] *How many fewer inches of rain fell in June than in May?* [1]

4 **ENRICH** If your student has mastered the concept of a bar graph, connect making a bar graph to predicting an outcome. Put different colored counters, such as checker pieces, into a box or bag. Have your student put 2 red pieces and 4 black pieces in the bag. Have him or her draw a simple bar graph labeled "Red" and "Black." As your student draws a piece from the bag, have him or her record it on the bar graph. Have your student predict which color he or she will draw next from the bag. Ask, *Which color do you think you will draw next?* Have your student compare the prediction with the result until the last piece is drawn. For example, say, *Look at your bar graph. You know how many pieces you started with. What color will the last piece be?*

5 **DISTRIBUTE** Distribute Student Learning Page 12.A and have your student complete it for more practice.

Branching Out

TEACHING TIP

Mix the use of bar graphs and groups of objects according to your student's learning style. Kinesthetic learners will benefit from seeing the groups (or piles) of objects. In this case, encourage your student to manipulate the objects while you draw a pictograph or bar graph. Then discuss the relationship between the objects and the pictograph or bar graph to be sure he or she understands the purpose of the graphs.

CHECKING IN

Have your student tally familiar things to collect and analyze data. For example, have your student list the cartoon television programs he or she likes and the shows with live actors that he or she likes. Observe as he or she collects the data, completes the tally, and uses a bar graph, checking whether or not he or she understands how to record and count data.

FOR FURTHER READING

Math in the Kitchen, by William Amato (Children's Press, 2002).

Math Made Easy: A First-Grade Workbook, by Sue Phillips and Sean McCardle (Dorling Kindersley, 2001).

Collect and Use Data

At a town picnic, 15 children chose these foods.

Make a bar graph. Color a box for each food.

Favorite Foods										
hot dog	███									
pizza										
hamburger										
ice cream										
	1	2	3	4	5	6	7	8	9	10

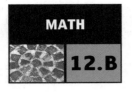

What's Next? You Decide!

Now it's your turn to choose what to do next in the lesson. Read the activities and decide which one you want to do—you may want to try them both!

Visit the States

MATERIALS

❑ 1 U.S. map

❑ markers or crayons

STEPS

Make a bar graph to find out which letter begins the most names of states.

❑ List the letters *A, C, D, F, H, I, K, L, M, N, O, P, R, S, U, V,* and *W* down one side of a sheet of paper.

❑ Use the map and make a tally mark for each state next to the letter it begins with.

❑ Make a bar graph to show the data.

Find the Favorite Sport

MATERIALS

❑ markers or crayons

STEPS

Find out the favorite sport of your friends and family members.

❑ Make a tally chart with the labels "Football," "Baseball," "Soccer," and "Basketball."

❑ Ask your family members which of the four sports are their favorites.

❑ Tally each answer on your chart.

❑ What are the results?

In Your Community

To reinforce the skills and concepts taught in this section,
try one or more of these activities!

Take a Shape Walk

Reinforce your student's knowledge of shapes by taking a shape walk through your community. As you walk, ask your student to look for geometric shapes in nature, signs, buildings, and any other objects you encounter. Encourage your student to look closely at an object and identify as many shapes as possible. For example, your student should not only see the circles in a stoplight but the rectangular shape of the box as well. Also make sure that your student explains why he or she knows an object is a particular shape, indicating that an object is, for example, a triangle because it has three connecting sides. Before you begin your walk, you may want to have your student make a list of the shapes he or she learned about in this section.

Use Addition, Subtraction, and Fractions at the Grocery Store

Your student has learned to use pictures and symbols for addition, subtraction, and fraction problems. Take him or her to the grocery store so that he or she may continue to practice. Have your student help you collect the groceries, but present some of the items on your grocery list as a series of addition, subtraction, and fraction problems. If you need three apples, you could tell your student you would like 2 + 1 apples. If you need two cans of soup, you could tell your student you need 5 − 3 cans of soup. To present your student with a fraction problem, ask for a specific number of an item, then ask your student to return half of it to the shelves. First ask your student to try to find the answers without using the actual items. If your student needs help, then allow him or her to use the objects to solve the addition, subtraction, or fraction problems.

Create an Entrepreneur

Many people have pleasant memories of operating a lemonade stand when they were young. Give your student a head start on his or her entrepreneurial career—plus a valuable addition, subtraction, and money lesson—by helping your student open a lemonade stand in your community. Your student will be exposed to adding the amounts of each sale, subtracting to find correct change, and exploring ways to make correct change. The experience will also be a good opportunity for your student to meet people in your community. Make sure that you have paper and a pencil available for your student to work out addition and subtraction problems if necessary. For more practice with addition, subtraction, and money, keep a log of the expenses and total sales for the day and have your student attempt to figure out how much money was made or lost. Be sure to keep the mathematical problems simple for your student and to guide him or her when necessary.

Build Something That Will Measure Up

An important part of sewing and building is accurate measurement. Think of a sewing or building project with your student. Test your student's estimation skills by asking him or her to estimate the quantity of materials needed for your project. Then take a trip to your local fabric store or hardware store for your materials. Have your student measure the desired length of all the materials that will need to be cut at the store. Then have him or her estimate the necessary amounts of materials that are already cut. Finally, return home and complete the project to see how your student's measurements measure up!

We Have Learned

Use this checklist to summarize what you and your student
have accomplished in the Math section.

❏ **Exploring Numbers and Patterns**
❏ same, more, or fewer
❏ understanding numbers and patterns to 10
❏ ways to show and compare numbers

❏ **Patterns and Numbers to 100**
❏ exploring tens and ones
❏ representing numbers to 100
❏ ways to show and compare numbers
❏ number patterns to 99

❏ **Understanding Addition**
❏ parts and wholes, addition sentences
❏ using counters, pictures, or symbols to add
❏ adding horizontally and vertically
❏ adding zero and sums to 18

❏ **Understanding Subtraction**
❏ parts and wholes, subtraction sentences
❏ using counters, pictures, or symbols to subtract
❏ subtracting horizontally and vertically
❏ zero in subtraction and subtracting from 18

❏ **Exploring Two-Digit Addition and Subtraction**
❏ adding two-digit numbers
❏ subtracting two-digit numbers
❏ ways to add and subtract

❏ **Fractions**
❏ exploring equal parts

❏ exploring halves, thirds, fourths
❏ fractions of a group

❏ **Money**
❏ pennies, nickels, dimes, quarters
❏ exploring ways to make 25 cents
❏ counting and comparing amounts up to $1.00

❏ **Measurement**
❏ inches and centimeters
❏ weight in pounds
❏ cups, pints, and quarts

❏ **Time**
❏ time to the hour, half hour, and minute
❏ using a calendar, months and seasons

❏ **Geometry**
❏ open and closed figures
❏ understanding and relating space and plane shapes
❏ squares, triangles, circles, rectangles
❏ hexagons, pentagons, quadrangles, rhombuses
❏ matching and combining shapes

❏ **Data Collection**
❏ collecting data and making graphs
❏ interpreting bar graphs

We have also learned:

_____

_____

Science

Science

Key Topics

SCIENCE

LESSON
3.1

Comparing Groups of Animals

Elephants, birds, goldfish, snakes, salamanders, and butterflies—they're all animals, but they sure don't look the same!

OBJECTIVE	BACKGROUND	MATERIALS
To teach your student about the various groups of animals	Animals of all kinds live on Earth. Scientists use a system of classification to group together animals with similar traits. In this lesson, your student will learn about the major groups of animals and some traits of the animals in each group.	<ul><li>Student Learning Pages 1.A–1.B</li><li>6–8 stuffed animals that represent mammals</li><li>1 copy Web, page 356</li><li>1–4 animal magazines with pictures of mammals and insects</li><li>1 pair scissors</li><li>glue</li><li>1 feather</li><li>1 bird identification book</li><li>1 photo of a fish</li><li>1 copy T Chart, page 355</li><li>markers or crayons</li><li>1 butterfly net</li><li>1 large, clean bucket</li><li>1 posterboard</li></ul>

VOCABULARY

MAMMALS animals with hair

FUR thick hair found on some mammals

BIRDS animals with feathers

FISH animals that live in water and have gills and scales

SCALES the hard protective outer covering found on fish and reptiles

GILLS structures that allow fish to breathe in water

REPTILES animals that live on land and have scales

AMPHIBIANS animals that live both on land and in water

INSECTS animals that have six or more legs and no internal bones

Let's Begin

1 **REVIEW** Review with your student what he or she knows about animals. Perhaps he or she has been to a zoo or has a pet. Although your student may be familiar with animals, remember

SCIENCE

LESSON 3.1

TAKE A BREAK

Take as much time as necessary for your student to understand the material covered in this lesson. You may wish to go through the lesson in one sitting, or you may prefer to take little breaks throughout. Let your student guide you!

ENRICH THE EXPERIENCE

With your student visit the virtual zoo at http://www.thebigzoo.com and search for mammals. Click on the name of each animal to see pictures of the great variety among mammals.

to help your student with any unfamiliar words, terms, or concepts in a noncritical and nonjudgmental manner. This will help him or her become more willing and confident when exploring unfamiliar territory.

2 **INTRODUCE** Collect a variety of stuffed toy animals that represent **mammals** and display them for your student. Explain that all of these animals are grouped together because they're the same in some ways. Invite your student to suggest ways that these animals are the same. Explain that they all have hair covering at least part of their skin. Some mammals have thick hair called **fur.** The fur covers their body and keeps them warm. Invite your student to point out the stuffed animals that have fur. Explain that baby mammals are born alive and look like tiny versions of their parents. Tell your student that most mammals live on land, including dogs, cats, and rabbits. However, some mammals, such as whales, live in water. Ask your student to identify where each of the animals represented by a toy animal lives.

3 **EXPAND** Give your student several animal magazines, scissors, glue, and a copy of the Web found on page 356. Tell your student to write "Mammals" in the center of the Web. Have your student look through the magazines for pictures of mammals, cut them out, and paste them in the circles of the Web. Ask your student to tell you what he or she knows about each of the animals pictured.

4 **OBSERVE** Tell your student that **birds** form another group of animals. Invite your student to tell you what he or she knows about birds. Explain that birds have **feathers.** Give your student a feather to observe and describe. Point out that it's very light. Explain that one function of feathers is to help keep birds warm. Feathers also help some birds to fly. Other birds, such as the ostrich, can't fly. Show your student a picture of an ostrich and explain that the ostrich can run very fast. Point out that to make babies, birds lay eggs. Bird eggs have hard shells. After a certain amount of time, baby birds hatch out of the eggs. Ask, *Can you name a difference between mammals and birds?* [mammals have hair, birds have feathers; most mammals are born alive, birds lay eggs]

5 **IDENTIFY** Give your student a bird identification book. Point out birds that can be seen in your neighborhood, perhaps robins, cardinals, hawks, or pigeons. Invite your student to look through the book and point out ways that birds are the same and different.

6   **DESCRIBE** Explain to your student that **fish** are a group of animals that live in water. Most fish hatch from eggs, and most are covered with **scales** that provide protection. All fish have special body parts called **gills** that allow them to breathe in water. Show your student a picture of a fish. Explain that the fins help keep the fish upright in the water and going in the right direction. Ask, *What body part do you think helps the fish move forward?* [the tail] Challenge your student to point out the fish's tail, fins, eyes, mouth, and gills.

7   **EXPLAIN** Tell your student that snakes, turtles, and dinosaurs all belong to the same group of animals, the **reptiles.** Explain that most reptiles also lay eggs and have scales to protect their bodies. Many kinds of reptiles, such as lizards and turtles, have four feet and a tail. These reptiles move by walking or crawling. Snakes are special types of reptiles that don't have any legs. Snakes move by sliding their bodies over the ground. Ask, *How else can turtles move besides walking?* [they can swim]

8   **DISTRIBUTE** Give your student a copy of the T Chart found on page 355. Have him or her write in the titles "Fish" and "Reptiles" above the two columns. Then have your student list at least three characteristics for each group. After finishing, have your student explain what he or she has written.

9   **EXPLAIN** Ask, *Do you think fish are the only animals that live in water?* [no] Explain that some kinds of animals, called **amphibians,** live both in water and on land. These include frogs, salamanders, and toads. Most amphibians hatch from eggs. Tell your student that amphibians have smooth wet skin, so they need to live close to water or in a moist place. If they dry out too much, they won't survive. Explain that amphibians have legs. When amphibians are on land they move by walking or hopping. Ask, *Can you name an animal that has smooth, wet skin, lives on land and in water, and hops?* [frog]

10   **CHALLENGE** Tell your student that all the animals discussed so far have bones inside them for support. Give your student the opportunity to feel his or her own bones. Then point out that **insects** form a very large group of animals that don't have skeletons inside them. Most of these animals are small. Remind your student that babies of mammals, birds, and fish look like small versions of their parents when they are born or hatch.

ENRICH THE EXPERIENCE

Take your student to visit a zoo, pet store, or farm to see the variety of animals. Challenge him or her to name the group to which each animal belongs.

Explain that most young insects don't look like miniature adult insects. When they hatch from eggs they usually look like little worms. Invite your student to name some insects he or she has seen and to describe his or her experiences with them.

11 **CREATE** Tell your student that all insects have at least six legs. Many have wings and can fly. Some insects, such as beetles, have a hard, protective outer covering. Have your student make a collage of pictures of butterflies, bees, ladybird beetles, mosquitoes, and moths using cut out magazine pictures, glue, and paper. Have your student draw any additional insects he or she would like to add.

12 **DISTRIBUTE** Give your student Student Learning Page 1.A. Assist him or her in completing the activity as needed.

13 **ASSIST** Then distribute Student Learning Page 1.B. Help your student read through the activities on Student Learning Page 1.B. Note that you can get fish scales for the first activity from your local grocery store if needed. Be sure to wash them thoroughly before giving them to your student.

Branching Out

TEACHING TIP

The American Veterinary Association Web site has animal activity sheets for children that can be printed as worksheets. Go to http://www.avma.org and click on Care for Animals, then Kid's Corner.

CHECKING IN

To assess your student's understanding of the lesson, have your student give you a verbal description of the characteristics of each animal group as you name them. Then have him or her compare the animal groups to one another. Finally, present several scenarios for your student to solve, such as *I'm an animal with six legs and I fly. What am I?* or *I have scales and can move on land. What am I?*

ENRICH THE EXPERIENCE

With your student, go to the Zoobooks virtual petting zoo at http://www.zoobooks.com. Click on Kids and then Pets to get to the virtual zoo. Challenge your student to decide which group each animal belongs to.

FOR FURTHER READING

Animals in Cold Places, by Moira Butterfield (Raintree/Steck Vaughn, 1999).

Big Bug Fun, by Joanne Oppenheim (Scholastic Trade, 2003).

Friends of a Feather, by Arlen Cohn (Accord Publishing, 1999).

Group Yourself as an Animal

Read the words. Circle the ones that are true about you.

_____

scales	smooth, wet skin
hair on skin	feathers
fur	wings
lives in water	hard body covering
fins	flies
lives on land	walks or runs
lives in water and on land	slides along the ground
gills	six legs

What animal group are you in? _____

What's Next? You Decide!

Now it's your turn to choose what to do next in the lesson. Read the activities and decide which one you want to do—you may want to try them both!

Look at Fish Scales

MATERIALS

- ❏ 4–6 fish scales
- ❏ 1 paper plate
- ❏ 1 hand lens

STEPS

- ❏ Put the fish scales on the plate.
- ❏ Touch them. How do they feel?
- ❏ Look at them with the hand lens.
- ❏ Draw what you see.
- ❏ How do scales protect fish?

Make a Farm Scene

MATERIALS

- ❏ 2 small boxes
- ❏ 1 ball green yarn
- ❏ 1 pair scissors
- ❏ 3–5 plastic farm animals
- ❏ 1 cup water in bowl
- ❏ 3–5 plastic pond animals

STEPS

- ❏ Make a barn and a house from the boxes.
- ❏ Use cut-up yarn for grass.
- ❏ Put the plastic animals in the farm.
- ❏ Fill the bowl with water. Use it for a pond.
- ❏ Fill the pond with the plastic animals.
- ❏ What group does each animal belong to?

Exploring Plant Life

Plants are living things . . . just like us.

SCIENCE

LESSON 3.2

OBJECTIVE	BACKGROUND	MATERIALS
To help your student learn more about plants	Plants are very important to life on Earth. They need certain things to live and grow. In this lesson, your student will learn how plants use air, sunlight, and water and how they make seeds.	■ Student Learning Pages 2.A–2.B ■ 1 tomato ■ 1 watermelon or peach ■ 1 knife ■ 1 pinecone ■ 1 sunflower ■ 3 potted plants ■ 1 carrot ■ 1 cup ■ markers or crayons

VOCABULARY

SEEDS the parts of a plant that grow into new plants

FLOWERS the parts of some plants that make seeds

CONES the parts of some plants that make seeds

STEM the part of a plant that grows above ground and supports the plant parts

LEAVES the flat, green parts of a plant that grow from the stem

ROOTS the part of a plant that holds the plant in the ground and absorbs water and minerals from the soil

Let's Begin

1 **INTRODUCE** Introduce your student to **seeds.** Explain that seeds are the beginnings of new plants. All plants grow from seeds. Tell your student that seeds come in different sizes, shapes, and colors. Cut open a tomato and a watermelon or a peach. Point out the seeds of a tomato to your student. Then show your student the watermelon seeds or peach pit. Tell your student that these are all types of seeds that new plants can grow from. Ask your student to describe how the seeds are the same and different.

2 **EXPLORE** Explain to your student that different plants make seeds in different ways. Some plants make seeds in **flowers.** A flower is the part of a plant that has colored petals. The flowers of plants come in all different colors, shapes, and sizes. Some plants form seeds inside of **cones.** Show your student a sunflower and a pinecone. Point out the middle part of the

sunflower where the seeds come from. Explain that the seeds that grow into pine trees come from inside pinecones. Ask, *What needs to happen before the seeds from flowers and cones can grow into a new plant?* [they need to go into soil]

3 **DISCUSS** Tell your student that seeds have to have good soil to be able to grow. Seeds reach the soil in many different ways. Some are blown by the wind. Some float in water. Some seeds have special hooks that stick to the fur of animals. These seeds travel on the animals and grow in new places. Tell your student that the picture shows how the seeds of a dandelion travel on the wind. Ask, *Name ways seeds travel to new soil.* [wind, water, animals]

Dandelion seeds are blown by the wind to get to good soil.

4 **RELATE** Tell your student that a plant is a living thing just like an animal or a person. This means that it needs certain things to grow and survive. Explain that plants need sunlight, water, and air. Without these things a plant will die. Show your student the importance of water to a plant's life using two potted plants. Put the plants in the same place. Together with your student regularly water one of the plants while not watering the other. Observe with your student the differences between the two plants over one to three weeks. Emphasize to your student that the plant that receives water is much healthier than the plant that doesn't. Be sure to water the second plant before it dies.

5 **EXPLAIN** Explain to your student how a seed grows into a plant. Tell your student that after a seed gets to good soil, it begins to soak up water. Soon, little roots start to grow down deep into the soil and a shoot grows up. The roots get food from

the soil to help the plant grow. The shoot develops leaves so that the plant can use sunlight to help it grow. Use the pictures to illustrate for your student the different steps in a seed's development into a plant. Ask, *Can you name the things that help a plant grow?* [water, sunlight, air, good soil, roots, leaves]

6 **SHOW** Explain to your student that plants have different parts. These parts include the flower, **stem, leaves,** and **roots.** The leaves help the plant use sunlight to grow. The roots help the plant get water and food from the soil. And the stem helps carry this food from the roots to other parts of the plant. Show your student a potted plant and help him or her identify its stem, leaves, and roots.

7 **EXPERIMENT** Point out that roots are an important part of the plant. Roots keep the plant anchored into the ground. Roots absorb the water and nutrients that the plant needs to live and grow from the soil. Tell your student that the orange part of a carrot, the part we eat, is the root of the carrot plant. Slice a one-inch piece off the top of a carrot. Then put this piece of carrot in a cup with a little bit of water. Over the next few days watch with your student as green shoots grow from the top of the carrot root. Ask, *What do you think the orange part of the carrot is doing?* [getting water from the cup so the green shoots can grow]

8 **EXPLORE** Remind your student that sunlight is one of the important things that a plant needs to live and grow. Ask, *Do you remember which part of the plant uses sunlight?* [leaves] Show your student the importance of sunlight by placing a small potted plant next to a sunny window. Keep the plant there for at least a week. Then observe with your student how the plant has bent toward the window. Explain that the plant is growing toward the window so that it can get more of the sunlight it needs. Ask, *What do you think would happen if we turned the plant so that it bends away from the window?* [it will begin to bend toward the window again] Try this experiment and have your student observe.

First a seed grows roots, then a shoot, then leaves.

9 **EXPLAIN** Invite your student to be quiet for 20 seconds and listen to himself or herself breathe. Ask, *How do you breathe air into your body?* [through the openings in the nose or mouth] Just like us, plants have openings in their bodies to breathe. These openings are very tiny and are located on the leaves. When a plant breathes, it uses parts of air to make its food. Ask, *How do you think dirty and polluted air affects plants?* [it might make it hard for plants to breathe and make food]

10 **EXPAND** Remind your student that a plant absorbs sunlight through its leaves. Explain that there are many different kinds of leaves. A plant that lives in a very windy place needs to have small, strong leaves. A plant that lives in a place that doesn't get

a lot of sunlight needs large leaves to catch the light. Have your student go outside and look at the leaves of a few different trees. Look at the shape, color, and size of the leaves. Invite your student to describe how they are the same and different.

11 **RELATE** Explain to your student that all plants need water, but that there are some plants that can live with very little water. In dry places, such as deserts, it may rain only once every few years. The plants that live in these dry places have to be able to collect as much water as they can and store it until the next rain. Cacti are one kind of plant that can survive in very dry places. They have thick stems that help them store water when it rains. They also have sharp needles called spines that protect them from heat and cold and also protect them from animals. Help your student use the library or the Internet to find a picture of a cactus.

12 **DISTRIBUTE** Distribute Student Learning Page 2.A. Go on a plant walk with your student. Help him or her notice some of the different plants that are living and growing there. Have your student choose two plants he or she sees on the walk to draw and write about.

Branching Out

TEACHING TIPS

❑ When you're making dinner, have your student help you in the kitchen. Use this time to point out different fruits, vegetables, and cereals that come from plants. Emphasize to your student how we use plants every day.

❑ Help your student become familiar with plants by having him or her be in charge of watering his or her family's houseplants. He or she can water them regularly and tell you if they look like they're outgrowing their pots or if their leaves are turning brown.

❑ Take a walk with your student around your neighborhood. Have him or her take along a notebook and writing instrument and count the number of different plants or vegetation that he or she spies. He or she doesn't have to know their names, just that there are a lot of different types of greenery growing!

CHECKING IN

To assess your student's understanding of the lesson, show your student a potted plant. Ask him or her to label the different parts of a plant and to describe their functions. Ask your student to tell how new plants grow. Have him or her name some of the things that a plant needs to live and grow.

Take a Plant Walk

Go on a walk with an adult. Draw a picture of two different plants that you see on your walk. Write a sentence about each plant.

What's Next? You Decide!

Now it's your turn to choose what to do next in the lesson. Read the activities and decide which one you want to do—you may want to try them both!

Watch How Plants Get Water

MATERIALS

❏ 1 piece celery

❏ 1 knife

❏ 1 large glass or cup filled with water

❏ red or blue food coloring

STEPS

❏ Ask an adult to help you cut a stalk of celery.

❏ Put some drops of food coloring in the water.

❏ Put the celery in the water.

❏ Watch over the next few days. See how the colored water moves up the celery.

Grow Your Own Plant

MATERIALS

❏ 1 plastic cup filled with soil

❏ 2–3 seeds

❏ 1 calendar

STEPS

❏ Dig a little hole in the soil.

❏ Put two or three seeds in the hole and cover them with soil.

❏ Water your seeds.

❏ Check on your plant every day and write down what you see.

❏ When your plant sprouts, put it where it can get light.

❏ Watch your plant grow!

Living Together in Nature

*The living world is like a giant jigsaw puzzle
made from interconnected pieces.*

SCIENCE

LESSON
3.3

OBJECTIVE	BACKGROUND	MATERIALS
To teach your student how animals and plants live together	Learning how animals and plants live together helps us appreciate the harmony and balance of the natural world. It also helps us understand how each living thing affects its surroundings. In this lesson, your student will discover how animals and plants depend on each other and learn about different natural habitats.	■ Student Learning Pages 3.A–3.B ■ 1 clipboard ■ several sheets blank paper ■ markers or crayons ■ 1 length string, 1–3 yards ■ 1 hand lens ■ 1 tree field guide ■ 1 simple flower, such as a tulip or lily

VOCABULARY
HABITATS   natural places where wild animals and plants live
NESTS   animal homes built to shelter baby animals
POLLEN   the part of a flower that helps make seeds

Let's Begin

1 **DISCUSS** Explain to your student that the places where animals and plants live are called **habitats.** Point out that habitats can be very different. They can range from a small rotten log to a garden to a huge ocean. Ask your student to name some of the things he or she would expect to find in a garden habitat. [flowers, green plants, grass, snails, bushes, insects, squirrels, rabbits, birds, and so on] Explain to your student that living things find everything they need to live in their habitats. Have your student consider the garden habitat. Ask, *Can you name some things that animals need to live?* [food, water, place to hide, warmth] *Can you name some things that plants need to live and grow?* [sunlight, water, air, soil]

2 **EXPLORE** Observe a nearby habitat with your student. Visit a local park, a garden, an empty lot, or a field. Bring along a clipboard or another writing surface, several sheets of blank paper, crayons or markers, string, and a hand lens. Invite your student to choose a study area and use a loop of string to mark out the perimeter of his or her space. Show him or her how to

SCIENCE

LESSON 3.3

TAKE A BREAK

Your student can learn about animal homes at http://www.kidport.com. Click on Reference Library, then Science, then Animal Homes.

FOR FURTHER READING

Crinkleroot's Guide to Knowing Animal Habitats, by Jim Arnosky (Aladdin Paperbacks, 2000).

Draw, Write, Now—Book 6: Animal Habitats, by Marie Hablitzel and Kim Stitzer (Barker Creek Publishing, 1999).

Oh Say Can You Seed? All About Flowering Plants, by Bonnie Worth and Aristicles Ruiz, ill. (Random House, 2001).

lift a stone to look for small creatures underneath. Encourage your student to notice where plants are found, what animals do, what they eat, and where they hide. Ask your student to select four plants and animals he or she sees (although, don't disturb them!) and draw them in detail. When you have finished, be sure to clean up the site.

3 **REVEAL** When you return indoors, discuss your student's drawings and ideas. Perhaps your student drew a flower, an insect, a rock, and a bird. Ask, *How did the things you drew work together?* [the insect may have hidden under the rock, the bird may have eaten the insect, the insect may have climbed inside the flower] Explain to your student that when animals and plants live together, they depend on each other to meet their needs. Sometimes they get their food from each other. Many animals eat plants for food. Tell your student that animals also use plants to build **nests** or make homes. Ask your student to name some animals that build nests or homes in trees. [birds, squirrels, wasps]

4 **GUIDE** Go outdoors with your student to explore the habitat around a tree. Give your student a hand lens and Student Learning Page 3.A. Help your student identify the tree using a tree field guide. Invite him or her to complete the learning page.

5 **CHALLENGE** Explain to your student that plants depend on animals to make more plants. Find a wildflower in your neighborhood or get a simple flower from a flower shop. Flowers with easy-to-see parts such as lilies or tulips are best. Have your student observe the inside of the flower with a hand lens. Point out the yellow **pollen.** Explain that plants use pollen to make seeds. When animals go into flowers looking for food, they carry pollen away on their bodies. Then the pollen rubs off onto the next flower they go to. This process helps the plant make its seeds. Ask, *Can you name some animals that help spread pollen between flowers?* [bees, butterflies]

Branching Out

TEACHING TIP

Explain to your student that you can often study animal activities by looking at the clues they leave behind. For example, you may learn about their behavior by looking at empty nests, chewed leaves or seeds, or animal tracks.

CHECKING IN

To assess your student's understanding of the lesson, ask your student to describe a habitat in his or her own words. Then ask him or her to name several ways animals depend on plants to survive, and vice versa.

Notice a Tree Habitat

Draw four animals in the habitat. Write their names on the lines.

1. _____ 3. _____

2. _____ 4. _____

What's Next? You Decide!

Now it's your turn to choose what to do next in the lesson. Read the activities and decide which one you want to do—you may want to try them both!

Go Ponding

MATERIALS

❑ 1 dip net or food strainer tied to a pole
❑ 1 white pan
❑ 1 plastic cup
❑ 1 hand lens

STEPS

❑ Go with an adult to the shore of a pond.
❑ Swish your dip net through the water.
❑ Hold the net upside down over the pan.
❑ Pour water over the net.
❑ Look at the tiny plants and animals in the pan with the hand lens.
❑ Return them to the water when you are done.

Take a Sock Walk

MATERIALS

❑ 1 pair long wool socks
❑ 1 hand lens

STEPS

❑ Go with an adult to a field with lots grass and plants.
❑ Put the socks on over your shoes.
❑ Walk around the field. What happens?
❑ Take off the socks.
❑ Look at the seeds with the hand lens.
❑ How do animals help seeds travel?

Discovering Weather

*The changing seasons mirror the way we
grow and change throughout our lives.*

SCIENCE

LESSON 3.4

OBJECTIVE	BACKGROUND	MATERIALS
To help your student learn more about weather and the seasons	Every day we are affected by weather. It determines what kinds of clothes we wear and what we are able to do. In this lesson, your student will learn some of the ways weather is measured and how the seasons affect weather.	■ Student Learning Pages 4.A–4.B ■ 1 outdoor thermometer

VOCABULARY
THERMOMETER a tool used to measure temperature **WEATHER INSTRUMENT** a tool that helps people read weather conditions

Let's Begin

1 EXPLAIN Explain to your student that the sun provides light and heat to Earth and is very important to Earth's weather. It warms our air and water. Ask your student to imagine what the ground outside looks like after it rains. Often there are puddles on the ground. Explain that the puddles don't stay there forever. That's because the sun's heat dries the water, which then evaporates into the air. Soon the water collects into clouds and falls again from the sky. Ask, *Why is the sun so important?* [it warms the water and the air, it gives light]

2 SUPPLEMENT While this lesson may only take an hour or two to cover, you can supplement the material covered with activities as your student shows interest. For example, take a trip outside with your student and have him or her describe characteristics of the current season. Have your student show examples in nature for each characteristic.

3 OBSERVE Remind your student that the weather is always changing. Some days are sunny, while others are cloudy, rainy, or windy. One way we describe the weather is by measuring the temperature, or how hot or cold the air is. Explain that the tool we use to measure the temperature is called a **thermometer.** Show your student a thermometer and how to read the numbers in degrees.

SCIENCE

LESSON 3.4

4 **EXPAND** Tell your student that a thermometer is a **weather instrument,** or a tool that helps us read the weather conditions. Another weather instrument is a rain gauge. It measures how much rain falls from the sky. A wind sock tells us which way the wind is blowing. Ask, *Can you name one weather instrument and how it's used?* [a thermometer to measure temperature, a rain gauge to measure the amount of rain, a wind sock to find the direction of wind]

5 **INTRODUCE** Point out that weather is affected by the four seasons of the year: winter, spring, summer, and fall. Explain that winter is the coldest part of the year. It's also a time when there is less daylight and longer nights. Point out that in many places it snows during winter. Ask, *What holiday do you know about that happens in winter?* [Christmas, Hanukkah, New Year's, Valentines Day, Martin Luther King Day, and so on]

6 **REVEAL** Explain that spring comes after winter. During spring, the weather begins to warm up and it can rain a lot. The days also get longer. New leaves begin to grow on trees and the seeds of smaller plants begin to grow out of the ground. Ask, *Why is spring an exciting season?* [because new plants are growing]

7 **MODEL** Explain that summer is the hottest season and has the most daylight. Summer comes after spring. Ask, *What is your favorite thing to do for fun in the summer?* Then reveal that fall comes after summer. The weather starts to cool and the days grow shorter. The leaves of many trees change colors and fall off the branches. Ask, *Have you seen the leaves of a tree change colors? What colors were the leaves?* [red, yellow, orange, brown, and so on]

8 **EXPLAIN AND DISTRIBUTE** Explain that in some places the weather in each season changes a lot, while in others it only changes a little. Ask, *Does the weather change a lot or just a little from season to season where you live?* Then distribute Student Learning Page 4.A. Read the directions with your student. Have him or her complete the exercise.

Branching Out

FOR FURTHER READING

Around the Year, by Tasha Tudor (Simon and Schuster, 2001).

Kick Up a Storm: A Book About Weather, by Nancy White (Scholastic Trade, 2000).

TEACHING TIP

Watch a television weather report with your student. Explain that the weatherperson uses different weather instruments, such as thermometers and rain gauges, to get information about the weather.

CHECKING IN

To assess your student's understanding of the lesson, ask him or her to name the four seasons and describe the weather during each season. Then have your student read the temperature on a thermometer.

Name the Four Seasons

Write "winter," "spring," "summer," or "fall" next to each picture. Then write a sentence about your favorite season.

1. _____

3. _____

2. _____

4. _____

5. Favorite season: _____

_____

What's Next? You Decide!

Now it's your turn to choose what to do next in the lesson. Read the activities and decide which one you want to do—you may want to try them both!

Make Your Own Rain Gauge

MATERIALS

- ❑ 1 plastic or wood box
- ❑ sand to fill box
- ❑ 1 empty tin can
- ❑ 1 ruler

STEPS

You can measure how much rain falls with a rain gauge.

- ❑ Fill the box with sand.
- ❑ Put the tin can in the box.
- ❑ Put the box outside.
- ❑ After it rains, use the ruler to measure how much water fell into the can.

Record the Weather

MATERIALS

- ❑ markers or crayons

STEPS

- ❑ Write down the days of the week.
- ❑ Every day during the week, write one to three words about the weather. Use words such as *sunny, cloudy, windy, cool,* and *warm.*
- ❑ Draw a picture of the weather for each day. Draw a sun if it's sunny, a cloud if it's cloudy, rain if it's rainy, and so on.
- ❑ At the end of the week, look at your weather record. How did the weather change?

SCIENCE

LESSON
3.5

Comparing Different Climates

From arctic to desert, our planet has many different climates.

OBJECTIVE	BACKGROUND	MATERIALS
To introduce your student to several types of climates	Because we are most familiar with our own area's climate, we may not realize that climates differ greatly depending on location and landforms. In this lesson, your student will learn about three distinct climates—desert, tropical rain forest, and arctic.	■ Student Learning Pages 5.A–5.B ■ 1 picture of a desert environment ■ 1 picture of a tropical rain forest environment ■ 1 world map or globe ■ 1 picture of an arctic environment ■ 1 copy Web, page 356 ■ 1 large glass container ■ gravel, sand, and soil ■ 3–4 small cacti

VOCABULARY
CLIMATE the weather patterns of an area over long periods of time **HUMID** when the air holds a lot of water **ARCTIC** the area around the North Pole

Let's Begin

1 **INTRODUCE** Ask your student to describe the weather where you live. Explain that an area's **climate** refers to the type of weather it has. Point out that climates are different in different parts of the world. Show your student a picture of a desert. Explain that a desert is a very dry place where rain and snow seldom fall. In some deserts, rain may not fall for years at a time. Explain that in most deserts, the temperature during the day is very hot, but at night it's much cooler. In some parts of the world, deserts are cold all the time. Explain that the plants and animals that live in a desert have special body parts that make it possible for them to survive in the dry heat. Have your student observe the picture of a desert and explain what he or she notices about the appearance of the soil, rocks, and plants.

2 **EXPLAIN** Show your student a picture of a tropical rain forest. Ask, *What can you see that's different in a tropical rain forest*

than in a desert? [there are more plants; things are greener]
Explain that many different plants and animals live in a tropical
rain forest. The climate is very hot and wet, and it rains almost
every day. Explain that the trees soak up water from the ground
and then release it through their leaves. As a result, the air is
humid and feels damp and sticky. In a tropical rain forest, the
temperature doesn't change much from night to day or season to
season. Ask, *Have you ever been in a bathroom after someone has
just finished taking a hot shower? What was the air like?* Point out
that the humidity in the bathroom was similar to a rain forest.

3   **EXPLORE**   On a globe or map of the world, show your student
the North Pole. Explain that the area near the North Pole is
called the **Arctic,** and it has a very cold climate. The land is
frozen and covered with snow most of the year. During most
of the winter, the Arctic is dark, even during the daytime hours.
Temperatures are very cold. The air is dry but some snow falls.
During the short summer, the days are long and there is very
little darkness. The air gets warmer in the summer but it's still
cool. Show your student a picture of the Arctic. Ask, *What
animals do you think live in the Arctic?* [polar bears, seals]

4   **DISTRIBUTE**   Distribute Student Learning Page 5.A and have
your student complete the activity.

5   **COMPARE**   Distribute a copy of the Web found on page 356.
Have your student write "Desert," "Tropical Rain Forest," or
"Arctic" in the center. In each circle, have him or her draw
or write something that tells about that climate.

Branching Out

TEACHING TIP

Help your student create a desert terrarium. Together place about two
inches of gravel in the bottom of a large glass container. Add an inch
and a half of a sand-soil mixture. Obtain small cacti from a local nursery
and plant them. Add a thin layer of sand. Place the terrarium in a sunny
place where your student can observe. Water it about twice a month.

CHECKING IN

To assess your student's understanding of the lesson, present different
climate characteristics and have your student name the climate(s) they
describe. For example, say, *the air is dry here* [desert and arctic], *many
plants and animals live here* [tropical rain forest], and so on.

FOR FURTHER READING

*Biomes of the Past and
Future,* by Karen J.
Donnelly (PowerKids
Press, 2003).

*First Reports—Biomes:
Coral Reefs, Deserts,
Grasslands,
Mountains, Oceans,
Rain Forests, Tundra,
Wetlands,* by Susan H.
Gray and Shirley W.
Gray (Compass Point
Books, 2000).

Find the Animals

Connect the dots to find the animals.

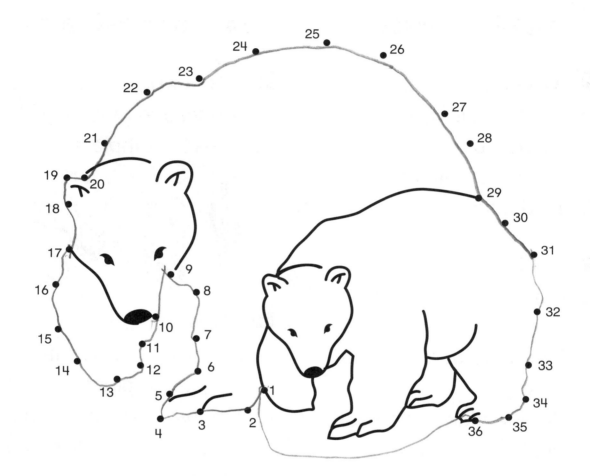

1. What animals did you find? _____

2. What climate do they live in? _____

What's Next? You Decide!

Now it's your turn to choose what to do next in the lesson. Read the activities and decide which one you want to do—you may want to try them both!

Watch for Water

■ MATERIALS

- ❑ 1 potted plant, such as a geranium
- ❑ 1 large plastic bag
- ❑ 1 twist tie

■ STEPS

- ❑ Put the plant inside the large plastic bag.
- ❑ Close the bag with the twist tie.
- ❑ Put the plant in the sun. Wait for one hour.

- ❑ Look at the bag again. What happened to the air in the bag?

Make a Model Cactus

■ MATERIALS

- ❑ 1 package modeling clay
- ❑ 10–15 toothpicks

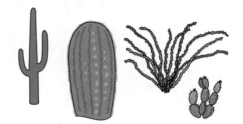

■ STEPS

What keeps animals from eating desert plants?
- ❑ Choose a desert plant.
- ❑ Shape the clay like your plant.
- ❑ Break the toothpicks in half and stick them into the clay. Keep the sharp ends out.
- ❑ What would happen if an animal took a bite out of the plant?

Studying Earth's Resources

*May the footprints we leave behind show that we've walked
in kindness toward Earth and every living thing.*
—Native American saying

OBJECTIVE	BACKGROUND	MATERIALS
To help your student learn about the importance of Earth's resources in our lives	Earth's resources are important to all living things on the planet. When people take too many natural resources or use them too quickly, it can negatively affect the future of all living things. In this lesson, your student will learn about Earth's resources and how to use them wisely.	■ Student Learning Pages 6.A–6.B ■ 1 photo of Earth

VOCABULARY
RESOURCES things that are used to meet a need **POLLUTION** the dirtying of Earth's resources **RECYCLING** making ready for reuse

Let's Begin

1   **INTRODUCE** Introduce the concept of **resources** to your student. Explain that a resource is something that's used to meet a need. Earth provides natural resources that people depend on to live. Water, air, and land are some of the resources people use. Challenge your student to think of one way he or she used Earth's resources today.

2   **REVEAL** Together, see if you and your student can produce a ballpark count of how many times in a day he or she uses water. Explain that water is very important to people. We need clean water to drink. We also need water to bathe, brush our teeth, and wash our clothes, cars, and dishes. We even have fun in water—we use it for swimming, boating, and fishing. Mention that sometimes people are wasteful with water. One way your student can help save water is by turning off the faucet while brushing his or her teeth. Look at the picture of Earth with your student. Point out that the blue parts are water that fills the oceans, lakes, rivers, and streams. Ask, *Does it look like there's more land or more water on Earth?* [more water]

3   **EXPLORE** Explain to your student that air is another of Earth's resources. Invite your student to inhale and exhale three deep

?

DID YOU KNOW?

Only one percent of all the water on Earth is drinkable freshwater. The rest is saltwater or frozen in glaciers.

breaths with you. Ask, *Can you think of one way we use air?* [to breathe] Emphasize the importance of clean air for staying healthy. Explain that people do some things that make our air dirty. The smoke and gases from our cars cause air **pollution.** Explain that one way we can help keep our air clean is by walking, riding a bicycle, or taking a public bus or train instead of driving a car. Take a walk with your student to a nearby store, park, or library instead of driving.

4 **EXPLAIN** Point out that land is also a resource. We use land in many different ways. Our houses, apartments, and buildings are built on land. We also use land to grow food. Explain that the garbage we throw away goes to places called landfills that take up space. By throwing away less garbage, we can keep more land clean. Point out that one way to create less garbage is by donating used clothes, toys, and other household items instead of throwing them away. Go through some old clothes and toys with your student and find a few items to bring to a local service agency.

5 **RELATE** Explain that another very important way we can help protect Earth's resources is by **recycling.** We can recycle cans, paper, glass, and plastics. When we recycle these items, they are made into new things instead of going into landfills. Show your student the recycle symbol. The recycle symbol means either that an item can be recycled or that it's been made from recycled material. Have your student look around your home for food containers or other items that show the recycle symbol. Distribute Student Learning Page 6.A. Help your student identify the recyclable items.

The recycle symbol tells us when something is recyclable or made of recycled material.

6 **EXPAND** Tell your student that people aren't the only ones who depend on Earth's resources. Air, water, and land are also very important to plants and animals. When people pollute or misuse resources, they hurt plants and animals. Explain that when people cut down trees and pollute water, they damage the homes of the animals that live there. Explain that we need to use our resources wisely to protect all living things—people, plants, and animals.

FOR FURTHER READING

Recycling (*True Books: Environment*), by Rhonda Lucas Donald (Children's Press, 2002).

Where Have All the Pandas Gone? Questions and Answers About Endangered Species, by Melvin Berger (Scholastic Reference, 2002).

Branching Out

TEACHING TIP

If your city or town recycles, have your student participate in collecting or sorting recyclable items. Help your student learn which items are recyclable and which aren't. You may even wish to visit the local recycling center.

CHECKING IN

To assess your student's understanding of the lesson, ask your student to name three of Earth's resources and why they are important to his or her life. Then ask him or her to tell you what recycling means and what kinds of things we can recycle.

Learn to Recycle

Circle the things that can be recycled.

What's Next? You Decide!

Now it's your turn to choose what to do next in the lesson. Read the activities and decide which one you want to do—you may want to try them both!

Save Water

MATERIALS

❑ 1 gallon jug
❑ 1 gallon drinking water

STEPS

❑ Fill a gallon jug with clean drinking water.
❑ For one day, each time you need water take it only from the jug.
❑ When you want a drink, need to wash your hands, or brush your teeth, use the water in the jug.
❑ At the end of the day look at how much water you used.
❑ Was one gallon enough for the whole day?

Clean Your Town

MATERIALS

❑ 2 garbage bags
❑ 1 pair work gloves

STEPS

❑ With an adult, go to a park, field, or street where there is garbage on the ground.
❑ Bring two garbage bags and wear work gloves.
❑ Pick up the garbage and put it in one bag.
❑ Put any cans, glass, plastic, or paper in another bag and recycle it.
❑ Don't pick up anything that's sharp or unfamiliar.
❑ Wash your hands when you're done.

Discovering the Forms of Matter

Everything from a tiny grain of sand to the air we breathe is made of matter.

OBJECTIVE	BACKGROUND	MATERIALS
To introduce your student to the forms of matter	Learning about matter helps us understand the natural world. In this lesson, your student will learn about the three forms of matter, how heat effects matter, and mixtures of matter.	■ Student Learning Pages 7.A–7.B ■ 3 paper cups ■ 1 package modeling clay ■ vanilla extract ■ 1 bowl ■ several household objects ■ paper towels ■ 1 desk lamp

VOCABULARY

MATTER anything that you can touch, occupies space, and has weight

SOLIDS forms of matter that hold their shape and have a fixed size or volume

LIQUIDS forms of matter that take up space and take the shape of their container

GASES forms of matter that have no shape or size

MIXTURE a combination of different types of matter

Let's Begin

1 **INTRODUCE** Tell your student that **matter** is anything that takes up space. Point to several different objects in the room and explain that these things are all made of matter. Explain that matter can come in three forms—**solids, liquids,** and **gases.** Solids are things such as rocks and snowballs. They take up space and keep their shape. Liquids are things such as milk that flow when poured. Gases, such as air, often can't be seen but still occupy space. Have your student put some clay into a paper cup and fill a second cup halfway with water. Put a drop of vanilla into a third cup. Ask your student to try pouring the matter from each cup into a bowl. Have your student notice and smell each one. Ask, *What form of matter is in each cup?* [clay: solid; water: liquid; vanilla: forms a gas that can be smelled]

TAKE A BREAK

The vocabulary words are the foundation of the lesson, so take as much time as necessary when discussing them. Remember to help your student in a noncritical and nonjudgmental manner.

SCIENCE

LESSON 3.7

2 **DISTRIBUTE AND COMPLETE** Distribute Student Learning Page 7.A. Gather household objects such as a block, chalk, vinegar, orange juice, an air-filled resealable bag, or an air-filled balloon. Help your student read the directions and complete the activity.

3 **EXPLORE** Explain that heat causes matter to change its form. To show how heat is related to the motion of matter, have your student rub his or her hands together quickly. Ask, *What happens to your palms?* [they get warmer]

4 **MODEL** Show the paper cup filled halfway with water to your student again. Ask, *What form of matter is this?* [liquid] Place the cup inside a freezer. Return after the water has frozen. Peel off the paper. Place the ice on a paper towel. Ask, *What form of matter is this?* [solid] Place the ice and paper towel under a desk lamp. Have your student watch as it melts back into a liquid. When the paper towel is wet, remove the ice that remains. After 10 minutes have passed have your student feel the paper towel. Explain that the heat from the lamp changed the water into a gas called water vapor. Ask, *What happens to a puddle on a sunny day?* [it gets smaller as the water turns to gas from the heat]

5 **DISCUSS** Explain to your student that mixing things together is another way we can change matter. A **mixture** is a combination of different types of matter. Point out that mixtures can form in liquids, solids, or gases. Explain that a tossed salad, milk, rocks, and fizzy drinks are all mixtures. Pour out a glass of soda. Point out the bubbles of gas in the liquid. Explain that air is a mixture of many gases. Tell your student that what makes the parts of a mixture special usually doesn't change. As a result, you can often separate the parts of a mixture. Ask, *How could you separate the parts of a salad?* [pick out bits of tomato by their red color, find onions by their strong smell, and so on]

Branching Out

TEACHING TIP

If your student has trouble understanding that gases take up space, use this simple demonstration. Wad up a dry paper towel and push it into the bottom of a cup. Fill a sink with water. Push the cup into the water with its mouth pointing down. Don't tilt the cup as you lift it up. The paper towel will still be dry. You could also blow up a balloon and have your student note that the space taken up by the gas (carbon dioxide) causes the balloon to expand.

CHECKING IN

To assess your student's understanding of the lesson, play a guessing game. Tell your student to look around the room and choose three pieces of matter, one in each form. Have your student describe each thing to you so you can guess what it is. Ask, *What form of matter is it?*

FOR FURTHER READING

Solids, Liquids and Gases, by the Ontario Science Centre (Kids Can Press, 2000).

What Is the World Made Of?, by Kathleen Weidner Zoehfeld (HarperCollins Publishers, 1998).

Describe Matter

Choose three different things in your home. Write their names in the chart. Describe each thing. Then decide if it's a solid, a liquid, or a gas. Put a check mark in the correct box.

Name of Thing	Describe It (color, shape, size)	Solid	Liquid	Gas
1.				
2.				
3.				

SCIENCE

7.B

What's Next? You Decide!

Now it's your turn to choose what to do next in the lesson. Read the activities and decide which one you want to do—you may want to try them both!

Make Mystery Matter

■ MATERIALS

- ❑ 1 measuring cup
- ❑ $\frac{1}{4}$ cup cornstarch
- ❑ 1 resealable bag
- ❑ 2 tablespoons water
- ❑ 1 plastic spoon

■ STEPS

- ❑ Pour the cornstarch into the resealable bag.
- ❑ Add the water.
- ❑ Knead the mixture in the bag with your fingers.
- ❑ Pour the matter into the measuring cup.
- ❑ Try pushing on it with a spoon.
- ❑ Put some in your hand. Try rolling it into a ball.
- ❑ When does it act like a liquid? A solid?

Separate Mixtures

■ MATERIALS

- ❑ 1 coffee filter
- ❑ 1 black, washable marker
- ❑ 1 plastic cup, 16 ounces

Coffee filter
Plastic cup

■ STEPS

Black ink is a mixture of colors.

- ❑ Draw a spot with the black marker in the center of the coffee filter.
- ❑ Set the filter over the top of the cup. It should hang over the sides.
- ❑ Place a few drops of water onto the ink. Watch the ink spread out.
- ❑ What hidden colors did you find in the black ink?

Exploring Movement and Magnets

Life is a steady flow of movement.

SCIENCE
LESSON 3.8

OBJECTIVE	BACKGROUND	MATERIALS
To teach your student how movement occurs and how magnets act on other objects	Movement is a natural part of life that we usually take for granted. In this lesson, your student will learn that movement results from a push or a pull and that magnets can push and pull some things.	<ul><li>Student Learning Pages 8.A–8.B</li><li>1 wooden block</li><li>2 bar magnets</li><li>1 metal paper clip</li><li>4–6 objects not attracted to magnets, such as cotton, paper, cork, and chalk</li><li>4–6 objects attracted to magnets, such as a nail, washer, spoon, and staples</li><li>1 toy car</li><li>1–3 old magazines</li><li>1 pair scissors</li><li>glue</li></ul>

VOCABULARY

MOVEMENT a change in the position of an object in space

PUSH to cause to move away from

PULL to cause to move toward

SPEED how fast something moves from one place to another

MAGNET an object that can push or pull some kinds of metal

ATTRACT to pull something toward

REPEL to push something away

Let's Begin

1   **DEMONSTRATE** Set a wooden block on a table or a desk. Ask your student to move the block away from him or her without taking it off the desk. Ask, *What did you do to the block?* [pushed it away] Then have your student bring the block back toward him or her in the same manner. Ask, *What did you do this time?* [pulled it toward me] Explain to your student that he or she easily caused the **movement** of the block by giving it a gentle **push** or **pull.** Point out that larger or heavier things can be harder to move. They would need a very strong push or pull.

FOR FURTHER READING

Find Out About: Pushes and Pulls (*Find Out About Series*), by Terry Jennings (BBC Publications, 1999).

Magnets (*Everyday Science*), by Peter D. Riley (Gareth Stevens Publishing, 2002).

Explain that animals and people can move on their own. Invite your student to name three things that can't move without a push or a pull and three things that can move by themselves.

2   **EXPLAIN** Ask your student to walk across the room. Then have him or her run across the room. Ask, *How were the two times you moved across the floor different?* [running was faster than walking] Explain that how fast or slow an object moves from one place to another is its **speed.** Invite your student to give examples of fast and slow moving objects. Ask, *Do moving things such as animals and cars always move at the same speed?* [no] Challenge your student to explain one way a moving object changes speed. [a driver steps on a brake to slow down movement; a horse moves its legs faster to speed up movement] Then distribute Student Learning Page 8.A. Help your student read the directions.

3   **EXPLORE** Give your student a bar **magnet.** Explain that a magnet can move some things. Place a paper clip on the table. Invite your student to use the magnet to pull the paper clip. Explain that when magnets pull something, we say they **attract** the object. Ask, *Do you think magnets attract all objects?* [no] Give your student various objects that are and aren't attracted to magnets. Have your student try the magnet with each one. Ask, *What kinds of objects does the magnet attract?* [metal objects] Explain that magnets attract some metals, but not all metals. Iron is one kind of metal that magnets attract. Give your student an empty soda can to test with the magnet. Ask, *Is the can made of iron? How can you tell?* [no, the magnet doesn't attract it, so it's not iron]

4   **EXPAND** Explain that magnets can push, or **repel,** other magnets. Magnets repel when the ends that are alike are near each other. Give your student two bar magnets. Have him or her hold the two ends marked *N* near each other. Ask your student to describe what happens using the word *repel.*

Branching Out

TEACHING TIP

Give your student a toy car. Have him or her experiment with different ways to make it move slowly and quickly. Have him or her describe how its speed changes as it moves.

CHECKING IN

To assess your student's understanding of the lesson, have him or her look through old magazines to find pictures of objects that are pushed or pulled, such as a glass of water, a pencil, a grocery cart, and a scooter. Have him or her cut out the pictures, glue them on paper, and identify each as an object that's pushed or pulled.

Find the Speed

Look at each picture. Write "fast," "slow," or "fast and slow" on the line.

1. _fast_

2. _slow_

3. _fast_

4. _fast and Slow_

5. _slow_

6. _Fast_

7. _Fast and Slow_

8. _Slow_

What's Next? You Decide!

Now it's your turn to choose what to do next in the lesson. Read the activities and decide which one you want to do—you may want to try them both!

Make a Balloon Rocket

MATERIALS

- ❏ nylon string
- ❏ 1 plastic straw
- ❏ 1 long balloon
- ❏ tape

Straw Tape Nylon string

Balloon

STEPS

Ask an adult to help you with this activity.

- ❏ Put the string through the straw.
- ❏ Tie one end of the string to a doorknob and the other to a chair.
- ❏ Blow up the balloon. Tape the balloon to the straw.
- ❏ Let go of the balloon. What pushes or pulls it?

Make Magnetic Movement

MATERIALS

- ❏ 1 metal paper clip
- ❏ 1 magnet
- ❏ 1 tub or tray

STEPS

- ❏ Make a paper boat. Ask an adult to help you.
- ❏ Tape the paper clip to the boat.
- ❏ Fill the tray or tub with a few inches of water. Float your boat on the water.
- ❏ Put the magnet near the boat. Move the magnet slowly. What happens to the boat? Why?

Investigating Sound

Our world is filled with sounds, from the cry of a baby to the soft rustling of wind.

OBJECTIVE	BACKGROUND	MATERIALS
To teach your student how sounds are produced and how they travel	From the alarm clock that wakes us in the morning to the fire signal that warns us of danger, we use sound to learn about the world around us. In this lesson, your student will learn about sound vibrations and how sound travels through different materials.	■ Student Learning Pages 9.A–9.B ■ 1 plastic or metal ruler ■ 1 pan filled with water ■ 2 rocks ■ 1 coiled spring toy ■ 1 piece plastic tubing, about 2 feet long ■ 2 funnels ■ tape ■ 1 radio ■ foam earplugs ■ 1 blanket ■ 1 rubber band

VOCABULARY

SOUNDS   the waves of energy produced when matter moves
VIBRATES   when something moves back and forth quickly

Let's Begin

1   **INTRODUCE** Tell your student to sit quietly and listen carefully. Ask, *What **sounds** do you hear around the house?* [possible answers: footsteps, cars in the street, heating or cooling sounds] Make a list of the sounds he or she mentions. Place a plastic or metal ruler on a table with one end hanging over the edge. Flip the free end with your hand. Ask your student to watch as the ruler moves back and forth. Explain to your student that all sounds start when something moves back and forth quickly, or **vibrates.** Recall the household sounds your student mentioned. Help your student figure out what moved to cause each sound. [a foot on the floor, the engine of a car, air through a vent]

2   **EXPLORE** Drop a rock into a pan of water. Ask your student to watch as the ripples spread out in all directions. Explain to your student that sound moves in waves much like the ripples in the water. However, instead of moving up and down, sound waves

DID YOU KNOW?

Different parts of musical instruments vibrate. Plucking the strings of a banjo makes them vibrate. Striking the skin of a drum makes it vibrate. Horns make music by vibrating the air in pipes.

move back and forth. Use a coiled spring toy to demonstrate this. Hold one end of the spring, and have your student hold the other. Stretch the toy along a table. Tap the part of the spring nearest you. Call the resulting ripple effect to your student's attention. Explain that the toy shows how sound waves move through air and objects.

3 **REVEAL** Explain to your student that we can hear sound because air can move. Point out that whenever anything vibrates, it pushes against the air around it. The air particles bump into each other. Tell your student that vibrating air passes on sound waves to our ears. When sound waves enter our ears, we hear sound. Explain that he or she wouldn't be able to hear sounds in outer space because there is no air there. Ask, *What do we need to hear sounds?* [air]

DID YOU KNOW?

Whales, dolphins, and other ocean animals use sound to communicate with each other. Because sound travels so well underwater, whales that are miles apart can hear each other.

4 **EXPERIMENT** Make a listening tube to find out whether sounds travel through other materials besides air. Obtain a piece of plastic tubing. Attach a funnel to each end of the tube with tape. It should fit tightly over the tips of the funnels. Have your student place a funnel over one ear and hold the other funnel against a table. Tap on the table. Next, put the funnel against the side of a pan of water. Click two rocks together above and below the surface of the water. Have your student listen. Ask, *Does sound travel easily through solids and liquids?* [yes] Explain that sound moves faster through solids and liquids than through air. Then distribute Student Learning Page 9.A. Be sure to show your student how to use the earplugs safely.

Branching Out

TEACHING TIP

Take as much time as needed with this lesson for your student to understand the concepts of sound. Let your student set the pace.

CHECKING IN

To assess your student's understanding of the lesson, ask him or her to draw a picture showing how sound gets from its source to the ear.

FOR FURTHER READING

Bangs and Twangs: Science Fun with Sounds, by Vicki Cobb (Millbrook Press, 2000).

Sounds All Around, by Wendy Pfeffer (HarperCollins, 1999).

Block Sound

Loud noises can hurt our ears. Turn on a radio. Try different ways to block the sound. Write a sentence about sound.

Try blocking the sound with a blanket.

Try blocking the sound with earplugs.

1. Which blocked more of the radio sounds, the blanket or the earplugs? _____

2. Sentence: _____

_____

_____

_____

_____

_____

What's Next? You Decide!

Now it's your turn to choose what to do next in the lesson. Read the activities and decide which one you want to do—you may want to try them both!

Make a Cup Roar

▲ MATERIALS

- ❏ 1 paper cup
- ❏ 1 foot-long string
- ❏ 1 pair scissors

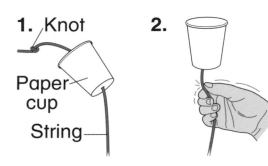

1. Knot
Paper cup
String
2.

▲ STEPS

- ❏ Poke a tiny hole in the bottom of the paper cup with the scissors.
- ❏ Tie a knot in one end of the string.
- ❏ Push the other end of the string through the hole.
- ❏ Wet the string with water.
- ❏ Hold the cup tightly with one hand.
- ❏ Rub your thumb down the length of the string.
- ❏ Can you hear the roaring sound?

Make a Bottle Band

▲ MATERIALS

- ❏ 5 empty glass bottles
- ❏ 1 metal spoon

▲ STEPS

- ❏ Fill the bottles with water to different heights.
- ❏ Blow across the top of each to make a sound.
- ❏ Tap each bottle with the spoon.
- ❏ Put the bottles in order from the highest to lowest sound.
- ❏ Play a song!

SCIENCE

LESSON
3.10

Learning About Bones and Muscles

Without your bones and muscles, you'd just be a lump on the ground!

OBJECTIVE	BACKGROUND	MATERIALS
To give your student an understanding of the importance of bones and muscles	Bones and muscles work together to hold the shape of the body and to help it move. Bones also protect the organs inside the body. In this lesson, your student will learn about the specific jobs of bones and muscles.	■ Student Learning Pages 10.A–10.B ■ 1 flashlight ■ 1 mirror ■ 1 set of chicken leg bones (dried) with the meat removed ■ 1 ball ■ 1 cracker

VOCABULARY
BONES the hard internal body parts that support the body **SKELETON** all the bones in the body **JOINT** a place where two bones meet **MUSCLES** the tissues that move and support the body

Let's Begin

1 **EXPLORE** Invite your student to feel his or her shin and head. Point out that these body parts are hard. Ask, *What makes these parts of your body so hard?* [bones] Then darken the room. Have your student hold out one hand with the palm down and the fingers spread out. Hold a flashlight under your student's fingers and turn it on. Ask, *What is the dark area in your fingers?* [bones] Point out that all the **bones** put together make up the **skeleton.** Explain that three functions of bones are to support the body, protect the internal body parts, and help the body move.

2 **DISCOVER** Let your student be the guide as to how much time to spend on the lesson. As your student shows interest, you may wish to cover the concepts all in one sitting or go back to the lesson over a period of time. Help your student make a connection to the lesson and ask, *What do you think would happen if we didn't have bones?* [we couldn't stand up or move and could get hurt easily]

DID YOU KNOW?

A baby is born with 270 bones that are softer than an adult's bones. By the age of about 25, an adult has 206 bones. These bones are hard and will last throughout life.

3 **DEMONSTRATE** Have your student open and close a door. Point out the hinges that make this action possible. Challenge your student to find a place on his or her body that moves like a door opening and closing. Explain that this is one type of **joint.** Every place in the body where two bones meet is a joint, but not all joints are the same. Invite your student to explore the ways that his or her body can move. Compare the movement of the elbow, knee, hip, spine, and ankle to the movement of the doorway hinges. Have a discussion with your student about the importance of each type of joint in helping your body move in many ways. Encourage your student to write three sentences identifying and describing three ways in which his or her joints move.

4 **OBSERVE** Explain that bones can't move by themselves. **Muscles** help them move. Have your student stand up and let one arm hang down loosely. With the other hand, have him or her feel the long muscle in the front of the upper arm, the biceps. Have your student bend his or her arm upward and then tighten the fist and arm muscles. Ask, *What happened to your muscle?* [it got shorter and thicker] Have your student continue to feel the muscle and then slowly lower the arm. Ask, *What happened to the muscle now?* [it got longer and thinner]

5 **EXPAND** Explain to your student that muscles work in pairs to move bones, help lift things, and help lower things. Have your student put one hand under a table, palm up, and push up on the table. With the other hand, have your student feel the same arm muscle as in the previous exercise. Ask, *What happened to this muscle when you pushed on the table?* [it got shorter and thicker] Ask, *What does this muscle do?* [it helps lift things] Then have your student sit at the table and feel the long muscle in the back of his or her upper arm, the triceps. Have your student place a palm on the top of the table and push down. With the other hand, have him or her feel this muscle again. Ask your student to describe how this muscle changed. Ask, *What does this muscle do?* [it helps push things down] Then distribute Student Learning Page 10.A.

TAKE A BREAK

Give your student a mirror and allow him or her to make various funny faces to see how the facial muscles work. Then have your student draw the funniest face he or she made.

FOR FURTHER READING

Watch Me Grow: Fun Ways to Learn About Cells, Bones, Muscles, and Joints: Activities for Children 5 to 9, by Michelle O'Brien-Palmer (Chicago Review Press, 1999).

Your Muscles and Bones (*How Your Body Works*), by Anita Ganeri (Gareth Stevens Publishing, 2002).

Branching Out

TEACHING TIP

Give your student a set of chicken leg bones and let him or her explore how the joint works. Invite your student to compare this joint to his or her own knee or elbow joint.

CHECKING IN

To assess your student's understanding of the lesson, have your student complete various actions, such as kicking a ball or eating a cracker. Then have him or her point out on his or her body which bones, muscles, and joints were involved in the activity.

Match Your Bones and Your Actions

Look at the skeleton. Match the bones to the way they help you move. Write the letter of the set of bones next to the activity they help you with.

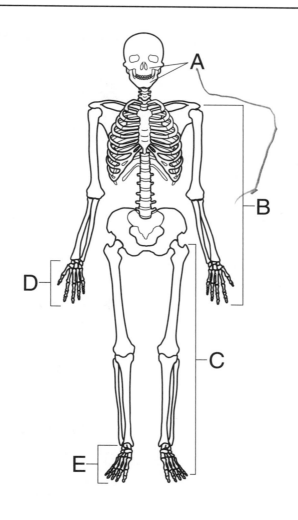

1. Kick a soccer ball _____

2. Run across the playground _____

3. Pet a dog _____

4. Talk to a friend _____

5. Swing on the jungle gym _____

What's Next? You Decide!

Now it's your turn to choose what to do next in the lesson. Read the activities and decide which one you want to do—you may want to try them both!

Model Your Backbones

▲ MATERIALS

- ❑ 1 plastic straw
- ❑ 1 pair scissors
- ❑ 1 pipe cleaner

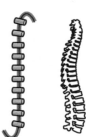

▲ STEPS

Your backbone protects your spinal cord. It also helps you move.

- ❑ Cut the straw into 10 pieces. Slide the pieces over the pipe cleaner.
- ❑ Bend the top and bottom of the pipe cleaner.
- ❑ How is the model like your spine?

Experiment with Joints

▲ MATERIALS

- ❑ masking tape

▲ STEPS

Try doing things without moving your joints!

- ❑ Keep your elbow straight. Try to pick up a pencil.
- ❑ Have an adult tape your thumbs to your hands. Try to pick up the pencil. Try to write your name.
- ❑ Keep the tape on your thumbs for an hour. What things are hard to do?
- ❑ Why do you think joints are important?

Going with the Flow

SCIENCE

LESSON 3.11

Your heart and lungs work in steady rhythm— without a break—for as long as you live.

OBJECTIVE	BACKGROUND	MATERIALS
To teach your student how the heart and lungs work	The heart and blood move nourishment around the body and carry away wastes. The lungs bring in fresh air with every breath. In this lesson, your student will learn how blood moves and how the heart and lungs work to keep us alive and healthy.	■ Student Learning Pages 11.A–11.B ■ 1 hand mirror ■ 1 sheet blank paper ■ markers or crayons ■ 2 funnels ■ 1 piece flexible plastic tubing, about 2 feet long ■ 1 plastic soda bottle with cap ■ 1 plastic straw ■ 2 balloons ■ 2 rubber bands ■ 1 lump modeling clay ■ 1 plastic squeeze bottle

VOCABULARY

HEART an organ that pumps blood through the body

BLOOD the liquid that flows inside the body and moves wastes and food

BLOOD VESSELS small tubes that carry blood

LUNGS spongy organs in the chest filled with air sacs that exchange gases

WINDPIPE a long tube in the throat that connects the nose and mouth to the lungs

Let's Begin

1 **INTRODUCE** Tell your student that the **heart** is a muscle found in the center of the chest. Each person's heart is about the size of his or her closed fist. Have your student place his or her fingers on both sides of his or her head in front of the ears. Tell your student to close his or her eyes, sit quietly, and listen to the heart beating. Explain to your student that the heart pumps **blood** all around the body. Explain also that the blood moves through small tubes called **blood vessels.** Point out that a good place to see these tubes is in the folds of skin under the eye. Give your student a hand mirror. Have your student use the mirror to gently observe and draw what he or she sees.

DID YOU KNOW?

Not all blood is red. Some animals, such as insects, have green blood, and lobsters have blue blood that contains copper.

2 **EXPLORE** Try the following to show your student just how hard the heart works. Have your student put his or her palms together, crossing the fingers of each hand over the back of the other hand and crossing the thumbs. Have your student squeeze his or her hands together 70 times. Ask, *Are you getting tired?* [probably] Explain that the heart pumps about 70 to 90 times each minute every day of a person's life. Now make a tool with your student to listen to the heart. Attach a funnel to each end of a piece of flexible plastic tubing. Fit the tubing tightly over the tips of the funnels using masking tape. Tell your student to put the mouth of one funnel over his or her chest and the mouth of the other over an ear. Have your student move the first funnel around until he or she finds his or her heartbeat. Then have your student jump up and down quickly and listen again. Ask, *Does your heart beat slower or faster after exercise?* [faster]

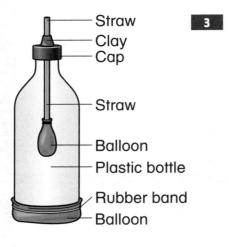

Straw
Clay
Cap

Straw

Balloon
Plastic bottle

Rubber band
Balloon

3 **MODEL** Make a model to show your student how the **lungs** work. Cut off the bottom of a plastic soda bottle, which will represent a person's chest. Punch a hole in the cap and insert a plastic straw. Use a lump of clay to make the seal airtight. Unscrew the cap and attach a balloon to the lower end of the straw with a rubber band. This balloon represents a lung. Cut off the neck of a second balloon and stretch it over the opening at the bottom of the bottle. Use a rubber band to hold the second balloon in place. Tell your student that this balloon represents the muscle below the lungs. To show how the lungs work, pull down on the bottom balloon to fill the model lung with air, and then push up to empty it. Have your student hold the bottle with the straw facing him or her while you push up to empty the balloon. Ask, *Can you feel air flowing out of the model lung?* [yes]

4 **GUIDE** Distribute Student Learning Page 11.A. Direct your student's attention to the picture of the chest showing the heart and lungs. Tell your student that when we breathe in, the air that enters the nose and mouth passes down a long tube called the **windpipe** and goes into the lungs. Explain that the heart and lungs work together to get fresh air into the blood and to the rest of the body. Have your student color the heart, lungs, and windpipe.

Branching Out

FOR FURTHER READING

The Heart: The Kids' Question and Answer Book, by J. Willis Hurst and Patsy Bryan, ill. (McGraw-Hill, 1998).

My Lungs, by Kathy Furgang (PowerKids Press, 2001).

TEACHING TIP

Show your student the pumping action of the heart. Fill a plastic squeeze bottle with water. Have your student watch as you squeeze the bottle and squirt out water. Similarly, the heart pumps blood by squeezing itself.

CHECKING IN

To assess your student's understanding of the lesson, ask him or her to describe how blood moves through the body. Have him or her describe the jobs of the heart and lungs as well.

Peek Inside Your Chest

Look at the picture. Color the lungs blue.
Color the heart red. Color the windpipe green.

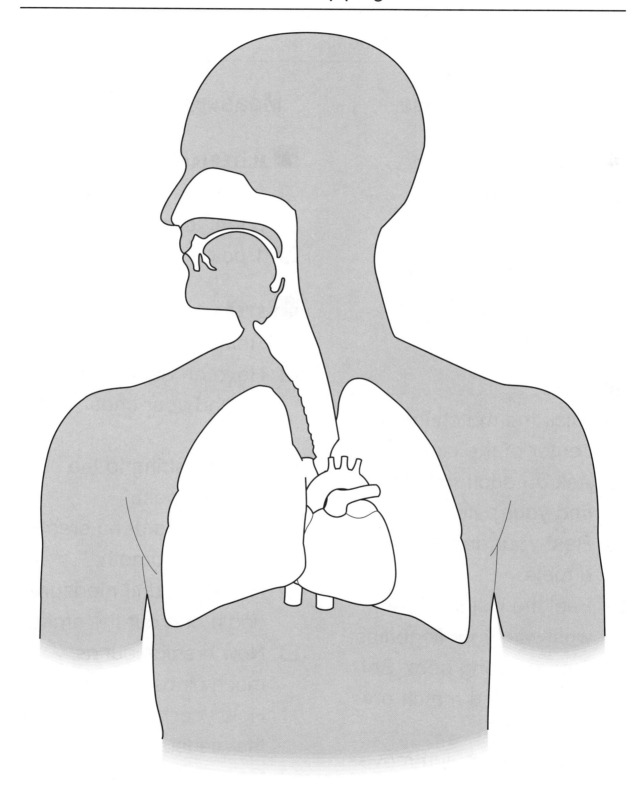

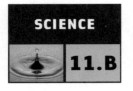

What's Next? You Decide!

Now it's your turn to choose what to do next in the lesson. Read the activities and decide which one you want to do—you may want to try them both!

See Your Pulse

MATERIALS

- ❏ 1 small lump clay
- ❏ 1 wooden match

Match

Clay

STEPS

- ❏ Stick the match into the center of the clay.
- ❏ Ask an adult to help you find your pulse.
- ❏ Rest your arm flat on a table.
- ❏ Feel the inside of your wrist with your fingertips.
- ❏ Find a strong beat. Set the clay and match on that spot.
- ❏ Watch the match move.

Measure Your Breath

MATERIALS

- ❏ 3 lengths string, each 3 feet long
- ❏ 1 pair scissors

STEPS

- ❏ Relax completely.
- ❏ Have an adult measure around your chest with string.
- ❏ Cut the string to the size of your chest.
- ❏ Now take a deep breath. Hold your breath.
- ❏ Have an adult measure again and cut the string.
- ❏ Now breathe out as much air as possible. Hold your breath. Repeat the measurement.
- ❏ Compare the strings.

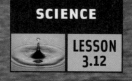

Finding Likenesses and Differences

Look around at other people. Are we the same or are we different?

OBJECTIVE	BACKGROUND	MATERIALS
To show your student how people are similar and how they are different	People are everywhere on Earth, and each of us is unique in one way or another. Yet all human beings have many important things in common. In this lesson, your student will identify some of the ways in which people are different and some of the ways they are the same.	<ul><li>Student Learning Pages 12.A–12.B</li><li>2–4 magazines or books with pictures of people</li><li>1 hand lens</li><li>2 copies Web, page 356</li><li>markers or crayons</li></ul>

VOCABULARY
ALIKE similar **DIFFERENT** not alike **FINGERPRINTS** the patterns of lines on a person's fingertips

Let's Begin

1 **COMPARE** Explain to your student that people are alike in many ways. Invite your student to name ways that the people he or she knows are **alike.** Discuss similarities such as the general structure of the body, the ability to move and breathe, and the need to eat food. Invite your student to think of some of the activities he or she does with friends. Point out that your student and his or her friends are alike in that they enjoy doing the same things. Ask your student to draw a picture of himself or herself with friends. Have your student describe how the picture shows that they are alike.

2 **EXPAND** Point out that people are alike in another way—they have the same kinds of emotions, or feelings. Discuss with your student different kinds of emotions, such as happiness, sadness, nervousness, love, anger, and so on. Ask your student to suggest ways these emotions are expressed. For example, people may express happiness by smiling or laughing and express sadness by crying. Have your student describe times when he or she has felt some of these emotions. Have him or her write a short paragraph about a time when he or she felt a certain emotion. Then have your student describe times when he or she has seen

TAKE A BREAK

Let your student's interest direct the lesson. You may wish to spend a short time on the activities or return to them over a period of time. Let your student be the guide!

other people express emotions. Together look through books or magazines. Have your student point out and describe the various emotions he or she sees people expressing.

People are alike in that we all feel emotions.

3 **CONTRAST** Discuss how some people your student knows are **different.** Point out that some differences are easy to see. For example, some people may be tall and others short; some may have curly hair and others straight. Mention that other differences are harder to see. Some people may enjoy sports while others may like to draw or read. Invite your student to make a list of the things he or she likes to do.

4 **EXPAND** Tell your student that every person has a different set of **fingerprints** and that a person's fingerprints stay the same throughout life. Give your student a hand lens so he or she can look closely at the patterns of tiny lines on his or her fingertips. Then distribute Student Learning Page 12.A.

5 **DISCUSS** Discuss with your student the importance of differences and similarities among people. Explain that sometimes it can be hard to understand people who are different at first, but that it's important not to leave people out just because they're different. Point out that differences in things such as talents and preferences make the world a successful and interesting place. Ask, *How do you feel when you meet someone who's different from you?*

FOR FURTHER READING

All Kinds of People: What Makes Us Different (*Spyglass Books*), by Jennifer Waters (Compass Point Books, 2002).

The Colors of Us, by Karen Katz (Holt, Rinehart and Winston, 1999).

Incredible Me!, by Kathi Appelt (HarperCollins Publishers, 2003).

Branching Out

TEACHING TIP

Give your student two copies of the Web found on page 356. On one, have him or her write "Different" in the middle. In the surrounding circles, have your student write or draw various ways that people are different. On the other Web, have him or her write "Alike" in the middle and fill in the surrounding circles with words or drawings that show how people are the same.

CHECKING IN

Give your student two pictures of people to compare. Have him or her list ways the people are the same.

Figure It Out

Look at each picture. Answer the questions.

1. How are the boys alike?

_____

2. How are they different?

_____

3. How are the girls alike?

_____

4. How are they different?

_____

What's Next? You Decide!

Now it's your turn to choose what to do next in the lesson. Read the activities and decide which one you want to do—you may want to try them both!

Make a Mobile

MATERIALS

- ❑ 2–5 magazines with pictures of people at work
- ❑ 1 pair scissors
- ❑ glue
- ❑ index cards
- ❑ masking tape
- ❑ string
- ❑ 1 hanger

STEPS

- ❑ Look in the magazines for pictures of people at work.
- ❑ Cut out the pictures. Glue each picture onto an index card.
- ❑ Tape a piece of string to each card. Tie each string to the hanger.
- ❑ Hang your mobile.

Make a Fingerprint Garden

MATERIALS

- ❑ 1 smock
- ❑ 1 stamp pad
- ❑ 1 sheet paper

STEPS

- ❑ Put on the smock.
- ❑ Press the tip of your finger onto the pad.
- ❑ Press your finger onto the paper and leave your fingerprint.
- ❑ Finish with the rest of your fingers.
- ❑ Now draw flowers around your fingerprints.

Keeping Your Body Healthy

Your body is very special, and you can do things to keep it healthy and safe.

OBJECTIVE	BACKGROUND	MATERIALS
To teach your student about staying healthy and safety rules	Children are exposed to germs and dangerous situations every day. The more your student knows about how people get sick or have accidents, the more likely he or she will be to avoid illness and injury. In this lesson, your student will learn about the causes of diseases and how to be healthy and safe.	■ Student Learning Pages 13.A–13.B ■ 1 paper towel ■ markers or crayons

VOCABULARY

GERMS organisms that are too small to be seen and that can cause disease

MEDICINE a substance that kills germs or reduces the symptoms of illness

VACCINES medicines that help prevent disease

SAFETY RULES rules for keeping the body safe

ACCIDENTS events that cause injuries

Let's Begin

1 **INTRODUCE** Explain to your student that **germs** are what make people sick. Point out that germs are so small we can't see them, but that they're all around, floating in the air and resting on every surface. Explain that germs can get into the body through the nose, eyes, mouth, or cuts in the skin. Ask, *Why do you think it's important to put a bandage on a cut right away?* [to keep germs from getting into the cut] Explain that germs can spread from one person to another when we cough, sneeze, or shake hands. Germs can cause the flu, colds, and many other illnesses. Invite your student to describe the last time he or she was sick with a cold or a cough.

2 **EXPAND** Tell your student that there are ways to keep germs from spreading. Some examples are covering our mouths and noses when we cough or sneeze, washing our hands with soap and water frequently, not sharing drinking glasses or silverware, and not putting things such as pencils or toys in our mouths. Model for your student the following steps to take when washing one's hands in public: use warm water and liquid soap when possible, rub the hands for 20 to 30 seconds, scrub under the fingernails, rinse thoroughly, turn off the faucet with a paper

Covering your mouth when you cough helps keep germs from spreading.

towel, and then dry the hands completely. Have your student practice washing his or her hands following these steps. Then distribute Student Learning Page 13.A. Have your student number the steps in their correct order.

3   **EXPLAIN**   Ask your student to describe a time when he or she has taken **medicine.** Explain that sometimes medicine can kill the germs that make a person sick. Medicines are usually swallowed but are sometimes given as shots. Remind your student that he or she should only take medicine when a parent says it's okay. Explain that some medicines called **vaccines** are taken to prevent germs from attacking the body. Tell your student about any vaccines he or she may have had. Invite your student to share his or her experiences of taking different kinds of medicines.

ENRICH THE EXPERIENCE

Visit your local fire station with your student. Ask the fire-fighters to explain fire safety rules and what to do in case of a fire.

4   **DISCUSS**   Explain to your student that **safety rules** help keep him or her from getting hurt. Ask, *Can you think of any safety rules?* Discuss the following rules: wait for a bus on the curb; never walk too close to a bus or car; don't be noisy in a bus or car; keep your hands, arms, and head inside a bus or a car; keep chair legs on the floor; be careful with scissors; be careful in the kitchen and ask an adult for help; wear a helmet when riding a bike or skating; don't play with matches or fire; in case of a fire, get out of the house quickly and then call for help; if your clothes are burning, stop, drop, and roll. Have your student find out if your family has a plan for where to meet in case of a fire. If not, have your student talk with family members and make a plan.

5   **EXPAND**   Tell your student that all of these safety rules are designed to help avoid **accidents.** Discuss some types of accidents that could happen at home or outside and the safety rules that are meant to prevent them. Invite your student to describe any accidents he or she has had and how they might have been avoided.

Branching Out

FOR FURTHER READING

Wash Your Hands!, by Tony Ross (Kane/Miller Book Publishers, 2000).

What Are Germs?, by Dr. Alvin Silverstein, Virginia Silverstein, and Laura Silverstein Nunn (Franklin Watts, 2002).

TEACHING TIP

Have your student give a safety presentation to your family. Ask him or her to talk about spreading and preventing germs and about safety rules.

CHECKING IN

To assess your student's understanding of the lesson, write each of the safety rules mentioned in the lesson on separate index cards. Place the cards facedown. Have your student draw a card and hand it to you. Read the card out loud and have your student act out the safety rule. Repeat until all the rules have been acted out.

Wash Your Hands Well

These steps aren't in the correct order. Number the steps from 1 to 6 in the correct order.

Step _____
Throw away the paper towels.

Step _____
Rub soap on your hands.

Step _____
Dry your hands with paper towels.

Step _____
Wet your hands with warm water.

Step _____
Rinse your hands of all the soap.

Step _____
Scrub your fingernails.

What's Next? You Decide!

Now it's your turn to choose what to do next in the lesson. Read the activities and decide which one you want to do—you may want to try them both!

Make a Book

 MATERIALS

- ❑ 6–10 sheets construction paper
- ❑ markers or crayons
- ❑ 1 hole puncher
- ❑ 3–4 lengths yarn, 4 to 6 inches long

STEPS

- ❑ Draw a picture on each sheet of construction paper. Draw a way to keep germs away or a safety rule.
- ❑ Write a title for your book on one page.
- ❑ Have an adult help you punch holes in each sheet of paper.
- ❑ Tie the sheets of paper together with yarn.

Get Rid of Germs

MATERIALS

- ❑ hand lotion
- ❑ 1 package glitter
- ❑ 3–4 paper towels
- ❑ soap

STEPS

- ❑ Suppose that glitter is germs.
- ❑ Rub some lotion on your hands.
- ❑ Hold your hands over a paper towel. Rub glitter all over your hands.
- ❑ Try to get the glitter off with a paper towel. Then with cold water. Then with soap and warm water.

Learning About Food

Meals aren't just a time to nourish our bodies. They're also a special time to spend with the people we love.

OBJECTIVE	BACKGROUND	MATERIALS
To help your student learn more about food and eating well	Food is an important part of our lives. Food gives us energy and keeps us strong and healthy. In this lesson, your student will learn about different kinds of food and where they come from. He or she will also learn how food helps his or her body.	■ Student Learning Pages 14.A–14.B ■ 3 different fruits ■ markers or crayons ■ 1 can vegetables

VOCABULARY

GRAINS the seeds of wheat, corn, rice, oats, and other cereal plants
SERVINGS portions of food or drink
DAIRY having to do with food made from milk

Let's Begin

1 **INTRODUCE** Explain that our bodies need food to stay healthy. Food comes in many different colors and shapes and has many different smells and tastes. One way we can describe our food is by where it comes from. Some of our food comes from plants, and some of our food comes from animals. Challenge your student to name one food that comes from a plant and one food that comes from an animal.

2 **COMPARE** Explain to your student that fruits and vegetables are two kinds of foods that come from plants. Ask your student to name some fruits and vegetables. Tell your student that apples, oranges, and strawberries are all fruits. Corn, lettuce, and peas are all vegetables. **Grains,** such as wheat, also come from plants. They are used to make bread and cereal. Hold a fruit taste test with your student. Get three different fruits, such as an apple, an orange, and a grape. Have your student close his or her eyes. Give your student a piece of each fruit one at a time. See if he or she can guess which fruit it is.

3 **EXPAND** Explain to your student that bananas are a kind of fruit. They have vitamins that are important to our bodies. People eat bananas in many different ways. Some people eat

bananas in their cereal. Some people make banana bread and banana cream pie. Bananas grow in places with warm weather. The bananas we buy at stores in the United States are grown in other countries. Ask, *Where do bananas come from?* [plants]

Bananas are fruits. They come from plants.

4 **INVESTIGATE** Tell your student that people also eat foods that come from animals. Meat and eggs both come from animals. The milk we drink also comes from animals, such as cows. Milk is used to make cheese and ice cream. Look around the kitchen with your student. Help your student identify some of the foods that come from animals. Distribute Student Learning Page 14.A. Have your student write "plant" or "animal" next to each picture as appropriate. Then have your student write one sentence about his or her favorite food.

5 **EXPAND** Explain to your student that turkey meat comes from turkeys that are raised on farms. People eat turkey in many different ways. Some people eat thin slices of turkey in sandwiches. Some families eat a special turkey dinner on holidays such as Thanksgiving. Some people eat turkey with vegetables such as potatoes, peas, or corn. Invite your student to think about special dinners he or she eats with the family on different holidays. Ask, *What do we eat for special meals? Which foods come from animals? Which foods come from plants?*

6 **SHARE** Remind your student that food is very important to our bodies. Explain that some foods are especially good for our bodies. We call these healthy foods. Fruits and vegetables are healthy foods. Fruits and vegetables give our bodies important vitamins. It's important for us to eat two to four **servings** of fruit and three to five servings of vegetables every day. Tell your student the name of your favorite fruit and favorite vegetable. Then invite your student to share with you the names of his or her favorite fruit and vegetable.

?
DID YOU KNOW?

Some people consider tomatoes to be fruits and others consider them to be vegetables. Botanists say that tomatoes are fruits because they have seeds. Still, most people consider tomatoes to be vegetables. Either way, tomatoes are used in many of the foods we eat, such as pasta sauce, salsa, and ketchup.

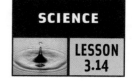
7 **DRAW** Tell your student that the foods we eat help keep our bodies strong. Explain to your student that **dairy** foods are made from milk. Milk has calcium, which helps keep our bones and teeth strong. Calcium also helps our bodies grow. Tell your student that we should eat two to three servings of dairy foods every day. Cheese, pudding, yogurt, cottage cheese, and ice cream are all dairy foods that help keep us strong. Meats, such as turkey and chicken, have protein and also help keep our muscles strong. It's recommended that we eat two to three servings of protein every day. If your family eats meat and dairy products, invite your student to draw his or her favorite foods from the dairy group and the meat group. Remind your student that foods from the dairy group and meat group come from animals. Mention that some people don't eat meat or dairy products; however, they get the nutrients found in these foods from other sources.

8 **EXPLAIN** Explain that just as a car needs gas to move, our bodies need food. Food gives us the energy we need to do things. Tell your student that grains are foods that give us a lot of energy. Remind your student that breads, cereals, rice, and noodles are all made from grains. We should eat at least six servings of grains every day. Ask, *What are some activities you need energy for?* [riding a bicycle, running, walking, playing sports, reading, talking, and so on]

Bread is a grain. It gives us energy.

9 **IDENTIFY** Show your student the picture of a farmer on a farm. Explain that most of the food at grocery stores comes from farms. Fruits, vegetables, and grains are all grown on farms. Farmers also keep animals on their farms that give us milk, eggs, and meat. Cows, chickens, and turkeys are all animals that farmers raise to provide us with food. Farmers send their food to other places using airplanes, trains, and trucks. For example, an orange farmer in Florida might send his or her fruit to stores in Minnesota. Visit a grocery store with your student. At the store,

Farmers work to give us food to eat.

remind your student that the food there comes from farms. Invite your student to notice the fruit and vegetable, bread, dairy, and meat sections. Have him or her tell whether the foods come from plants or animals.

10   **RELATE**   Explain that many foods that come from farms are sent to a factory before they get to a store. Show your student a can of vegetables. Tell him or her that the vegetables were grown on a farm and then sent to a factory. At the factory, the vegetables were packaged in cans. The cans were sealed and labels were put on the cans. The canned vegetables were then sent to a grocery store. Have your student look again at the foods in the kitchen. Ask, *Which foods do you think were sent to factories?*

11   **EXPAND**   Explain that some foods are not always good to eat. Sweets are one of these foods. Sweets, such as candy, cakes, and cookies, have a lot of sugar. Explain that eating sweets once in a while is okay but that eating too many sweets is not healthy. Point out that sugar can hurt your student's teeth. Ask, *What can you do to keep your teeth strong and healthy?* [brush every day with a toothbrush and toothpaste]

12   **TRACK**   Explain that it's important to eat foods from all the different groups. We need a combination of grains (such as breads, noodles, and cereals), fruits and vegetables (such as spinach and green beans), meats (such as fish and chicken), and dairy (such as milk and yogurt). We should try not to eat too many sweets. Have your student keep a picture journal of the foods he or she eats for one day. Help him or her make a five-column chart on a sheet of paper. Title the columns "Grains," "Fruits and Vegetables," "Meat," "Dairy," and "Sweets." Remind your student to draw pictures of the foods he or she eats for breakfast, lunch, dinner, and snacks.

FOR FURTHER READING

Eat Healthy, Feel Great, by William Sears and Martha Sears (Little, Brown and Company, 2002).

The Grain Group (*The Food Guide Pyramid*), by Helen Frost (Pebble Books, 2000).

My Farm, by Alison Lester (Houghton Mifflin Company, 1999).

Branching Out

TEACHING TIP

Help your student try some new kinds of fruits and vegetables. Go to the fruit and vegetable section of a grocery store and find a fruit or vegetable your family doesn't usually eat. Take it home and try it with your student. Emphasize that there are many different kinds of foods. It's fun and exciting to try something new!

CHECKING IN

To assess your student's understanding of the lesson, show your student one type of food from each group. Use foods you already have in your kitchen. Ask your student to name the food group each food belongs to. Then have your student tell you if the food comes from plants or animals.

Discover Where Food Comes From

Write "plant" or "animal" on the line below each picture. Then write one sentence about your favorite food.

1. __plant__

2. _____

3. _____

4. _____

5. Favorite food:

_____

_____

_____

What's Next? You Decide!

Now it's your turn to choose what to do next in the lesson. Read the activities and decide which one you want to do—you may want to try them both!

Make a Food Picture

MATERIALS

- ❑ 1 posterboard
- ❑ markers or crayons
- ❑ 1 grocery store ad
- ❑ 1 pair scissors
- ❑ glue

STEPS

- ❑ Write "Food" in the middle of the posterboard.
- ❑ Find pictures of foods that come from both plants and animals in the ad.
- ❑ Cut out the pictures.
- ❑ Glue the pictures to the posterboard.
- ❑ Hang your poster in a place where your family can see it.

Make a Salad

MATERIALS

- ❑ lettuce
- ❑ 1 sliced tomato
- ❑ 1 sliced cucumber
- ❑ salad dressing
- ❑ 1 salad bowl
- ❑ forks

STEPS

Ask an adult to help you make a salad!

- ❑ Wash the vegetables.
- ❑ Tear the lettuce into small pieces.
- ❑ Mix the vegetables in the salad bowl.
- ❑ Eat the salad with your family.

In Your Community

To reinforce the skills and concepts taught in this section,
try one or more of these activities!

Community Gardens

Community gardens are outdoor spaces on public or private lands where community members can grow vegetables, flowers, or other kinds of plants. They are often found in empty lots in urban areas where people often don't have the space to create a garden at home. Find out if one of these gardens exists in your community and, if so, plan a visit with your student. Observe the types of plants that are growing with your student and talk with the gardeners about how they care for the plants. Perhaps next season you and your student might wish to participate in the community garden together.

Nature Walk

Go to the library with your student and check out a local plant and animal guidebook. Pick a location to explore that's likely to contain a wide variety of plant and animal life, such as a nature preserve. If there aren't any nature preserves or other open spaces near you, find a place where your student is likely to be exposed to the greatest amount of plant and animal life, such as a pet store or greenhouse. Have your student look up in the guidebook each plant or animal he or she sees to learn more about it.

A Healthy Dose of Information

Your local health food store can be a good place for your student to learn about the importance of a healthy diet. Contact the store to see if a qualified representative would be willing to spend time with you and your student. The representative should know about foods that help you stay strong, how food provides energy, where specific foods come from, and which foods are important for a healthy diet. Have your student write down three questions he or she would like to ask in preparation for your visit.

Fun at the Science Museum

Plan a trip to a local science museum or children's museum. Find out the title of the feature exhibit and get information about the museum's exhibits on matter, sound, motion, the human body, and weather. Science museums often feature exhibits that are interactive and allow your student to participate in hands-on activities. Discuss with your student which exhibits he or she would like to explore. If you don't have a science museum near your home, you may want to plan a special trip to the nearest city and visit several museums.

Meet with a Personal Trainer

Call a local fitness gym, Pilates studio, or physical therapy clinic and try to arrange a meeting with one of the staff members. These professionals can talk with your student about bones and muscles, how they grow, and how to keep them healthy and strong. Arrange for a demonstration of the special equipment used and see if the staff member can show your student some basic exercises that can be beneficial to children. Before your visit, have your student write down at least two specific questions he or she would like to ask.

Visit a Weather Station

Find out where the nearest weather station is to your home. Arrange to visit the weather station with your student for a tour. Explain that you are interested in having your student see and learn about the different weather instruments that are used there. Arrange to talk to a weather expert if you can. Have your student prepare questions about the local climate, how the weather is predicted, and how the weather changes with the seasons.

We Have Learned

Use this checklist to summarize what you and your student
have accomplished in the Science section.

❏ **Animals and Plants**
❏ mammals, birds, fish, reptiles, amphibians, insects
❏ seeds and how plants grow
❏ habitats and how animals and plants help each other

❏ **Weather**
❏ weather and the sun
❏ weather instruments and reading air temperature
❏ how weather changes each season

❏ **Climates**
❏ desert
❏ tropical rain forest
❏ arctic

❏ **Earth's Resources**
❏ how we use resources
❏ what can be recycled

❏ **Forms of Matter**
❏ solids, liquids, gases
❏ heat and matter
❏ mixtures

❏ **Motion**
❏ pushing, pulling, speed
❏ magnets: attract and repel

❏ **Sound**
❏ vibrations and what we need to hear sound
❏ sound waves

❏ **Your Body**
❏ bones and muscles
❏ heart and lungs
❏ differences and similarities in people

❏ **Staying Healthy**
❏ germs and illness
❏ medicine, vaccines, safety

❏ **Food**
❏ foods from plants and animals
❏ food groups
❏ how food gives us energy
❏ where food comes from

We have also learned:

_____

_____

_____

_____

_____

_____

_____

_____

SHEPHERD'S HUT
CIRCA 1900

Social Studies

Social Studies

Key Topics